In *The Cambridge Companion to Jane Austen* leading scholars from around the world present Austen's works in two broad contexts: that of her contemporary world, and that of present-day critical discourse. Beside discussions of Austen's novels there are essays on religion, politics, class-consciousness, publishing practices, and domestic economy, which describe the world in which Austen lived and wrote. More traditional issues for literary analysis are then addressed: style in the novels, Austen's letters as literary productions, and the stylistic significance of her juvenile works. The volume concludes with assessments of the history of Austen criticism and the development of Austen as a literary cult-figure; it provides a chronology, and highlights the most interesting recent studies of Austen in a vast field of contemporary critical diversity.

THE CAMBRIDGE
COMPANION TO
JANE AUSTEN

CAMBRIDGE COMPANIONS TO LITERATURE

THE CAMBRIDGE
COMPANION TO
JANE AUSTEN

EDITED BY

EDWARD COPELAND
Pomona College

AND

JULIET McMASTER
University of Alberta

CAMBRIDGE
UNIVERSITY PRESS

Published by the Press Syndicate of the University of Cambridge
The Pitt Building, Trumpington Street, Cambridge CB2 1RP
40 West 20th Street, New York, NY 10011–4211, USA
10 Stamford Road, Oakleigh, Melbourne 3166, Australia

First published 1997
Reprinted 1997, 1998

Printed in the United Kingdom at the University Press, Cambridge

A catalogue record for this book is available from the British Library

Library of Congress cataloguing in publication data

The Cambridge companion to Jane Austen / edited by Edward Copeland
and Juliet McMaster
p. cm. – (Cambridge companions to literature)
Includes bibliographical references and index.
ISBN 0 521 49517 2 (hardback) – ISBN 0 521 49867 8 (paperback)
1. Austen, Jane, 1775–1817 – Criticism and interpretation.
2. Women and literature – England – History – 19th century.
I. Copeland, Edward. II. McMaster, Juliet. III. Series.
PR4036.C3 1997 823'.7–dc20 98-23387 CIP

ISBN 0 521 49517 2 hardback
ISBN 0 521 49867 8 paperback

CONTENTS

CONTENTS

NOTES ON CONTRIBUTORS

RACHEL M. BROWNSTEIN is Professor of English at Brooklyn College and the Graduate Centre, CUNY. She is the author of *Becoming a Heroine: Reading about Women in Novels* (1982) and *Tragic Muse: Rachel of the Comédie-Française* (1993).

JOHN F. BURROWS is Emeritus Professor of English and Director of the Centre for Literary and Linguistic Computing at the University of Newcastle, NSW, Australia. He has published two monographs and several essays on Jane Austen's fiction. His other writings lie chiefly in the field of Australian literature and, since 1983, in that of computational stylistics. He is best known for *Computation into Criticism: A Study of Jane Austen's Novels and an Experiment in Method* (1987).

EDWARD COPELAND, F. S. Jennings Professor of English at Pomona College, Claremont, California, is the author of a study of novelists contemporary with Jane Austen, *Women Writing about Money: Women's Fiction in England, 1790-1820* (1995), and of essays on Austen, Smollett, Cleland, Richardson, and Burney. He is co-editor with Carol Houlihan Flynn of The Clarissa Project: volume 16, *The Critical Commentary – New Essays*.

MARGARET ANNE DOODY is Andrew W. Mellon Professor of Humanities and Professor of English at Vanderbilt University Nashville, where she is presently Director of the Comparative Literature Program. She is the author of two novels and a number of critical and biographical works, including *A Natural Passion: A Study of the Novels of Samuel Richardson* (1974), *The Daring Muse: Augustan Poetry Reconsidered* (1985), and *Frances Burney: The Life in the Works* (1988).

JAN FERGUS, Professor of English at Lehigh University, has published *Jane Austen and the Didactic Novel* (1983) and *Jane Austen: A Literary Life* (1991). She is Book Review Editor for *Eighteenth-Century Studies*, and is completing a study of the audience for prose fiction in eighteenth-century English entitled *Readers and Fictions*.

CAROL HOULIHAN FLYNN, is Professor of English at Tufts University, and the author of *Samuel Richardson: A Man of Letters* (1982), a novel, *Washed in the Blood* (1983), *The Body in Swift and Defoe* (1990), and essays on Smollett, Sterne, Cleland, and Fielding. She is co-editor with Edward Copeland of The Clarissa Project: volume 16, *The Critical Commentary – New Essays*.

ISOBEL GRUNDY is Henry Marshall Tory Professor at the University of Alberta. Her publications include *Samuel Johnson and the Scale of Greatness* (Georgia, 1986); with Patricia Clements and Virginia Blain, *The Feminist Companion to Literature in English* (Yale, 1990); and an edition of Eliza Fenwick's *Secrecy, or The Ruin on the Rock* 1795 (Broadview, 1994). She has edited Lady Mary Wortley Montagu's *Romance Writings* (forthcoming), and is writing her life.

CLAUDIA L. JOHNSON, Professor of English at Princeton University, is author of *Jane Austen: Women, Politics, and the Novel* (Chicago, 1988), *Equivocal Beings: Politics, Gender, and Sentimentality in the 1790s: Wollstonecraft, Radcliffe, Burney, Austen* (Chicago, 1995), and essays and reviews on eighteenth-century literature and music. She is editing the forthcoming Norton Critical Edition of *Mansfield Park*.

GARY KELLY is Professor and Head of the Department of English, Keele University, England. He has published *The English Jacobin Novel* (1976), *English Fiction of the Romantic Period* (1989), and *Women, Writing, and Revolution* (1993). He has edited Wollstonecraft's two novels and Sarah Scott's *Millenium Hall*.

DEIRDRE LE FAYE is the author of *Jane Austen: A Family Record* (1989), the definitive factual biography, and editor of the new (3rd) edition of *Jane Austen's Letters* (1995). She has also published (with Maggie Black) *The Jane Austen Cookbook* (1995), and numerous articles on Austenian subjects in *Notes and Queries, Review of English Studies*, and *The Book Collector*.

JULIET McMASTER, University Professor at the University of Alberta, is the author of *Thackeray: The Major Novels* (1970), *Trollope's Palliser Novels* (1978), *Dickens the Designer* (1987), and *Jane Austen the Novelist* (1995). She is also co-editor with Bruce Stovel of *Jane Austen's Business: Her World and her Profession* (1995), and General Editor of the Juvenilia Press.

BRUCE STOVEL is a member of the English Department at the University of Alberta. Co-editor with Juliet McMaster of *Jane Austen's Business: Her World and her Profession* (1995), he has published many essays and reviews on Austen, Richardson, Fielding, Swift, Sterne, Charlotte Lennox, Frances Burney, Scott, Evelyn Waugh, Kingsley Amis, Brian Moore, and Margaret Laurence.

JOHN WILTSHIRE, Reader in English at La Trobe University, Melbourne, Australia, is the author of *Jane Austen and the Body* (1992). He specializes in eighteenth-century literature and in medical and health-care narrative. He is an editor of the journal *Hysteric: Body, Medicine, Text*.

PREFACE

The problem for anyone who addresses readers of Jane Austen is always the same: *Which* readers of Jane Austen? They come uniquely self-defined. The old division between Janeites and anti-Janeites is now replaced by new divisions, perhaps not so hostile as the old ones, but sufficiently distinct to make general introductions a moot question. The new Janeites, energetic members of the Austen societies, for example, have eager feelings for Austen, but limited tolerance for bookish harangues; and the academics, also with energy in abundance, are bookish enough about Austen, but have few feelings of the Janeite kind. Generational divisions prevail as well: older readers who are jealously protective of Austen, their cultural icon, and younger readers who are equally enthusiastic for Austen, their new-found subversive. Meanwhile, first-time readers arrive at the novels with conflicting motives: 'I'm reading Jane Austen for graduate school', or, 'I read Jane Austen because I want to understand my mother.'

One approach, however, addresses an issue that Austen readers of all stripes embrace with equal enthusiasm, the contextual setting of Austen's works. Students first encountering her works and old hands reading her novels both sense that Austen's culture is receding from them at an unsettling speed. Novels that once seemed so accessible to readers now produce a growing consciousness that profound differences between Austen's culture and today's must be addressed. North American students in particular find themselves mystified, for example, by the economics of Austen's novels, by her class distinctions, by the role of the church. They are startled to find that Austen's works possess political resonance. Readers mystified by 'Sir', 'Lady', and 'Reverend' now want more than a simple key to the players. The old Janeite question, 'How do they make whip't syllabub?' has altered almost universally to '*Why* do they make whip't syllabub?'

Jane Austen's stock in the literary marketplace has never been higher than late in our twentieth century, when even Hollywood has seen fit to attach itself to her rapid rise in popularity, and adaptations on stage, screen, and television are emerging in such quick succession that the newsmedia can hardly keep pace. Faced within the same few months with a Hollywood adaptation of *Emma* as the teenage fashion movie *Clueless*, full-scale screen versions of *Persuasion* and *Sense and Sensibility*, and the second BBC television serial of *Pride and Prejudice* in ten years, journalists have been feverishly turning to literary critics to ask which Austen novel they should read first and fastest in order to catch up with the culture. The pace has certainly picked up since the classic movie of 1939, starring Greer Garson and Laurence Olivier as Elizabeth and Darcy.

A *Cambridge Companion to Jane Austen* can't hope, any more than the journalists, to capture the burgeoning Austen boom on the wing. This collection seeks rather to recover and illuminate elements of *her* culture, so that her novels may speak the more lucidly to ours.

Essays in the *Companion*, by a group of contributors who have already distinguished themselves in Austen studies and elsewhere, cover a broad range. Deirdre Le Faye, Austen's biographer and the editor of her letters, provides a chronology of Austen's life, as a map of the life and career by which the student and scholar can locate other historical events. Jan Fergus fills this in with detailed guidance on the 'professional writer', and Austen's engagement in the publishing practices of her day. The six published novels, Austen's major works, are discussed in two swathes, as she composed them: the first three, *Northanger Abbey*, *Sense and Sensibility*, and *Pride and Prejudice* – all drafted in the 1790s – receive group treatment in Rachel Brownstein's searching essay on irony and romance. The last three, *Mansfield Park*, *Emma*, and *Persuasion*, all composed in the ripe Chawton years, are John Wiltshire's subject. This division allows for a fresh approach to the major works, which have been examined often enough individually, but which reveal new themes and motifs when so grouped.

Austen's other works, the ones not designed for publication, receive separate treatment. Margaret Anne Doody's essay on the short fiction presents a provocative glimpse of the other kind of writer Austen might have become, but for her necessary adaptation to the new values of the Regency; and Carol Houlihan Flynn examines the letters as literary productions, and as documents that register Austen's marginalized position as a woman writer.

The subsequent essays address aspects of Austen's cultural context, and her reception in our own culture today. Juliet McMaster examines class and class consciousness in the novels; Edward Copeland presents an informed guide to money, income, and material culture; and Gary Kelly discusses Austen's development of the Anglican novel, the genre she developed to articulate her own and her immediate society's mediated middle-of-the-road position in religion and politics. John Burrows examines Austen's style in relation to that of her contemporaries, and Isobel Grundy, in a far-reaching essay, demonstrates the multiple literary sources, influences, and light allusions that inform Austen's writing in her letters and fiction.

In our own day, Austen has become not just an author, but a 'figure', a writer avidly claimed by readers lay and academic, by critics of different stripes and schools. Claudia Johnson examines the Janeites and anti-Janeites, the 'cults and cultures' that have grown to surround this retiring country spinster and her 'little bits ... of ivory'; and finally Bruce Stovel provides a guide to the burgeoning critical tradition from her time to our own.

ACKNOWLEDGEMENTS

The Cambridge Companion to Jane Austen draws on the talents of a number of outstanding scholars, and the first debt we would like to acknowledge is that to our contributors, for their patience under our editorial onslaughts as well as for their scholarly expertise. We are grateful too for the skilled research assistance of Erika Rothwell and Nicholette Walker, of the English Department at the University of Alberta. A version of Margaret Anne Doody's paper on the short fiction appeared in *Persuasions*, the annual journal of the Jane Austen Society of North America (number 16, 1994); and Deirdre Le Faye's 'Chronology' of Jane Austen's life appears in longer form in *Jane Austen: A Family Record* (London: The British Library, 1989). We are grateful to the publishers for permission to reprint. Thanks are also due to John Murray, for permission granted to Jan Fergus to quote from the Murray Archives in her essay on 'The professional woman writer'.

TEXTS AND ABBREVIATIONS

References to Jane Austen's works are to these editions:

The Novels of Jane Austen, ed. R. W. Chapman, 5 vols., 3rd edition (London: Oxford University Press, 1933), reprinted with revisions, 1969.

Minor Works, ed. R. W. Chapman (London: Oxford University Press, 1954), reprinted with revisions by B. C. Southam, 1969.

Jane Austen's Letters, collected and edited by Deirdre Le Faye (Oxford: Oxford University Press, 1995).

Catharine and Other Writings, ed. Margaret Anne Doody and Douglas Murray (Oxford: Oxford University Press, 1993).

Abbreviations:

C&OW	*Catharine and Other Writings*
E	*Emma*
L	*Jane Austen's Letters*
MP	*Mansfield Park*
MW	*Minor Works*
NA	*Northanger Abbey*
P	*Persuasion*
PP	*Pride and Prejudice*
SS	*Sense and Sensibility*

1

DEIRDRE LE FAYE

Chronology of Jane Austen's life

1764   *April 26*   Marriage of Rev. George Austen and Cassandra Leigh.
October 9   Marriage of James Leigh-Perrot (Mrs. Austen's brother) and Jane Cholmeley.

1765   *February 13*   James Austen born at Deane.
Summer   Mr. and Mrs. Hancock (Mr. Austen's sister) and their daughter Eliza return from India.

1766   *August 26*   George Austen the younger born at Deane.

1767   *October 7*   Edward Austen born at Deane.

1768   *July/August*   Austen family move to Steventon.
?Autumn   Mr. Hancock returns alone to India.
?Winter   Marriage of Jane Leigh (Mrs. Austen's sister) and Rev. Dr. Edward Cooper.

1770   *July 1*   Edward Cooper the younger born in London.

1771   *June 8*   Henry-Thomas Austen (hereafter 'HTA') born at Steventon.
June 27   Jane Cooper born at Southcote, near Reading.
?Autumn   Cooper family move to Bath, 12 Royal Crescent.

1773   *January 9*   Cassandra-Elizabeth Austen (hereafter 'CEA') born at Steventon.
March 23   Mr. Austen becomes Rector of Deane as well as Steventon. Pupils live at Steventon from now until 1796.

1774   *April 23*   Francis-William Austen (hereafter 'FWA') born at Steventon.

1775   *November 5*   Mr. Hancock dies in Calcutta.
        December 16   Jane Austen (hereafter 'JA') born at Steventon.

1777   *Winter*   Mrs. Hancock and Eliza go to the Continent.

1779   *June 23*   Charles-John Austen (hereafter 'CJA') born at
        Steventon.
        July 3   James Austen matriculates at St. John's College, Oxford.
        Summer   Mr. and Mrs. Thomas Knight II (cousins of
        Mr. Austen) visit Steventon.

?1780   The Coopers move to 14 Bennett Street, Bath.

1781   Marriage of Eliza Hancock to Jean-François Capot de Feuillide, in
        France.

1782   *Summer*   First mention of JA in family tradition.
        December   First amateur theatrical production at Steventon –
        Matilda.

1783   Edward Austen (hereafter 'EAK') adopted by Mr. and Mrs.
        Thomas Knight II.
        Spring   JA, CEA, and Jane Cooper go to Mrs. Cawley in Oxford.
        May 3   Rev. I. P. G. Lefroy instituted to Ashe.
        Summer   Mrs. Cawley moves to Southampton and the girls fall ill.
        October 25   Mrs. Cooper dies in Bath.

1784   *July*   *The Rivals* performed at Steventon.
        July   Dr. Cooper moves to Sonning.

1785   *Spring*   JA and CEA go to the Abbey School, Reading.

1786   EAK abroad on Grand Tour from 1786–90.
        April   FWA enters Royal Naval Academy, Portsmouth.
        June 25   Eliza de Feuillide's son Hastings born in London.
        November   James Austen goes to the Continent.
        December   JA and CEA have now left school.

1787   JA starts writing her *Juvenilia*.
        Autumn   James Austen returns from the Continent.
        December   *The Wonder* performed at Steventon.

1788   *January*   *The Chances* performed at Steventon.
        March   *Tom Thumb* performed at Steventon.
        A 'private theatrical exhibition' also performed at Steventon some
        time later this year.
        July 1   HTA matriculates at St. John's College, Oxford.
        Summer   Mr. and Mrs. Austen take JA and CEA to Kent and
        London.
        September   Mrs. Hancock and Eliza de Feuillide return to
        France.
        December 23   FWA sails to East Indies.
        Winter   *The Sultan* and *High Life Below Stairs* performed at
        Steventon.

1789   *January 31*   First issue of *The Loiterer* appears – published
        weekly by James Austen in Oxford until March 1790.
        Spring   Lloyd family rent Deane parsonage.

1790   *April*   James Austen takes up residence as curate of Overton.
        Autumn   EAK returns to England from Grand Tour.

1791   *June 21*   Death of Mr. Francis Austen of Sevenoaks
        (Mr. Austen's uncle).
        July   CJA enters Royal Naval Academy, Portsmouth.
        September 15   James Austen becomes vicar of Sherborne
        St. John.
        December 27   Marriage of EAK and Elizabeth Bridges, in Kent;
        they live at Rowling.

1792   *January*   The Lloyds leave Deane for Ibthorpe.
        February 26   Death of Mrs. Hancock, in London.
        March 27   Marriage of James Austen and Anne Mathew,
        at Laverstoke; they presently take up residence at Deane
        parsonage.
        August 27   Death of Dr. Cooper, at Sonning.
        October   JA and CEA visit the Lloyds at Ibthorpe.
        December 11   Marriage of Jane Cooper and Capt. Thomas
        Williams, RN, at Steventon.
        ?Winter   CEA engaged to Rev. Tom Fowle.

1793   *January 21*   Louis XVI of France guillotined.
        January 23   EAK's first child, Fanny, born at Rowling.

February 1 Republican France declares war on Great Britain and Holland.
Spring HTA becomes Lieutenant in Oxfordshire Militia.
March 14 Marriage of Edward Cooper and Caroline Lybbe-Powys; they live at Harpsden until 1799.
April 15 James Austen's first child, Anna, born at Deane.
June 3 JA writes last item of *Juvenilia*.
Winter FWA returns home from Far East.
December JA and CEA visit Butler-Harrison cousins in Southampton.

1794   *February 22* M. de Feuillide guillotined in Paris.
Midsummer JA and CEA visit the Leighs at Adlestrop.
?August JA and CEA visit Edward and Elizabeth at Rowling.
September CJA leaves Royal Naval Academy and goes to sea.
October 23 Death of Mr. Thomas Knight II.
?Autumn JA possibly writes *Lady Susan* this year.

1795   JA probably writes *Elinor and Marianne* this year.
May 3 Death of Anne Mathew at Deane; Anna sent to live at Steventon.
Autumn Rev. Tom Fowle joins Lord Craven as his private chaplain for the West Indian campaign.
December 1795/January 1796 JA's flirtation with Tom Lefroy on his visit to Ashe Rectory.

1796   *January* Tom Lefroy leaves Ashe for London.
Tom Fowle sails for West Indies.
April JA and CEA visit the Coopers at Harpsden.
?Summer James Austen courting Eliza de Feuillide.
June Capt. Thomas Williams knighted.
August EAK and FWA take JA to Rowling via London; she returns to Steventon late September/early October.
October JA starts writing *First Impressions*.
End November James Austen engaged to Mary Lloyd.

1797   *January 17* Marriage of James Austen and Mary Lloyd at Hurstbourne Tarrant; Anna returns to live at Deane.
February Tom Fowle dies of fever at San Domingo and buried at sea.

August JA finishes *First Impressions*.

November 1 Mr. Austen offers *First Impressions* to publisher Cadell; rejected sight unseen.

November JA starts converting *Elinor and Marianne* into *Sense and Sensibility*.

Mrs. Austen, JA, and CEA visit the Leigh-Perrots in Bath, at Paragon Buildings.

EAK and family move from Rowling to Godmersham.

Winter Rev. Samuel Blackall visits Ashe. Mild courtship of JA.

December 31 Marriage of HTA and Eliza de Feuillide, in London.

1798　*April 6* Death of Mr. William-Hampson Walter (Mr. Austen's elder half-brother), in Kent.

August Mr. and Mrs. Austen, with JA and CEA, visit Godmersham.

JA possibly starts writing *Susan* (*Northanger Abbey*).

August 9 Lady Williams (Jane Cooper) killed in road accident.

October 24 JA and her parents leave Godmersham for Steventon.

Mrs. Austen ill until end November.

November 17 James Austen's son James-Edward born at Deane.

1799　*February* JA possibly visits the Lloyds at Ibthorpe.

March CEA returns to Steventon from Godmersham.

May 17 Mrs. Austen and JA arrive in Bath, with Edward and Elizabeth, and stay at 13 Queen Square.

End June They return home.

JA probably finishes *Susan* (*Northanger Abbey*) about now.

Late summer The Austens pay round of visits to the Leighs at Adlestrop, the Coopers at Harpsden, and the Cookes at Great Bookham.

August 14 Mrs. Leigh-Perrot charged with theft and committed to Ilchester Gaol.

October The Coopers move to Hamstall Ridware, Staffordshire.

1800　*March 29* Mrs. Leigh-Perrot tried at Taunton and acquitted. Probably stays at Steventon thereafter.

October EAK visits Steventon and takes CEA back to Godmersham with him via Chawton and London.

End November   JA visits the Lloyds at Ibthorpe; returns home mid-December.

December   Mr. Austen decides to retire and move to Bath.

1801   *January*   HTA resigns commission in Oxfordshire Militia and sets up as banker and army agent in London, living at 24 Upper Berkeley Street and with office at Cleveland Court, St. James's.

End January   JA visits the Bigg-Wither family at Manydown.

February   CEA returns to Steventon from Godmersham via London.

May   The Austen family leave Steventon; Mrs. Austen and JA travel to Bath via Ibthorpe, and stay with the Leigh-Perrots. James Austen and his family move to Steventon.

End May   The Austens lease 4 Sydney Place and then go on West Country holiday; probably visit Sidmouth and Colyton. JA's traditional West Country romance presumably occurs between now and the autumn of 1804.

September   The Austens visit Steventon and Ashe.

October 5   They return to Bath.

October 9   Hastings de Feuillide dies, in London.

1802   *Spring*   Mrs. Lybbe-Powys visits the Austens in Bath.

March 25   Peace of Amiens commences.

April   James and Mary, with Anna, visit the Austens in Bath.

Summer   CJA joins the Austens for holidays; visit Dawlish and probably Teignmouth, also probably Tenby and Barmouth.

September 1   JA and CEA arrive at Steventon.

September 3   CJA takes JA and CEA to Godmersham.

October 28   CJA brings his sisters back to Steventon.

November 25   JA and CEA visit Manydown.

December 2   Harris Bigg-Wither proposes to JA; she accepts.

December 3   JA rejects proposal; she and CEA return to Steventon and set off at once for Bath.

Winter   JA revises *Susan* (*Northanger Abbey*).

1803   *February*   Mrs. Lybbe-Powys visits the Austens in Bath.

Spring   JA sells *Susan* (*Northanger Abbey*) to Crosby of London.

May 18   Napoleon breaks Peace of Amiens; HTA and Eliza nearly trapped in France.

Summer   JA possibly visits Charmouth, Up Lyme, and Pinny.

July   FWA stationed in Ramsgate.

September to October Mr. and Mrs. Austen, probably accompanied by JA and CEA, stay at Godmersham.
October JA and CEA visit Ashe.
October 24 They return to Bath.
November The Austens visit Lyme Regis.

1804   JA probably writes *The Watsons* this year.
January Mrs. Lybbe-Powys visits the Austens in Bath.
Spring Mrs. Austen seriously ill.
HTA moves house to 16 Michael's Place, Brompton, and moves office to Albany, Piccadilly.
Summer The Austens, with HTA and Eliza, visit Lyme Regis.
October 25 The Austens return to Bath and move to 3 Green Park Buildings East.
December 16 Madam Lefroy of Ashe killed in a riding accident.

1805   *January 21* Death of Mr. Austen in Bath.
March 25 Mrs. Austen and her daughters move to 25 Gay Street, Bath.
April 16 Mrs. Lloyd dies at Ibthorpe, and thereafter Martha Lloyd joins forces with Mrs. Austen, JA, and CEA.
June Mrs. Austen, JA, and CEA travel to Godmersham via Steventon, taking Anna with them.
June 18 James Austen's younger daughter Caroline born at Steventon.
Summer Possible courtship by Edward Bridges.
September 17 JA and CEA go to Worthing, and stay there with Mrs. Austen and Martha Lloyd until at least early November.
October 21 Battle of Trafalgar – FWA unable to participate.

1806   *January* Mrs. Austen and her daughters visit Steventon.
January 29 Mrs. Austen returns to Bath and takes lodgings in Trim Street.
February JA and CEA visit Manydown, returning to Bath via Steventon mid-March.
July 2 Mrs. Austen and her daughters finally leave Bath, and go via Clifton to Adlestrop.
July 24 Marriage of FWA to Mary Gibson, at Ramsgate.
August 5 Adlestrop family go to Stoneleigh Abbey.
August 14 Mrs. Austen and her daughters go from Stoneleigh to visit the Coopers at Hamstall Ridware and stay about five weeks.

October   The Austens call at Steventon, and with FWA and Mary Gibson take lodgings at Southampton.
Winter   CEA visits Godmersham.

1807   HTA moves office from Albany to 10 Henrietta Street, Covent Garden.
March   The Austens move into house in Castle Square, Southampton.
April   HTA brings CEA back to Southampton from Godmersham via London.
May 19   Marriage of CJA to Fanny Palmer, in Bermuda.
August   The Coopers visit Southampton.
September   EAK arranges family gathering at Chawton Great House, followed by further family gathering in Southampton.

1808   *January to March*   JA and CEA staying at Steventon, Manydown, and with the Fowles at Kintbury.
May 15   HTA and JA at Steventon en route for London.
June 14   JA goes to Godmersham with James and Mary.
July 8   JA returns to Southampton.
September 28   CEA goes to Godmersham.
October 10   Death of Elizabeth Austen (Knight) at Godmersham.

1809   *February*   CEA returns to Southampton.
April 5   JA attempts to secure publication of *Susan* (*Northanger Abbey*).
May 15   Mrs. Austen and her daughters arrive at Godmersham.
June   HTA and Eliza move house to 64 Sloane Street, London.
July 7   Mrs. Austen and her daughters move into Chawton Cottage.
August   JA regains interest in composition.
October   EAK and Fanny visit Chawton.

1810   *July to August*   JA and CEA visit Manydown and Steventon.
November   EAK and Fanny visit Chawton.
Winter   *Sense and Sensibility* accepted for publication.
The Leigh-Perrots buy 49 Great Pulteney Street, Bath.

1811   *February*   JA planning *Mansfield Park*.

March JA staying with HTA in London and correcting proofs of *Sense and Sensibility*; CEA at Godmersham.

May JA returns to Chawton via Streatham.

August CJA and family return to England.

October 30 *Sense and Sensibility* published.

November JA visits Steventon.

?Winter JA starts revising *First Impressions* into *Pride and Prejudice*.

1812 *April* EAK and Fanny visit Chawton.

June 9–25 Mrs. Austen and JA visit Steventon – the last time Mrs. Austen does so; CEA goes to Godmersham.

June 17 America declares war on Great Britain.

October 14 Death of Mrs. Thomas Knight II; Edward Austen now officially takes name of Knight.

Autumn JA sells copyright of *Pride and Prejudice* to Egerton for £110.

1813 *January 28* *Pride and Prejudice* published. JA half-way through *Mansfield Park*.

April 21 EAK and family come to Chawton Great House and stay for four months.

April 22 JA goes to London to attend Eliza de Feuillide.

April 25 Eliza de Feuillide dies.

May 1 JA returns to Chawton.

May 19 HTA takes JA to London again, for a fortnight.

June HTA moves house to 10 Henrietta Street.

?July JA finishes *Mansfield Park*.

August 17 Anna Austen engaged to Ben Lefroy.

September EAK and JA travel via London to Godmersham; her last visit there.

November 13 EAK takes JA back to Chawton via London; *Mansfield Park* probably accepted for publication at this time.

1814 *January 21* JA commences *Emma*.

March 1 HTA takes JA to London.

April JA returns to Chawton via Streatham.

EAK and family stay at Chawton Great House for two months.

April 5 Napoleon abdicates and is exiled to Elba.

May 9 *Mansfield Park* published.

Midsummer JA visits the Cookes at Great Bookham.

HTA moves house to 23 Hans Place, London.

August   JA visits HTA in London.

FWA and family move into Chawton Great House and stay there for about two years.

September 3   HTA takes JA home to Chawton.

September 6   CJA's wife Fanny Palmer dies after childbirth.

Autumn   Hinton/Baverstock lawsuit against EAK commences.

November 8   Marriage of Anna Austen and Ben Lefroy at Steventon; they go to live in Hendon.

November 25   JA visits HTA in London.

December 5   HTA takes JA back to Chawton.

December 24   Treaty of Ghent officially ends war with America.

December 26   JA and CEA stay with Mrs. Heathcote and Miss Bigg in Winchester.

1815   *January 2–16*   JA and CEA stay at Steventon, also visiting Ashe and Laverstoke.

March   Napoleon escapes and resumes power in France; hostilities recommence.

March 29   *Emma* finished.

?March or April   JA and CEA probably visit HTA in London.

June 18   Battle of Waterloo finally ends war with France.

July   Mary Lloyd and Caroline stay at Chawton.

August 8   JA starts *Persuasion*.

August   Anna and Ben Lefroy move to Wyards, near Chawton. JA possibly goes to London to negotiate publication of *Emma*, returning early in September.

October 4   HTA takes JA to London; he falls ill, and she stays longer than anticipated.

November 13   JA visits Carlton House; receives invitation to dedicate a future work to the Prince Regent.

December 16   JA returns to Chawton.

End December   *Emma* published, dedicated to the Prince Regent.

1816   *Spring*   JA begins to feel unwell.

HTA buys back MS of *Susan* (*Northanger Abbey*), which JA revises and intends to offer again for publication.

March 15   HTA's bank fails; he leaves London.

May   EAK and Fanny stay at Chawton for three weeks.

May 22   JA and CEA go to Cheltenham via Steventon.

June 15 They return to Chawton via Kintbury.

Midsummer FWA and family move from Chawton Great House to Alton.

July 18 First draft of *Persuasion* finished.

August 6 Persuasion finally completed.

September CEA and Mary Lloyd go to Cheltenham.

December HTA ordained, becomes curate of Chawton.

1817   FWA and family living in Alton this year.

January 27 JA starts *Sanditon.*

March 18 Ceases work on this MS.

March 28 Death of Mr. Leigh-Perrot at Scarlets.

April 27 JA makes her will.

May 24 CEA takes JA to Winchester, where they lodge at 8 College Street.

July 18 JA dies in early morning.

July 24 Buried in Winchester Cathedral.

?Autumn HTA arranges publication of *Northanger Abbey* and *Persuasion.*

End December *Northanger Abbey* and *Persuasion* published together, with 'Biographical Notice' added by HTA.

2

JAN FERGUS

The professional woman writer[1]

You will be glad to hear that every Copy of S[ense] & S[ensibility] is sold & that it has brought me £140 besides the Copyright, if that sh^d ever be of any value. – I have now therefore written myself into £250 – which only makes me long for more.

These words of Jane Austen to her brother Frank, written on July 3, 1813 (*L* 317) after she had published two novels, are those of a professional author who is acutely conscious of her sales (as well as the possible future value of her copyright) and eager to increase her profits. Austen's professionalism here exists in startling contrast to her brother Henry's earliest biographical accounts of her, accounts that helped to create the long-standing myth of Austen as a genteel amateur, the spinster lady author who sketched her novels in moments of leisure. Henry wrote in his first 'Biographical Notice' (printed with *Northanger Abbey* and *Persuasion* in 1818):

Neither the hope of fame nor profit mixed with her early motives ... She could scarcely believe what she termed her great good fortune when 'Sense and Sensibility' produced a clear profit of about £150. Few so gifted were so truly unpretending. She regarded the above sum as a prodigious recompense for that which had cost her nothing ... [S]o much did she shrink from notoriety, that no accumulation of fame would have induced her, had she lived, to affix her name to any productions of her pen ... in public she turned away from any allusion to the character of an authoress.   (*NA, P* 6–7)

Henry's wish to project an image of a ladylike, unmercenary, unprofessional, private, delicate, and domestic author led him to repeat these statements fifteen years later, in the expanded 'Memoirs of Miss Austen' that were printed with Richard Bentley's edition of *Sense and Sensibility*. He then added an anecdote omitted earlier, that Austen refused to meet the writer Germaine de Staël, so as to emphasize Austen's ladylike disdain for publicity.[2] This distaste did not make her less professional, however. During probably the same visit to London (September, 1814) in which she avoided Madame de Staël, she kept a careful eye to business: she was 'in some hope', she wrote, 'of getting Egerton's account [for *Mansfield Park*] before I go away – so we will enjoy ourselves as long as we can' (L 274).

The image that Henry Austen creates – at odds with the evidence that both Austen's letters and her publishing decisions offer of her professionalism – is precisely the one that so annoyed Henry James, according to Brian Southam: 'the myth of the inspired amateur, the homely spinster who put down her knitting needles to take up her pen'.[3] That myth, and others like it, have prevented subsequent readers from understanding that, for Austen, being a professional writer was, apart from her family, more important to her than anything else in her life.

Austen wrote when opportunities for women to publish had never been greater, and from her childhood her aim was to see her works in print. She collected her juvenilia in volumes made to resemble published books as closely as possible. She wrote three novels before she was twenty-five, although she didn't manage to publish them till much later. Her literary career depended to some extent upon the other women novelists of her time, who created and sustained a market for domestic fiction by women, and whose attitudes towards writing, like Austen's own, became increasingly professional. Many of Austen's contemporaries, including Ann Radcliffe, Frances Burney, Charlotte Smith, Elizabeth Inchbald, Maria Edgeworth, and Amelia Opie, among others, received much greater fame and fortune as novelists in their own time than Austen did. But these novelists are only the most visible of a large mass of women who rushed into print at the end of the eighteenth century. The number of women writers increased dramatically throughout the century, as Judith Phillips Stanton's research has shown, but exploded at the end, rising by 'around 50 percent *every decade* starting in the 1760s'.[4]

THE CULTURAL CONTEXT: OBSTACLES TO AUTHORSHIP

This publishing explosion occurred despite the presence of many social obstacles to women's writing. Publishing her own writing could threaten a woman's reputation as well as her social position. For any woman, the fame of authorship could become infamy, and novels were particularly reprehensible, as their famous defence in *Northanger Abbey* indicates (37–8). Proper women, as Henry Austen makes clear, were modest, retiring, essentially domestic and private. Authorship of any kind entailed publicity, thrusting oneself before the public eye – thus loss of femininity. These prejudices led many women besides Austen to publish their first novels anonymously, among them Sarah Fielding, Frances Burney, and Ann Radcliffe; they affixed their names to their works only when their excellent reputations as novelists were established. And writing for profit – professional writing – could be even more disreputable than writing for fame; Henry Austen, in the first passage quoted from him, takes care to assert that at first Austen hoped for neither fame nor profit.

Before Austen's birth in 1775, literature had become firmly fixed in the marketplace, to the dismay of many. Alvin Kernan has succinctly summarized the change: 'An older system of polite or courtly letters – primarily oral, aristocratic, amateur, authoritarian, court-centered – was swept away at this time and gradually replaced by a new print-based, market-centered, democratic literary system.'[5] The public replaced the patron as a source of income. But the older aristocratic attitudes that saw print and payment as vulgar were surprisingly persistent among elite women and some men. Most male writers, however, were happy to be paid for their writing, and once they established themselves in this new literary marketplace, as reviewers, essayists, and so forth, with few exceptions they tended to discourage competition from women writers. They transferred (with renewed energy) much of the old aristocratic disdain for all print to hack writers – the male denizens of Grub Street – and to women who wrote. Women were attacked for having the temerity to write without having the necessary learning and taste. Only desperate financial need, preferably to support aged parents, a sick husband, or destitute children, could (according to literary men) excuse a woman's exposing herself in print to obtain money. Accordingly, women's prefaces often apologize for writing by alluding to distresses of this sort, causing reviewers frequently to condescend kindly to their work, though increasingly they bemoaned the number and grammar of 'female scribblers'.

A woman might also face legal obstacles to authorship if she were married. Married women had no legal existence. They could not own property or sign contracts. Although Charlotte Smith began to publish in order to support herself and her children after her feckless husband was imprisoned for debt, a contract for her novel *Desmond* (1792) survives signed not by her but by Benjamin Smith, who was at the time residing in Scotland under an alias.[6] The publishing records for Ann Radcliffe's *The Romance of the Forest* (1791) list William Radcliffe, her husband, as the work's author; he apparently received £40 for the second edition (1792).[7] Comparable restrictions survived in France within living memory: 'it was not until 1965 that married women were legally permitted to publish a work or to engage in any profession without the consent of their husbands'.[8] Unmarried women in the eighteenth century did not face these restrictions, but they generally lived under their fathers' authority, and fathers (like Frances Burney's) might tend to disapprove of their daughters' risking their modesty, their reputations, and possibly their marriageability by publishing. By contrast, Austen's father tried to help her publish the early version of *Pride and Prejudice, First Impressions*, writing to a possible publisher himself.

THE PROCESS OF PUBLISHING

The obstacles to women's writing make their success in publishing novels all the more remarkable. Admittedly, it was much easier then for authors to have novels published, nationally distributed, and reviewed in the major review journals than it is now. When Austen gave advice to her niece Anna Austen on a novel-in-progress, she assumed that the novel would be not only finished but published. Although today few would be likely to encourage young unpublished writers to expect to see their novels in print, Austen did not hesitate. In her own circle of family and friends, in fact, Austen knew several published authors, many of them women: for instance, her much older friend Anne Lefroy, whose 1804 obituary mentions that she had published poetry when quite young.[9] Austen's mother's first cousin Cassandra Cooke produced *Battleridge: An Historical Tale, Founded on Facts* (2 vols., 1799). Other slightly more distant Leigh cousins published during Austen's childhood: James Henry Leigh's poem *The New Rosciad* appeared in 1785, and Cassandra, Lady Hawke's novel *Julia de Gramont* came out in 1788. In the next year, Austen's brothers James and Henry, along with other friends, began publishing their weekly periodical essays, *The Loiterer*; the collected essays were brought out in 1790. All these books were reviewed in major review journals.[10]

This family access to print must have encouraged the youthful Austen and helps to account for the way that her advice to her niece takes printing for granted, reflecting the greater availability of publication in her lifetime. All writers, known or unknown, who wished to obtain payment for a novel had four options for publishing: (1) by subscription, (2) by profit-sharing, (3) by selling copyright, and (4) on 'commission', a system whereby the author was responsible for paying all the expenses of publication while the publisher distributed the copies and took a commission on all sold. Austen most frequently employed this last form, also known as publishing for oneself. The closest equivalent we have to this method is to employ a 'vanity press' – that is, to pay for printing one's own works. This form of publication, not respected now, means that books will be neither reviewed by the public press nor sold in shops; authors frequently distribute them free of charge. By contrast, in Austen's lifetime a book published on commission was perfectly respectable, as likely as any other book to be reviewed and sold.

Publication by subscription

Subscription was declining somewhat, for it was a cumbersome and demeaning business, and not always remunerative. Subscribers paid for a projected book, preferably in advance. A list of their names would be printed in the work when it appeared. An author solicited subscribers (usually by publishing proposals), kept records, and collected money – or asked friends to do so, rather a heavy tax on friendship because subscribers generally were reluctant to part with cash. Admittedly, Frances Burney made £1,000 – a tremendous sum – by selling subscriptions to *Camilla, or a Picture of Youth* (1796); 'Miss J. Austen, Steventon' is listed as a subscriber in the first volume. Burney also received £1,000 in copyright money for *Camilla*.[11] But her success in combining these two forms of publication was possible only because her reputation was preeminent. The Hookham records show how unlikely such rewards were for other women. A Mrs. Clutterbuck attempted to get subscribers through Hookham and Carpenter for a projected 'Beauties of St. Pierre' in June and July, 1798; she got five and had Hookham return the money (G/127).

Publication by profit-sharing

Profit-sharing became frequent only in the early nineteenth century. Publishers who chose this form of publication paid for printing and advertising, repaid themselves as the books were sold, and shared any profit realized over and above the costs. If the sale did not cover expenses, the firm absorbed the loss. Publishers generally offered profit-sharing to untried authors whose market they could not predict. In some cases, sharing profits could be more remunerative than publishing for oneself or selling copyright. If Austen had published all the editions of her works that appeared during her lifetime by profit-sharing, she would have made more money than she actually did.[12] Obviously, an author who published for himself took all the profits, not just half, but in practice this meant only about 50 per cent more money.

Sale of copyright

To most eighteenth-century British authors eager to dispose of their property, sale of limited copyright for a fee was by far the most prestigious and desirable option available, if they could find a purchaser. The fee offered a clear sum of money, generally payable within a year of publication, and it removed the writer comfortably and decorously from the marketplace as none of the other options did, for the publisher was obliged to pay the sum agreed upon however poorly the work sold. If sales were good and further editions were printed, a publisher who had purchased copyright might send the author an additional payment. Established authors, unwilling to leave themselves at the mercy of publishers' generosity, might contract for additional payments once a specified number of copies or editions were printed or sold, as Radcliffe had probably done when she sold the copyright of *The Romance of the Forest* for an unnamed sum to Hookham and Carpenter.

Publishing on commission

Austen's most frequent mode of publication was at her own risk, or 'on commission' as it was called. The author was ultimately responsible for the cost of paper, printing, and advertising; the publisher kept accounts, distributed the books to the trade, and charged a 10 per cent commission on each copy sold – a kind of royalty in reverse. If not enough copies were sold to cover costs, the author had to make up the difference. Austen herself assumed that this method required an initial outlay of capital: she wrote to her sister on the appearance of the second edition of *Sense and Sensibility* that 'I suppose in the meantime I shall owe dear Henry a great deal of Money for Printing &c' (*L* 250). But surviving publishers' records indicate that as a rule the publisher seems to have paid for production of a book, charging the expenses off against receipts some months later, after the work had sold. Even Hookham and Carpenter, fashionable booksellers but a relatively small publishing firm, operated this way. When Miss Mary Barker published 750 copies of her three-volume novel *A Welsh Story* in June, 1798, Hookham carried the cost of about £61 for paper, not quite £50 for composing, printing, and correcting, and £6 for advertising. Less than half the copies were disposed of by the end of September, so that the author owed the firm over £48 (G/138). This mode of publication could be more remunerative to an author than selling copyright, but clearly the risks were great – to publishers also, if they financed the outlay. Hookham and Carpenter may never have recovered the money owed them by Mary Barker. Her debt of £48 includes the commission gained on selling 180 copies, only about £5. If the work had sold out, their total profit on commission would have been less than £25 – a small sum for which to risk nearly £120.

MONEY AND THE MARKET

Probably the major reason for the explosion of women into print towards the end of the eighteenth century was their need for money. Publishing was one of the few means by which a woman of the middling or upper classes could earn cash. Laetitia-Matilda Hawkins' account of her first venture into print makes this motive clear: 'Some few years previous to this time [Samuel Johnson's death in 1784], being in want of a sum of money for a whim of girlish patronage, and having no *honest* means of raising it, I wrote a downright novel.'[13] Hawkins sold her novel to Thomas Hookham, probably for no more than 10 or 20 pounds – sufficient for 'a whim of girlish patronage' but not for full support. With few exceptions, as Edward Copeland's research has shown,[14] women could not live on their earnings from publishing novels alone; these funds had to supplement other sources of income.

One reason for most women's very limited income from publishing was that the novel-reading public at this time was small. In the 1790s, novels by unknown writers would be published in editions of just 750, 500, or (later) 1,000 copies, while proven novelists might sell 2,000 or 3,000 in one or more editions. The largest known edition for an Austen novel was 2,000, for *Emma* (1816), and it failed to sell out. It took Walter Scott's novels to enlarge the novel-reading public, beginning with the publication of *Waverley* in 1814. The limited market for novels was partly dictated by their cost. All Austen's novels were printed on hand presses similar in principle to those used by Gutenberg three hundred years earlier. These techniques and especially the great expense of handmade paper kept the price of books high,[15] making small editions more economical than large ones unless a strong and steady demand were assured. It was much cheaper to print a small edition of 750 copies and to recompose and reprint if it sold out than to risk a large edition of two or three thousand that might ultimately be sold as waste paper. The paper for even a small edition, like the 750 copies of Mary Barker's *Welsh Story*, absorbed more than half the costs.

Barker's book, unlike those of Austen's brothers and cousins, does not seem to have been reviewed.[16] Reviews were thought then as now to increase sales, though they may have had less influence upon purchases by individuals than upon purchases made by book clubs and book societies, which frequently subscribed to review journals.[17] On the whole, Austen received few reviews – during her lifetime, two for *Sense and Sensibility*, three for *Pride and Prejudice*, none for *Mansfield Park*, and ten for *Emma* (although two of these were written in German). Most were short and reasonably favourable. The longest, on *Emma*, was written by Walter Scott at her publisher John Murray's urging: 'Have you any fancy to dash off an article on "Emma"? It wants incident and romance, does it not? None of the author's other novels have been noticed [by Murray's own periodical, the

Quarterly Review] and surely "Pride and Prejudice" merits high commendation.'[18] Murray sent Austen a copy of the review, and her response survives – a surprising one: 'I return you the Quarterly Reveiw with many Thanks. The Authoress of *Emma* has no reason I think to complain of her treatment in it – except in the total omission of Mansfield Park. – I cannot but be sorry that so clever a man as the Reveiwer of *Emma*, should consider it as unworthy of being noticed' (*L* 313). Austen's response is professional. She regrets Scott's failure to mention *Mansfield Park*, no doubt because the novel had never been reviewed and, more important, because she may have known that sales of the second edition had already stalled by the time she wrote.

AUSTEN'S PUBLISHING CAREER

When Austen arrived in her final home at Chawton on July 7, 1809, she was thirty-four and unpublished, a condition that she was determined to alter. Her earlier attempts to publish *First Impressions* and *Susan*, versions of *Pride and Prejudice* and *Northanger Abbey*, had failed. Cadell and Davies, respectable publishers, had refused George Austen's offer on November 1, 1797 of the manuscript of *First Impressions*. Austen had sold the manuscript of *Susan* to the London publisher B. Crosby and Company and had received £10 for it by 'the Spring of the year 1803', according to her angry letter to the firm on April 5, 1809 (*L* 174). She adopted the pseudonym 'M[rs] Ashton Dennis' for this enquiry to Crosby about the delay in publishing *Susan*; this name allowed her to sign herself 'M.A.D.' Her letter makes clear her determination to publish.

Sense and Sensibility

At this point, Austen had three completed manuscripts available to her: *Susan* (although to publish it, she would have to return Crosby's £10), *First Impressions*, and *Sense and Sensibility*. She chose shrewdly to work on *Sense and Sensibility*. Its emphasis upon the importance as well as the costs of self-command made it her most orthodox novel both aesthetically and morally. *Susan* or *Northanger Abbey* constituted a bold experiment in burlesque over which Crosby had clearly vacillated, thinking it a profitable speculation at first, and then a poor risk. The manuscript version of *Pride and Prejudice* contained an extremely unorthodox heroine, and Austen may have feared either similar vacillation from another publisher, if she succeeded in selling the copyright, or a more ambivalent reception from reviewers and the reading public than *Sense and Sensibility* was likely to obtain. Mary Russell Mitford wrote to a friend in December, 1814, for instance, deploring 'the entire want of taste which could produce so pert, so worldly a heroine as the beloved of such a man as Darcy'.[19] Austen may have approached the publisher Thomas Egerton early in 1811 through Henry. Egerton had sold James' and Henry's *The Loiterer* in his Whitehall shop more than twenty years earlier and may have liked the novel well enough to feel that he would gain prestige by being associated with it. Perhaps more important, he must have felt that he could trust Henry Austen, at this time a banker, to settle the bill for costs.

Once Egerton had agreed to publish the novel on commission, he sent it to the printer Charles Roworth, perhaps in February or March, 1811. Roworth took his time: Austen wrote near the end of April that 'Mrs. K[night] regrets in the most flattering manner that she must wait *till* May [for *Sense and Sensibility*], but I have scarcely a hope of its being out in June. – Henry does not neglect it; he *has* hurried the Printer ...' (L 182). The delay was much worse than Austen anticipated; the novel was not advertised until the end of October. She experienced some delay from printers on *every* novel that she published for herself, though none was as lengthy as this. By contrast, Egerton was later able to issue *Pride and Prejudice* within a few months of purchasing it, doubtless because his own profit was at stake. He would earn less than £36 by publishing *Sense and Sensibility* on commission in an edition of 750 copies, by my calculations, whereas Austen herself made £140, as she wrote to her brother Frank (L 217). It was not worth Egerton's while to hurry the printers.

Although he stood to gain little by agreeing to publish *Sense and Sensibility* on commission, Egerton ran no risk; only the author did. Austen was, according to her brother Henry's 'Biographical Notice', 'so persuaded ... that its sale would not repay the expense of publication, that she actually made a reserve from her very moderate income to meet the expected loss' (NA, P 6). At this time, the expenses of publishing 750 copies of the novel would come to about £155, and advertisements would ordinarily take another £24 or so.[20] The novel retailed at 15s., but the books were accounted for to the author at the trade price of 9s. 6d. If every copy were sold, receipts at the trade price would be over £356, leaving a maximum profit of about £140 after deducting expenses of £179 and Egerton's 10 per cent commission on the sales.

Austen was risking, then, about £180 on the chance of earning £140. In fact, however, her risk was substantially less. The buyer's market for novels was small, but sales to circulating libraries were fairly certain. A novel normally would have to sell between one half and two-thirds of an edition to become profitable. For example, within five months of being issued in February, 1810, Maria Benson's *The Wife. A Novel* had sold 275 of the

500 copies printed, and in two more years another 49, realizing £7.6.4 to split with Longman, who had agreed to share profits with the author.[21] If only 275 copies of *Sense and Sensibility* had sold, Austen would have had £130, less Egerton's 10 per cent, to offset her expenses of £179; that is, she would have owed about £62. If the other 475 copies had been remaindered at the same price that Benson's novel was in 1813 (1s. 6d. each), Austen would have received another £32 or so. At worst, then, her loss was unlikely to be more than £30. Although she probably was unable to 'reserve' such a sum from her own 'moderate income' (her dress allowance had been £20 a year [L 31, 32]), she could perhaps set aside about half. And every additional copy of her novel that was sold at the full trade price of 9s. 6d. would reduce this possible debt. She would break even once 419 copies were bought, even allowing for Egerton's commission. Had Austen known earlier that even at worst her losses were likely to be manageable, she might have published sooner – perhaps when she inherited £50 in 1807. Fortunately, by 1811 Austen was prepared to invest money in herself, in her own authorship.

Pride and Prejudice

Egerton had almost certainly accepted *Sense and Sensibility* by February, 1811. This acceptance evidently made Austen optimistic enough about the possibilities of publication to begin her most ambitious novel to date, *Mansfield Park*. According to Cassandra's memorandum, this novel was begun 'somewhere about Feby 1811 – Finished soon after June 1813' (*MW* facing 242). No other novel took Austen so long to write. Probably part of the time was spent revising *First Impressions* into *Pride and Prejudice*. She perhaps began this revision when she discovered that *Sense and Sensibility* had sold well enough to break even; this point was quite likely to be reached within six months of issue, in May, 1812. By the following November, Austen had completed her revisions to *Pride and Prejudice*, made a fair copy, and sold the manuscript to Egerton for £110, as she wrote to Martha Lloyd: 'Its' being sold will I hope be a great saving of Trouble to Henry, & therefore must be welcome to me. – The Money is to be paid at the end of the twelvemonth.' Austen had been disappointed by Egerton's offer: 'I would rather have had £150, but we could not both be pleased, & I am not at all surprised that he should not chuse to hazard so much' (*L* 197). The offer was rather niggardly. By my calculations, Egerton made a profit of more than £450 on just the first two editions. Austen's unfortunate decision to part with the copyright of *Pride and Prejudice* was made, however, before she could predict that the first edition of *Sense and Sensibility* would sell out and bring her £140.

Issued at the end of January, 1813, *Pride and Prejudice* was Austen's most popular novel, both with the public and with her family and friends. By the spring of 1813, three favourable reviews had appeared (compared to two for *Sense and Sensibility*). Before May, 1813, *Pride and Prejudice* had become the 'fashionable novel', according to Anne Isabella Milbanke, who was to marry Lord Byron.[22] Its popularity eventually meant the end of Austen's anonymity. By the following September, her authorship was pretty well known, as she wrote to her brother Frank: '... the truth is that the Secret has spread so far as to be scarcely the Shadow of a secret now – & that I beleive whenever the 3[d] appears, I shall not even attempt to tell Lies about it. – I shall rather try to make all the Money than all the Mystery I can of it. – People shall pay for their knowledge if I can make them' (L 231). Although Austen joked about both, money was important to her, and anonymity had been so essential that she had had Cassandra write to Godmersham in September, 1811, 'to beg we would not mention that Aunt Jane Austen wrote "Sense & Sensibility"'.[23]

Because she had sold the copyright, Austen did not profit from her most popular novel as she should have done. Egerton probably issued a first edition of 1,000 copies of *Pride and Prejudice* and, in the following October, a second edition of perhaps 750, both of which were sold at 18s., three shillings more than *Sense and Sensibility*. Had Austen published such editions for herself, she would have made about £475, allowing for Egerton's commission of approximately £100, when they sold out – supposing that Egerton had brought them out as economically for her as he did for himself. Certainly he produced *Pride and Prejudice* more cheaply, using cheaper paper and less of it, even though the novel was longer than *Sense and Sensibility*.[24] And furthermore, he seems to have been guilty of overcharging for *Pride and Prejudice*, which cost three shillings more than *Sense and Sensibility*. The latter had in fact been slightly underpriced: Longman charged 16s. 6d. for a shorter three-volume novel like Benson's *The Wife* early in 1810, and retained that price for *She Thinks for Herself*, which appeared almost exactly when *Pride and Prejudice* did and was of comparable length. Austen seems to have been professionally alert to Egerton's manoeuvrings, for she wrote shrewdly to Cassandra on January 29, 1813: 'The Advertisement is in our paper to day for the first time; – 18s. – He shall ask £1 – 1 – for my two next, & £1 – 8 – for my stupidest of all' (L 201). For Austen, 'shall' in the second or third person is always emphatic: it 'commands or threatens', to use an eighteenth-century grammarian's formula.[25] By naming sums in excess of one pound – not yet appropriate for a three-volume novel – she jokingly suggests that she will imitate Egerton's sharp business practices. More seriously, she implies that she will not permit him to undercharge again when her own profit is at stake – and she did not. *Mansfield Park* retailed at 18 shillings.

The success of *Pride and Prejudice* certainly increased the demand for *Sense and Sensibility*, sold out by July 3, 1813, according to a letter written on that date to Frank (*L* 217). It had taken about twenty months to clear the edition. Austen wrote as a postscript to Frank on September 25, 1813, that 'There is to be a 2ᵈ Edition of S. & S. Egerton advises it' (*L* 232), and the second editions of both *Sense and Sensibility* and *Pride and Prejudice* were advertised together on October 29. On the whole, Egerton's advice to Austen was sound. She never lost money by publishing with him, although she had to wait until 1816 before receiving profits on the second edition of *Sense and Sensibility*.[26]

Mansfield Park

In her dealings with Egerton, Austen seems to have learned quickly that his interests were very different from hers. Her wry remark on the price that he charged for *Pride and Prejudice* shows her awareness that he was likely to profit from the novel more than she had – and more than she had profited from publishing *Sense and Sensibility* for herself. After the success of *Pride and Prejudice*, Egerton certainly offered to purchase the copyright of Austen's next novel, but she did not accept his offer. It was no doubt rather low – perhaps £150. She evidently had learned to prefer her own judgment of the value of her work to Egerton's, and she was prepared to risk an unfavourable response from the reading public. In other words, as Austen wrote to her brother, 'I have written myself into £250'; she chose to invest that money in underwriting her own work – wisely (*L* 217). She probably offered *Mansfield Park* to Egerton in January, 1814. On March 21, Austen expected a delay of at least a month before publication: 'Perhaps before the end of April, *Mansfield Park* by the author of S & S. – P. & P. may be in the world. – Keep the *name* to yourself. I shᵈ not like to have it known beforehand' (*L* 262).[27]

Egerton seems to have produced *Mansfield Park* quite cheaply, perhaps at Austen's request. The paper is thinner (thus less expensive) than the thin paper used for *Pride and Prejudice*, and because each page contains twenty-five lines, not twenty-three as in the earlier novels, further savings on paper were achieved. R. W. Chapman has conjectured that Egerton printed only 1,250 copies; later, Henry Austen reminded John Murray that he himself had 'expressed astonishment that so small an edition of such a work should have been sent into the world'.[28] This edition sold out in only six months, more quickly than that of *Pride and Prejudice*, which had taken eight or nine months to clear despite being almost certainly smaller. Using

Chapman's estimate of 1,250 copies, we must assume that Egerton produced *Mansfield Park* extremely cheaply indeed, based on what we know of Austen's earnings. Her profit exceeded £310, more than she received during her lifetime for any novel.[29]

Emma

Austen composed *Emma* in only fourteen months, from January 21, 1814, to March 29, 1815; she was clearly at the height of her genius. During this time, she also saw *Mansfield Park* through the press, made three visits to Henry in London, and three more to other friends. She wrote on November 18, 1814, that the first edition of *Mansfield Park* was sold out, and that her brother wanted her to come to London, 'to settle about a 2^d Edit: – but as I could not very conveniently leave home now, I have written him my Will & pleasure, & unless he still urges it, shall not go. – I am very greedy & want to make the most of it' (*L* 281). She did go, for on November 30, 1814, she wrote: 'it is not settled yet whether I *do* hazard a 2^d Edition. We are to see Egerton today, when it will probably be determined. – People are more ready to borrow & praise, than to buy ... but tho' I like praise as well as anybody, I like what Edward calls *Pewter* too' (*L* 287). Egerton must already have advised against a second edition. He may have pointed to a falling-off in demand for the first edition before it sold out. Austen had hoped in July, 1813, that *Mansfield Park* 'on the credit of P. & P. will sell well, tho' not half so entertaining' (*L* 217). Although in fact *Mansfield Park* sold out faster than *Pride and Prejudice*, perhaps word of mouth reduced later demand. The second edition was finally issued more than a year later on February 19, 1816, by John Murray, who brought out *Emma* at the end of 1815.

Unfortunately, Egerton's advice turned out to be good. Murray's second edition of *Mansfield Park* lost money. In addition, Murray produced Austen's books more expensively during her lifetime than Egerton had, which reduced her possible profit. Nonetheless, her decision to approach Murray was not, on the face of it, a bad one. Murray's imprint carried much more prestige than Egerton's. By the time Austen submitted *Emma* to him in August or September, 1815, he was Lord Byron's publisher and had co-published many of Walter Scott's works, including *Waverley* (1814). Furthermore, Murray was reputedly very open-handed to authors, offering large copy-right fees. Accordingly, once Murray received a favourable opinion of *Emma* from his editor William Gifford, who wrote that 'Of "Emma", I have nothing but good to say', Austen might well have expected a generous fee for the copyright.[30] Instead, on October 15, 1815, Murray offered the sum of £450 altogether for the copyrights of *Emma*, *Mansfield Park*, and *Sense and Sensibility*. Austen commented, accurately enough, 'It will end in my publishing for myself I daresay' (*L* 291). Despite illness, Henry dictated early in November an exasperated reply to Murray: 'The terms you offer are so very inferior to what we had expected, that I am apprehensive of having made some great error in my arithmetical calculation.' He went on to point out that his sister had made more than £450 by one small edition of *Sense and Sensibility* and a moderate one of *Mansfield Park*.[31] Henry's illness worsened, and Austen conducted most of the remaining negotiations for herself. In a letter of November 3, she requested a meeting with Murray, at which time he must have agreed to publish *Emma* on commission, and on November 23 she was already 'vexed' by printers' delays (*L* 295, 297). Murray responded civilly, promising 'no farther cause for dissatisfaction ... In short, I am soothed & complimented into tolerable comfort' (*L* 298).

Hindsight indicates that Murray's offer of £450 for the three copyrights was fair if not generous. Austen would have done well to accept it. First, she would have received that sum within a year. Instead, because losses on the second edition of *Mansfield Park* were set against the profits of *Emma*, Austen received during her lifetime only £38.18.0 profit on her greatest work.[32] Ultimately, her heirs received a total of about £385 more from the sole edition of *Emma*, from the second of *Mansfield Park* (both of which were remaindered in 1821), and from the sale in 1832 of the copyrights of the three novels for £42 each.[33] In short, Murray's estimate in 1815 of the market value of her copyrights was if anything exaggerated. Nonetheless, Murray treated Austen rather less generously than other writers. He frequently gave such large payments to his authors that he lost money by their works. For instance, he offered Helen Maria Williams 50 guineas in 1816 for her pamphlet, *Letters on Protestants*; the work sold out, but Murray still realized a loss of £18.2.6.[34] Austen's refusal to accept Murray's £450 suggests how highly she valued *Emma* and how willing she was to risk a different valuation from the public. Her recent profit on *Mansfield Park* may have encouraged her to insist that Murray publish the fairly large edition of 2,000 copies of *Emma*. Unfortunately, *Emma* was not as popular as her earlier works: in the first nine months it had sold only 1,248 copies. After four years, the total was 1,437, and the rest were remaindered.

Ironically enough, at about the same time that Austen was refusing Murray's money and insisting on publishing for herself, she was exposed to her only experience of 'patronage' – the support of polite letters by wealthy patrons. When *Emma* was in the press, the Prince Regent – who admired the novels – apparently learned of Austen's presence in London and sent his librarian to visit her. This officious and obtuse character, James Stanier Clarke, invited Austen to visit him at Carlton House and during the course of the visit imparted, in her words, 'the Information of my being at liberty to dedicate any future work to HRH. the P.R. without the necessity of any solicitation on my part' (L 296). On November 15, 1815, just over a month before *Emma* was issued, Austen wished to know 'whether it is incumbent on me to shew my sense of the Honour, by inscribing the Work now in the Press, to H.R.H. – I sh^d be equally concerned to appear either Presumptuous or Ungrateful' (L 429). The word 'incumbent' suggests her annoyance. She or perhaps Henry subsequently wrote the briefest possible dedication to be prefixed to *Emma*, and she was obliged to send an expensively bound copy to the Regent; he took no notice of it or the dedication and certainly sent no money. Austen's last letter to Clarke contains her very professional reply to his suggestion that she write 'an Historical Romance, founded on the House of Saxe Cobourg', which she acknowledged 'might be much more to the purpose of Profit or Popularity than such pictures of domestic Life in Country Villages as I deal in'. She concluded, however, 'No, I must keep to my own style and go on in my own way; And though I may never succeed again in that, I am convinced that I should totally fail in any other' (L 312).

Persuasion and Northanger Abbey

When Austen wrote this letter to Clarke on April 1, 1816, she had been writing *Persuasion* for nearly eight months, and the phrase 'though I may never succeed again' – though properly modest – may hint at a fear that this novel might fail to earn money, as her second edition of *Mansfield Park* was failing. At this time, 'Profit or Popularity' was of even more concern to her as a writer than it had been. Her family had suffered financial reverses. Her brother Henry's bank had failed on March 15, 1816; he took orders and became a curate in the Chawton neighbourhood. Austen herself had lost £13.7.0 of profit on *Mansfield Park* that had remained in her account with Henry, but fortunately the remainder of her earnings had already been invested in the 'Navy Fives'. Other members of her family were much more seriously affected. Her brother Edward lost £20,000, her uncle James Leigh-Perrot £10,000, her brothers James and Frank several hundreds each. As a result, neither Frank nor Henry could afford any longer to contribute to their mother's income.[35] These losses and threats may have kept Austen from any immediate attempt to publish *Northanger Abbey*, which Henry had probably reclaimed from the London publisher Crosby, returning his £10, fairly soon after the publication of *Emma*.[36] In any case, the strain of so many family reverses helped to undermine Austen's own health. Symptoms of Addison's disease, which eventually killed her, may have shown themselves early in 1816.[37]

When *Persuasion* was finally completed on August 6, 1816, almost precisely a year after it was begun on August 8, 1815, Austen put it aside for longer than any other novel, probably because of the family's financial troubles. In February, 1817, she received the first small profits on *Emma*. At this point, she had two completed but unpublished novels on her hands. Possibly she had expected that she could use earnings on *Emma* to underwrite the publication of *Northanger Abbey* or *Persuasion*, or both. Her meagre profit of about £39 may have caused her to write to her niece Fanny Knight on March 13, 1817: 'I have a something ready for Publication, which may perhaps appear about a twelvemonth hence' (*L* 333). Austen perhaps hoped that next year's profits would permit the publication of *Persuasion*. Since the failure of Henry's bank, she had been allowing her half-yearly dividends of £15 on the £600 in the 'Navy Fives' to accumulate in a new account at Hoare's bank; they amounted to £45 by the time she died.[38] She may have planned to draw upon these also, if necessary, to publish *Persuasion* and perhaps *Northanger Abbey* as well. In the same letter, she told Fanny that 'Miss Catherine is put upon the Shelve for the present, and I do not know that she will ever come out' (*L* 333). The phrase 'upon the shelf' is appropriately mercantile, whether applied to an unsuccessful debutante unable to come out into the market or to an unsaleable commodity like a book. Austen's mind and language seem to have been particularly attuned to the market after the disappointing failure to earn money from *Emma*.

Nonetheless, Austen did not permit herself to be discouraged from further publication by illness, by having two unpublished manuscripts by her, by the failure of her second edition of *Mansfield Park*, or by the relative unpopularity of *Emma*. She was forced to postpone publication, but it remained her goal, as is evident in her decision to begin a new novel, *Sanditon*, on January 27, 1817. She wrote twelve chapters before stopping on March 18, 1817, when presumably her health failed. She died four months later.

Although anxiety about money and ill health had prevented Austen from publishing *Persuasion* before her death, her sister Cassandra was evidently determined to see her sister's last works in print. She had Austen's will proved on September 10, 1817. After paying burial expenses of £92, £100 in legacies, more than £22 in probate costs, and £25 in debts, Cassandra owed duty on an estate of £561.2.0.[39] Once the estate was settled, Cassandra arranged to publish the two remaining novels with Murray; as a result, she had no duty to pay on those receipts. Possibly the family's financial problems lay behind the apparent insistence that Murray produce *Northanger Abbey* and *Persuasion* as cheaply as possible: only 1,750 copies were printed on very inexpensive paper. They appeared at the end of December, 1817, and 1,409 copies sold within a year. This four-volume dual publication on commission earned £518.6.5, more than any earlier Austen novel, even though the last 283 copies had to be remaindered at 3s. 1d. each – a far cry from the £1.4.0 retail price.[40] Overall, Cassandra collected £784.11.0 from Murray on this edition and on the final sales of *Emma* and *Mansfield Park*.[41] The sale of the five remaining copyrights to Richard Bentley in 1832 for £210 brought Austen's overall literary earnings to at least £1,625, most of which was received after her death. During her life she received something over £631, perhaps as much as £668 and loose change.[42] She earned, despite her increasing professionalism, rather less than has usually been thought, much less than contemporaries like Maria Edgeworth (£11,062.8.10) or Frances Burney (£4,280).[43]

This £630 or so that Austen 'wrote herself into', to use her own phrase, was not very substantial by any contemporary standard. As Edward Copeland points out elsewhere in this volume, lump sums of money were always translated into yearly incomes. Invested in the Navy Fives, part of Austen's earnings brought her £30 a year, not much more than her dress allowance of £20 a year during her father's lifetime and much less than the income of anyone else in her family.[44] This sum would not afford genteel maintenance to a single woman, even though women alone were certainly supposed to require very little: as Fanny Dashwood puts it, her mother- and sisters-in-law 'will live so cheap' (*SS* 12).

If we depart from Austen's practice, however, and calculate her earnings of just over £630 between 1811 and 1817 as a yearly income of £90, we cannot conclude that she wrote herself into even temporary wealth. Novelists like Amelia Opie and Mary Darby Robinson, who did not invest their earnings but applied them to daily expenses, found that even when they made as much as £150 to £200 a year for several years, those sums did not keep them out of debt despite other sources of income.[45] By contrast, Austen not only invested most of her earnings but allowed the dividends to accumulate in her account at Hoare's bank.[46] When she wrote to her niece Fanny Knight on March 13, 1817 that 'I have a something ready for Publication, which may perhaps appear a twelvemonth hence' (*L* 484), she had learned a month earlier that her profits on *Emma* were small because the second edition of *Mansfield Park* had sold so poorly. Her dividends amounted to £30 by January, 1817; in a year, they would come to £60. I imagine that, after the family catastrophe of Henry's bankruptcy a year before, and the weak sale of *Mansfield Park*, Austen was waiting to publish *Persuasion* (and perhaps *Northanger Abbey*) until she could underwrite the publication herself. We see here, I believe, and in her continuing (until March 18) despite failing health to write her new novel *Sandition*, perhaps the most poignant evidences of Austen's professionalism.

NOTES

1 The arguments in this essay summarize and expand those presented earlier in *Jane Austen: A Literary Life* (London: Macmillan, 1991).

2 [Henry Austen,] 'Memoir of Miss Austen', in Jane Austen, *Sense and Sensibility* (London: Richard Bentley, 1833), p. ix.

3 B. C. Southam, ed., 'Introduction', *Jane Austen: The Critical Heritage* (London: Routledge and Kegan Paul, 1968), p. 32.

4 'Profile of Women Writing in English from 1660 to 1800', *Eighteenth-Century Women and the Arts*, ed. Frederick M. Keener and Susan E. Lorsch (New York: Greenwood Press, 1988), p. 248.

5 Alvin Kernan, *Printing Technology, Letters & Samuel Johnson* (Princeton: Princeton University Press, 1987), p. 4.

6 Judith Phillips Stanton, 'Charlotte Smith's "Literary Business": Income, Patronage, and Indigence', in Paul J. Korshin, ed., *The Age of Johnson*, vol. 1 (New York: AMS Press, 1987), pp. 376–7.

7 Hookham and Carpenter published *The Romance of the Forest*. Their records are located in the Public Record Office, C104/75/1–3. They comprise three ledgers, the first labelled F (= 1), the second G (= 2), and the third Petty Ledger F (= 3). This information comes from the Petty Ledger, p. 191, where the name is spelled 'Mr Ratcliff'. All subsequent references to the ledgers will be indicated in the text by the alphabetical abbreviation of the ledger followed by page number.

8 Carla Hesse, 'Reading Signatures: Female Authorship and Revolutionary Law in France, 1750–1850', *Eighteenth-Century Studies*, 22:3 (1989), 486.

9 *Gentleman's Magazine*, vol. 84, part ii (Dec. 1804), 1178.

10 See Antonia Forster's *Index to Book Reviews in England, 1775–1800*, to be published by the British Library.

11 Frances Burney, *Camilla*, ed. Edward A. and Lillian D. Bloom (Oxford: Oxford University Press, 1982), pp. xix–xx.

12 Jan Fergus and Janice Farrar Thaddeus, 'Women, Publishers, and Money, 1790–1820', *Studies in Eighteenth-Century Culture*, 17 (1987), 198 and n. 38, 206–7.

13 Laetitia-Matilda Hawkins, *Memoirs, Anecdotes, Facts, and Opinions*, 2 vols. (London: Longman, Hurst, *et al.*, 1824), 1:156.

14 Edward Copeland, *Women Writing about Money: Women's Fiction in England, 1790–1820* (Cambridge: Cambridge University Press, 1995), ch. 7. See also calculations of various levels of income, pp. 24–33.

15 When Austen sold the copyright of *Susan* for £10 in 1803, novels cost about 3s. 6d. per volume; by 1813, they had doubled: Egerton charged 6s. per volume for *Pride and Prejudice*.

16 See Forster, *Index 1775–1800*.

17 Jan Fergus and Ruth Portner, 'Provincial Subscribers to the *Monthly* and *Critical Reviews*, and their Book Purchasing', O M Brack Jr., ed., *Writers, Books, and Trade: An Eighteenth-Century Miscellany for William B. Todd* (New York: AMS Press, 1994), p. 167.

18 Samuel Smiles, *A Publisher and his Friends: Memoir and Correspondence of the Late John Murray*, 2 vols. (London: John Murray, 1891), 1:228.

19 Mary Russell Mitford, *The Life of Mary Russell Mitford*, ed. A. G. L'Estrange and William Harness, 3 vols. (London: Richard Bentley, 1870), 1:300.

20 I have arrived at these figures by examining the Archives of the House of Longman, microfilmed by Chadwyck-Healey (Cambridge, England), hereafter cited as Longman; I have used Longman's costs for books of comparable length produced at the same time as Austen's to calculate the probable sizes and costs of editions she published with Egerton (whose records do not survive). Because my conclusions about Austen's editions and profits differ significantly from other accounts, I have documented my calculations in detail in the notes to ch. 5 of *Jane Austen: A Literary Life*; those interested may refer to those notes. The Longman records usefully supplement those of Austen's later publisher John Murray. For very different estimates of Austen's editions and profits, see (among others) Jane Aiken Hodge, 'Jane Austen and her Publishers', John Halperin, ed., *Jane Austen: Bicentenary Essays* (Cambridge: Cambridge University Press, 1975), pp. 75–85.

21 Longman reel 1, I/2/156.

22 Quoted by David Gilson, *A Bibliography of Jane Austen* (Oxford: Clarendon Press, 1982), p. 25.

23 Quoted by Le Faye in William and Richard Arthur Austen-Leigh, revised and enlarged by Deirdre Le Faye, *Jane Austen: A Family Record* (London: The British Library, 1989), p. 167.

24 These estimations are based upon Gilson's bibliographical analysis of the novel: despite being somewhat longer than *SS*, *PP* was printed in fewer sheets, 36.5 instead of 38, using slightly smaller type in the second and third volumes. With his own profits at stake, Egerton shaved costs.

25 Robert Lowth, *A Short Introduction to English Grammar* (1762), p. 58, quoted by K. C. Phillipps, *Jane Austen's English* (London: André Deutsch, 1970), p. 125.

26 See Austen's note of 'Profits of my Novels', reproduced in facsimile in *Plan of a Novel* (Oxford: Clarendon Press, 1926); hereafter cited as 'Note on profits'.

27 Sidney Ives, *The Trial of Mrs. Leigh Perrot* (Boston: Stinehour Press, 1980), p. iii; Deirdre Le Faye conjectures that this fragment was written to Frank Austen, *Jane Austen: A Family Record*, p. 188.

28 Bodleian MS Autog d 11/244^r; printed in William and Richard Arthur Austen-Leigh, *Jane Austen: Her Life and Letters. A Family Record*, 2nd edition (London: 1913; reissued New York: Russell and Russell, 1965), p. 311.

29 Austen must have made over £310 from *MP*, according to the letter from Henry to John Murray cited later in the text, for Henry asserts that she received from her small edition of *SS* (£140) and a moderate one of *MP* more than the £450 Murray had offered for the copyrights of *SS*, *MP*, and *E*. She also invested the bulk of profits from her novels in £600 worth of 'Navy Fives', according to her own 'Note on profits'. Scholars have assumed that this £600 represents clear profit, but in fact 'Navy Fives' always sold at a discount during the period when Austen could have purchased them. Her investment cost her less than £600, and her profits were accordingly smaller than has been assumed. Although we cannot calculate her earnings precisely without knowing the date on which she made her purchase, we can nonetheless infer the size of the first edition of *MP* and arrive at an approximation of Austen's profits on it. Accordingly, I calculate that she earned from £310 on *MP* to a little over £347.

30 Quoted by Gilson, *A Bibliography of Jane Austen*, pp. 66–7.

31 Bodleian MS Autog d 11/224^r; W. and R. Austen-Leigh, *Jane Austen: Her Life and Letters. A Family Record*, p. 310.

32 See 'Note on profits'.

33 Exactly 539 copies of *E* were remaindered at 2s. apiece on January 25, 1821, 498 copies of *MP* at 2s. 6d., and 282 copies of *NA* and *P* at 3s. 1d. (Murray Archives, BB 1/228–9; BB 1/242–3; BB 2/28–9; Copies Ledger B/151). British Library Add. Mss. 46611, ff. 305, 311, 313 records the sale of Austen's copyrights to Richard Bentley. Austen and her heirs also received profits on the second edition of *Sense and Sensibility*, which came to about £32 during her lifetime, according to her 'Note on profits', and an unknown sum afterwards; the existence of this edition no doubt helped to lower Murray's offer for the three copyrights.

34 Murray Archives, Copies Day Book (CB)/B/128.

35 Le Faye, *Jane Austen: A Family Record*, pp. 211, 222.

36 James Edward Austen-Leigh, *Memoir of Jane Austen*, ed. R. W. Chapman (1926; rpt. Oxford: Clarendon Press, 1967), p. 138. The *Memoir* was originally issued in 1870.

37 For this diagnosis, see Zachary Cope, 'Jane Austen's Last Illness', reprinted in *Collected Reports of the Jane Austen Society, 1949–1965* (1967; rpt. Folkestone: William Dawson and Sons, 1990), pp. 267–72.

38 Elizabeth Jenkins, 'Some Banking Accounts of the Austen Family', *Annual Report of the Jane Austen Society* (1954); rpt. *Collected Reports of the Jane Austen Society, 1949–1965*, intro. Elizabeth Jenkins (1967; rpt. Overton, Hampshire: Jane Austen Society, 1990), p. 59.

39 *Collected Reports, 1966–1975*, p. 39 (1967). Legacy duty came to £16.16.8; see Le Faye, *Jane Austen: A Family Record*, p. 233.

40 Murray Archives, Copies Ledger B/142,151.

41 Murray Archives, Customer Ledger D/550.

42 Austen had received during her lifetime more than £310 (and up to £347) from *MP*, £250 from *SS* and *PP*, £71.6.1 partial profits on *E* and the second edition of *SS*; Cassandra's £784.11.0 from Murray and £210 from Bentley bring the total to £1625.17.1 at least (see British Library Add. Mss. 46611, ff. 305, 311, 313). Some further payments from Egerton for the second edition of *SS* were certainly also received, and more profit on *MP* is very likely.

43 Fergus and Thaddeus, 'Women, Publishers, and Money, 1790–1820', p. 205, n. 27.

44 Her sister Cassandra had an income of £50 a year from the legacy of £1,000 left her by her fiancé Tom Fowle; her mother had by her own account £122 a year in 1820 (Richard A. Austen-Leigh, *Austen Papers, 1704–1856* [London: Spottiswoode, Ballantyne, 1942], p. 264); even her brother Henry after his bankruptcy obtained the curacy of Chawton at 52 guineas a year (Le Faye, *Jane Austen: A Family Record*, p. 212).

45 Jan Fergus and Ruth Portner, 'Women, Publishers', *passim*.

46 *Collected Reports of the Jane Austen Society, 1949–1965*, intro. Elizabeth Jenkins, 1976; reprinted by the Jane Austen Society, 1990, p. 59 (Report for 1954).

3

RACHEL M. BROWNSTEIN

Northanger Abbey, Sense and Sensibility, Pride and Prejudice

'For what do we live', Mr. Bennet exclaims to his favourite daughter late in *Pride and Prejudice*, 'but to make sport for our neighbours, and laugh at them in our turn?' (*PP* 364). The question is rhetorical – an answer, not a proper question – and Jane Austen's moral critics have sternly remonstrated with those who read it as the novelist's own answer. They explain it away as an epigram, only Mr. Bennet's philosophy, to be read ironically – by which they mean dismissively. And indeed Mr. Bennet is particularly obtuse, his wit ill-advised, when he says what he does while chuckling over the letter in which Mr. Collins reports that his patroness, Lady Catherine de Bourgh, disapproves of a marriage between Elizabeth and Darcy. Earlier in the novel, when her father read a letter from the same unctuous writer, Elizabeth was his pleased collaborator, asking, 'Can he be a sensible man, sir?', so Mr. Bennet could complacently reply, 'No, my dear; I think not. I have great hopes of finding him quite the reverse. There is a mixture of servility and self-importance in his letter, which promises well. I am impatient to see him' (64). Now Elizabeth is in love with Darcy; she has just refused to promise Lady Catherine de Bourgh not to marry him; she cannot possibly laugh at what her parent takes to be the absurd rumour of her impending marriage ('Mr. Darcy, who never looks at any woman but to see a blemish, and who probably never looked at *you* in his life!' [363]). When Mr. Bennet urges her to be 'diverted', not '*Missish*' (363–4), Elizabeth can only muster a strained smile and a nervous laugh. 'Her father had most cruelly mortified her, by what he said of Mr. Darcy's indifference, and she could do nothing but wonder at such a want of penetration, or fear that perhaps, instead of his seeing too *little*, she might have fancied too *much*' (364). Because it is glib as well as blind, her father's self-confidence threatens her own. When Elizabeth was first 'mortified' by Darcy's dismissal of her beauty ('tolerable; but not handsome enough to tempt *me*'), she forced a laugh and 'told the story ... with great spirit among her friends'; Mr. Bennet's daughter has, after all, 'a lively, playful disposition, which delighted in any thing ridiculous' (12). But now she is worried that Darcy's own 'notions of dignity' might make him accept his aunt's 'ridiculous' arguments against her; and she is weaker than she was, living now neither to make sport for her neighbours nor to laugh at them, but more anxiously and narrowly for love.

The sympathetic reader is inclined to deplore Mr. Bennet's failure of penetration as Elizabeth does, and reflect that it is of a piece with what we (along with her) have come to recognize as his general insufficiency – as the lax, irresponsible father who invited disaster by allowing Lydia to follow the soldiers to Brighton; the overly caustic parent who embarrassed Mary in public to stop her singing ('You have delighted us long enough' [101]), and flippantly recommended Wickham to Elizabeth as 'a pleasant fellow, [who] would jilt you creditably' (138); the husband guilty of breaching decorum by exposing his wife to the contempt of her daughters. At this point in the story, one tends not to reflect (as one might) that he behaved more reason-ably than not when he refused to lock up his wild daughter, silenced his doltish one, teased Elizabeth for a silly infatuation, and, years before, chose the detached pleasures of 'the true philosopher' over more foolish or vicious occupations when his pretty wife proved silly and 'all his views of domestic happiness were overthrown' (236). The courtship plot is approaching closure, and feeling seems more important than reason, especially as the dialogue of father and daughter in volume III follows a long passage in the free indirect style that gives us access to Elizabeth's thoughts. Mr. Bennet seems a flat, static comic character, merely the sum of his 'quick parts', in comparison to his daughter, who has depth and feeling as well as 'some-thing more of quickness than her sisters' (5).

Nevertheless, undercut as it is by his character and circumstances, Mr. Bennet's remark is part of what *Pride and Prejudice* says and means. The epigram leaps off the page; like the narrator's happy formulation about Charlotte Lucas, that 'without thinking highly either of men or of matrimony, marriage had always been her object' (122), it claims truth by thus leaping, and by moving with authority from the particular to the general. Rejecting great expectations (like Elizabeth's), it speaks to the portions of our brains that suspect romantic fiction – portions Jane Austen has cultivated. Its economical phrasing, its symmetry and sense, its philosophical detachment, are appealing not merely for their own sakes but because they are among this novel's values. Mr. Bennet's question reflects with striking accuracy the world of *Pride and Prejudice*, in which social interactions are the substance of life. Even the romantic plot begins as Elizabeth makes sport for Darcy, and she laughs at him in her turn; and towards the end, when Jane Bennet gets engaged, the narrator looks away from the main characters to tell us that 'the Bennets were speedily pronounced to be the luckiest family in the world, though only a few weeks before ... they had been generally proved to be marked out for misfortune' (350). In the world of Austen's novels, all the people who don't inherit property depend for their lives on what the neighbours say about them, spend their time exchanging gossip or 'news' about one another, and quite reasonably feel themselves to be (in the words of Henry Tilney of *Northanger Abbey*) 'surrounded by a neighbourhood of voluntary spies' (*NA* 198). It is tempting to read Mr. Bennet's remark as a self-conscious gesture by the novelist: like Jane Austen, he relishes people and gossip, and moves easily from observations about his fellows to moral philosophy. If his detachment is not exemplary, his disinterest is. When we consider the answers that other characters in *Pride and Prejudice* might give to the big question – if it occurred to them – of what we live for, Elizabeth's father's seems not half bad: living to make sport for our neighbours and to laugh at them in our turn is more generous and civil than living to make self-aggrandizing marriages or to attend to our own and our family's best interests, as most people in the novel, and elsewhere, do.

Most readers will agree that Jane Austen wants us to condemn those people – most people – but Mr. Bennet's philosophy still strikes most as insufficient, antithetical to the values of feeling, sympathy, and love that most people profess. Austen's irony thwarts readers in search of straight answers to big questions; her novels formulate only to undercut them. Meanwhile the seriousness of her irony baffles those readers who think wit must be either decorative or definitive. I begin here with Mr. Bennet because playful and purposeful irony seems to me the most important thing about Jane Austen. One of her acquaintances recalled of Austen that 'her keen sense of humour ... oozed out very much in Mr. Bennett's [*sic*] Style',[1] and his accents, or the more cynical tones of La Rochefoucauld, are audible in a gossipy letter she wrote to her sister Cassandra in 1799: 'Whenever I fall into misfortune, how many jokes it ought to furnish to my acquaintance in general, or I shall die dreadfully in their debt for entertainment' (*L* 38). But my argument here is not biographical; nor do I propose to take issue with Henry Austen's nervous insistence that his sister 'drew from nature; but, whatever may have been surmised to the contrary, never from individuals' ('Memoir', *NA*, *P* 7–8). Rather, I want to consider the conjunctions of romantic narrative and ironic commentary in Jane Austen's first three full-length novels, *Northanger Abbey*, *Sense and Sensibility*, and *Pride and Prejudice*.

These novels present themselves as a group on the basis of a 'memorandum' Cassandra Austen jotted down after her sister's death, stating that all three were drafted in the 1790s. Because they were published much later and no manuscripts survive, it is impossible to know how closely the drafts correspond to the novels as we know them, or what revisions were made and when Jane Austen made them, or which novels should rightly be considered her first, second, and third. *Sense and Sensibility* was the first of the works to be published, but a version of *Pride and Prejudice* called *First Impressions* was probably the first long novel she completed; *Northanger Abbey* remained in manuscript until after the novelist's death, but *Susan*, the first novel she sold to a publisher, who advertised but failed to print it, was evidently a version of the book that finally appeared in 1818. As the facts, such as they are, prevent a critic from relying on the standard plot of growth and development, they free her to devise another one. This essay will consider the ways irony interrogates romance and romanticism, in these three novels. I will conclude with *Pride and Prejudice* because it provides a happy ending, the balance of forces being most strenuous and perfect there: disengagement from romance is a simpler pleasure in *Northanger Abbey*, and in *Sense and Sensibility* both satire and sentiment are more problematic.

Jane Austen, in her twenties, is easily imagined as asking herself what we write novels for, and answering that she for one wrote to criticize and perfect the form. Her early novels are all brilliantly aware of themselves as novels – heroine-centred domestic fictions of a kind that became popular in the wake of Samuel Richardson's *Pamela* (1742) and *Clarissa* (1747–8). By the time she began writing, the genre had been widely criticized on moral and aesthetic grounds. Focused on the education and courtship of a virtuous virgin, courtship novels – many of them by women – reflected the concerns of a culture in change, which debated the nature of authority and personal distinction, and the value of sentiment and the sentient self. The woman-centred novel was deliberately didactic, conscious of setting standards of morality and behaviour in a world that wanted them. It was critical of mere materialism; it valued genteel manners, female subjectivity, women's lives, and affection in marriage, and above all the unique, superior, integral self. Novels about a young woman's courtship and marriage – crucial to the cultural revolution we call romanticism – were Jane Austen's favourite reading; the novels she wrote in her turn laugh at them in Mr. Bennet's spirit, conscious of being novels themselves. Embracing and parodying the novel form, Austen keeps a neighbourly distance from its tropes and premises, seeing them as analogues of her culture's conventions and values. Her sense of the novel's limits permeates her moral, witty fictions, offering itself – in lieu of any ideal romantic heroine, in place of any clear didactic message – as a model of human behaviour.

NORTHANGER ABBEY

The mixed mockery and defence of fiction in *Northanger Abbey* is evident from the first sentence, which (like the more famous first sentence of *Pride and Prejudice*) repeats so as to mock what the neighbours (other writers and readers) think and say. Here the subject is the idea of a heroine: 'No one who had ever seen Catherine Morland in her infancy, would have supposed her born to be an heroine' (*NA* 13). Clearly 'no one', i.e. everyone, is wrong. Catherine, named in the first sentence of a novel, is sure to be a heroine, whatever that means. Along with those conditional verbs, the initiating negative, the excessive emphasis, the peculiar pauses imposed by the comma and the queer 'an' before 'heroine' that forces one to say it (here, but nowhere else) with an extra-hard aspirate or no 'h' at all – all these serve to question the very idea of a heroine. Even if we know nothing about the books that Catherine's neighbours read, we have no trouble understanding that idea, or the reasons why Catherine would seem an unlikely heroine. She is plain, not beautiful, and happy and healthy rather than victimized and pathetic. Preferring rolling down a hill, and boys' games, to 'the more heroic enjoyments of infancy, nursing a dormouse, feeding a canary-bird, or watering a rose-bush' (13), she is unfeminine. Nurturing is not her game – until she grows up and begins to curl her hair and read the books that encourage a girl to behave like other girls – that is, like that extraordinary representation of conventional femininity, a romantic heroine. Mocking the implausible exaggerations and clichés of novelists, Jane Austen simultaneously suggests that these reflect society's expectations of genteel girls. As Catherine becomes a heroine inevitably, by growing up, Austen makes the point that social and literary conventions collaborate with biology to construct femininity – much as Simone de Beauvoir does in *The Second Sex*, where she memorably declares, 'One is not born, but rather becomes, a woman.'[2] If the novelist is less outraged by her insight than the twentieth-century polemicist is, she is also more chary than de Beauvoir of the romantic idea of the heroic or transcendent self.

Concluding her introduction of Catherine, the narrator writes that 'when a young lady is to be a heroine, the perverseness of forty surrounding families cannot prevent her. Something must and will happen to throw a hero in her way' (16–17). *Northanger Abbey* sets about to make a heroine of Catherine Morland in the manner of sentimental novelists, by arranging the young lady's entrance into the social world. Ineptly chaperoned by empty-headed Mrs. Allen, she is taken from her father's country parish, where heroes are hard to come by, to the resort city of Bath: location will turn out to be as important as a hero or a novelist in making a young lady a heroine. In Bath, ignorant Catherine sets about to learn what the manners of good society are and what they mean and mask, and how to behave herself and judge others; later, at Northanger Abbey, she is threatened by the more inchoate and intimate sinister forces of the eponymous abbey and her own imagination, and her education continues. That Catherine does not in fact change or learn very much – her mind being, first and last, 'warped by an innate principle of general integrity' (219), in Henry Tilney's wry formulation – is an ironic comment on novels of education. As Catherine reads and discusses gothic novels in Bath, and schemes to visit a castle in the neighbourhood, Austen elides the differences between didactic, moral domestic novels and the more sensational and fantastic gothic novels that were the rage in the 1790s. *Northanger Abbey*'s take on tropes of fiction, kinds of readers, and modes of reading is too thoroughly riddled with ironies to allow one to categorize it comfortably as parody or pastiche.

Austen's most sustained defence of fiction occurs at the end of the fifth chapter of the first volume of this novel. It is presented as a digression – an abrupt disengagement, really – from the account of Catherine's swiftly developing intimacy with Isabella Thorpe. The young ladies, the narrator reports, are such great friends that

> if a rainy morning deprived them of other enjoyments, they were still resolute in meeting in defiance of wet and dirt, and shut themselves up, to read novels together. Yes, novels; – for I will not adopt that ungenerous and impolitic custom so common with novel writers, of degrading by their contemptuous censure the very performances, to the number of which they are themselves adding – joining with their greatest enemies in bestowing the harshest epithets on such works, and scarcely ever permitting them to be read by their own heroine, who, if she accidentally take up a novel, is sure to turn over its insipid pages with disgust. (37)

The language in which other novelists are criticized is violent; the pleasure in departing from their practice is gleeful. Still, the writer insists that novels, 'which have only genius, wit, and taste to recommend them', are vastly superior to the 'threadbare strains' of reviewers and the productions of literary hacks, 'the nine-hundredth abridger of the History of England, or ... the man who collects and publishes in a volume some dozen lines of Milton, Pope, and Prior, with a paper from the Spectator, and a chapter from Sterne' (37–8). She makes a stirring declaration of solidarity with her fellows ('Alas! if the heroine of one novel be not patronized by the heroine of another, from whom can she expect protection and regard? ... Let us not desert one another; we are an injured body' [37]), naming individuals – 'Cecilia, or Camilla, or Belinda', novels, or heroines – as members of this 'body'. Novels are conflated with heroines, novelists praised for exhibiting 'the greatest powers of the mind ... the most thorough knowledge of human nature, the happiest delineation of its varieties, the liveliest effusions of wit and humour' (38). Austen's defence of the gothic novels that Catherine and Isabella read and talk about, which this declaration conspicuously ignores, will also rest on their truth to – their imbrication in – human nature. Favouring individuals over abstractions, moving swiftly from the specific to the philosophical and general, the narrator's rhetoric is very like Mr. Bennet's.

Catherine's necessary hero is introduced to her altogether prosaically, as a dancing partner, by the master of ceremonies whose job it is to make such introductions. Romantic fiction is implicitly debunked by this event, also by the fact that Catherine likes Henry Tilney immediately, and that that makes him like her: far from being overwhelmed by her heroinical qualities, 'a persuasion of her partiality for him [is] the only cause of giving her a serious thought' (243). The tropes of stock romance are parodied as, for instance, the requisite separation of the lovers is effected by Isabella Thorpe and her brother John, who physically restrain Catherine, each holding onto one arm, when she struggles to follow Henry and his sister down the street. Longing for the more elegant Tilneys, our heroine is entangled with the vulgar Thorpes, because she was so quickly taken up by the importunate, scheming Isabella – who as it turns out is being courted by her own brother James. The several brother-and-sister pairs, and Catherine's infatuation with both the sisters as well as one of the brothers, make for an ironically unerotic atmosphere in this romance: Henry's clever chaste comparison of marriage to a country dance reflects the novel's sassy sexlessness.

Named perhaps after Jane Austen's favourite brother, but perhaps after 80 per cent of the heroes of the novels she had read,[3] Henry Tilney is an unconventional romantic hero, 'not quite handsome', though 'very near it' (25), and womanishly knowledgeable about not only fiction but fabrics. He is dominated and intimidated by his overbearing father, the General, himself 'a very handsome man, of a commanding aspect, past the bloom, but not past the vigour of life' (80). It is General Tilney, not his son, who pointedly relishes Catherine's physical attractions, appreciating the elasticity of her walk – and causing her to walk on 'with great elasticity, though she had never thought of it before' (103). (Sir Thomas Bertram of *Mansfield Park*, another propertied paterfamilias, also makes a young woman blush by appreciating her body.) The General invites Catherine to Northanger Abbey: misinformed that she is an heiress, he means to marry her to his clergyman son. (His older son Frederick, who will inherit Northanger Abbey, is a military man like his father, and a rake.) The coincidence of the heroine's motive and the villain's, along with the hero's passivity, are among the nice ironies that make this romance so cheerful.

The sexy General is commanding, and when he instructs Catherine to ride in Henry's open curricle she agrees, even though she has already learned – and managed to get Mr. Allen to acknowledge – that it is improper for a young lady to ride alone with a gentleman in an open carriage. In the carriage Henry sets her up to expect 'all the horrors that a building such as "what one reads about" may produce' (157). He encourages her to expect to be lodged in a 'gloomy chamber – too lofty and extensive for you, with only the feeble rays of a single lamp to take in its size – its walls hung with tapestry exhibiting figures as large as life, and the bed, of dark green stuff or purple velvet, presenting even a funereal appearance'. Overriding her good-humoured, sensible protests that what he projects is impossible ('This is just like a book! – But it cannot really happen to me' [159]), he predicts what she will find in the secret chambers of the abbey in the matter-of-fact flat tones of the fiction that has captivated Catherine: 'In one perhaps there may be a dagger, in another a few drops of blood, and in a third the remains of some instrument of torture; but there being nothing in all this out of the common way, and your lamp being nearly exhausted, you will return towards your own apartment' (160). Catherine continues to protest that she is nothing like a gothic heroine, but she is drawn in by the familiar formulas; because she likes him, she falls for attractive Henry Tilney's skilful straight-faced teasing even though she was able to recognize it for what it was from the beginning, in Bath, when he solemnly discussed the durability and cost of muslin with Mrs. Allen, and she feared 'as she listened to their discourse, that he indulged himself a little too much with the foibles of others' (29).

Once they reach the abbey, and the cooperative elements provide the requisite storm, Catherine begins to imagine gothic horrors. For all its modern kitchens that are the General's particular pride, Northanger Abbey was 'a richly-endowed convent at the time of the Reformation' (142) and it is still redolent of the sinister spirituality and romance of a repudiated religion, therefore of stories like Ann Radcliffe's that are set on the dangerous, exotic continent of Europe. The General is imposing; his children are afraid of him; to Catherine, it is logical to imagine that he must have murdered his wife in the Abbey. Catherine is energetic, curious, and only seventeen; she has longed to visit an atmospheric old building the way she has wanted to dance, to walk, to learn to appreciate the picturesque, and to love a hyacinth. She is nothing like a quixotic, deluded, isolated reader who prefers romantic fantasies to the actual world: while Jane Austen enjoyed Charlotte Lennox's *The Female Quixote* (1752) and, later, Eaton Stannard Barrett's *The Heroine* (1815), *Northanger Abbey* departs from the Cervantean model. Not only is Catherine too modest to presume herself a heroine of romance, but it would be hard for any girl to do so in a world like hers, where people read novels, and discuss them together – Catherine and Isabella Thorpe, and also Henry Tilney, who finished *The Mysteries of Udolpho* in two days, his 'hair standing on end the whole time' (106), after he made off with his sister's copy of the novel when their reading aloud was interrupted. (The thorough inadequacy of Henry's would-be rival John Thorpe is clear from his ignorance of novels – as well as his loud, profane, slangy talk, which he directs at his horse when he takes Catherine out for a drive. Where Henry's style is personal and his tastes are feminine, macho Thorpe will only admit to having read risqué novels by men, *Tom Jones* and *The Monk*.)

Catherine is too naive and unselfconscious to keep anything like Henry's amused distance from novels; she especially admires Isabella for sounding like 'all the heroines of her acquaintance' (119), and has nothing but a new publication in mind when she expects 'that something very shocking indeed, will soon come out in London' (112). We are persuaded to think her absurd for having horrific 'visions of romance' (199) about the General – but then, on the other hand, they prove to be substantially correct. No wife-murderer, he is evil in a commonplace way – a greedy, scheming, rude social climber; when he discovers that she is not rich after all, he ejects poor Catherine from his house without ceremony, or explanation, or pocket money, at an uncomfortably early hour of the morning, forcing her to travel home alone in a public conveyance, therefore in some degree of danger. Insensitive, inhospitable, and selfish, obsessed with marrying his children for money, he is a villain of 'common life', not romance. The moral would seem to be that our heroine's instincts were good guides to truth – perhaps even that they were good because they were informed by gothic novels about vulnerable women persecuted by powerful men.

But one is warned away from that conclusion as, at the end, the question of a moral is explicitly begged. The happy ending rewards nearly everyone as the narrator, winking at the reader, marries Catherine and Henry and even finds among the incidental *dramatis personae* a husband for Miss Tilney, whose new title allows the General the pleasure of addressing his daughter as 'My Lady'. The narrator ostentatiously leaves 'it to be settled by whomsoever it may concern, whether the tendency of this work be altogether to recommend parental tyranny, or reward filial disobedience' (252). Mockingly rejecting these inversions of commonplace morals and the typical ones they parody, Austen offers, in place of any advice on living, this novel that compares and contrasts itself to its romantic, didactic fellows, its heroine to other heroines. The literary satire of *Northanger Abbey* modulates smoothly into commentary on most people's language, which is so very different from 'the best chosen language' (38) of novelists: Isabella Thorpe's lies and fluent endearments and inflated expostulations, her brother John's profane bluster, and the bland inanities of Mrs. Allen, who 'as she never talked a great deal, so she could never be entirely silent; and, therefore, while she sat at her work, if she lost her needle or broke her thread, if she heard a carriage in the street, or saw a speck upon her gown, she must observe it aloud, whether there were any one at leisure to answer her or not' (60). Henry Tilney is the novel's hero because he mocks commonplaces, pronouncing professorially on the style of women's letters and journals and the loose overuse of words like 'amazingly' and 'nice', and managing to put himself nearly in the frame of the story, alongside the narrator, when he first meets Catherine and anticipates the figure he'll cut in the journal he's sure she keeps:

> I know exactly what you will say: Friday, went to the Lower Rooms; wore my sprigged muslin robe with blue trimmings – plain black shoes – appeared to much advantage; but was strangely harassed by a queer, half-witted man, who would make me dance with him, and distressed me by his nonsense. (26)

(Poor Catherine doesn't know what to say, but recognizes this as clever.) Like Mr. Bennet, Henry is self-indulgent and sometimes goes too far, being too quick to see himself as others might see him. But he shines, in a world where it is not possible to transcend the common lot or the common language, by seeing conventions and fictions for the near relations they are, and appreciating and using them for his purposes. Briefly at a loss for language when he discovers Catherine's suspicions about his father, he charges her with having 'formed a surmise of such horror as I have hardly words to – ' (197). He manages, however, to reprimand her fluently, making a charming fine distinction, as he does so, between her conventional, outlandish fantasies and Catherine herself: 'Dearest Miss Morland, what ideas have you been admitting?' (198).

Catherine, Henry's counterpart, is this novel's heroine because she can give new meaning to available clichés. When she chats in the Pump-room with Eleanor Tilney, the narrator tells us, 'though in all probability not an observation was made, nor an expression used by either which had not been made and used some thousands of times before, under that roof, in every Bath season, yet the merit of their being spoken with simplicity and truth, and without personal conceit, might be something uncommon' (72). The meanings of 'common', a word related to 'communal', range from 'pervasive', to 'banal'; 'uncommon' can mean 'implausible' and also 'rare'. Both words occur frequently in *Northanger Abbey*, which contrasts the implausibilities of romance with the commonplaces of common life – ordinary life, the life we lead in common – only to show that the two have much in common. Mocking conventions and clichés, it suggests that they are inescapable – and that the best and most interesting way to live is with awareness of them, and in dialogue, as this novel is, with others.

SENSE AND SENSIBILITY

Sense and Sensibility (1811) and *Pride and Prejudice* (1813) are longer, more ambitious novels than *Northanger Abbey*: in both, the literary satire is subtler and the social satire broader, and the narrator's engagement with the heroine and the fiction is more complex. The similar symmetrical titles invite the reader to see the novels as a pair, proposing different views of romance and reality, the self and the neighbours, love and laughter.

Most of the laughter in *Sense and Sensibility* is hollow: those who laugh most are most unaware that they themselves make sport for their neighbours. When fastidious Marianne Dashwood corrects him for using a cliché, declaring that she abhors 'every common-place phrase by which wit is intended', bluff Sir John Middleton doesn't understand her – 'but he laughed as heartily as if he did' (*SS* 45). His jolly but coarse mother-in-law, Mrs. Jennings, makes clumsy, stupid jokes – at which nearly everyone laughs – about Elinor Dashwood's lover whose name starts with 'F', perverting wit by establishing 'its character as the wittiest letter in the alphabet' (125). Mrs. Jennings' silly second daughter, Mrs. Palmer, laughs all the time at nothing, hardest of all when her dour, sour, unpleasant husband ignores her: '"Mr. Palmer does not hear me," said she, laughing, "he never does sometimes. It is so ridiculous!"' (107). She anticipates the absurdity of his election to Parliament with more laughter: '"How I shall laugh! It will be so ridiculous to see all his letters directed to him with an M.P."' (113). Edward Ferrars, Elinor's lover, has a foppish brother Robert who is as amused by the church as Mrs. Palmer is by the state; when told that Edward has finally chosen a profession, 'He laughed most immoderately. The idea of Edward's being a clergyman, and living in a small parsonage-house, diverted him beyond measure; – and when to that was added the fanciful imagery of Edward reading prayers in a white surplice, and publishing the banns of marriage between John Smith and Mary Brown, he could conceive nothing more ridiculous' (298).

Elinor and Marianne Dashwood, the novel's earnest and self-conscious heroines, register the failings of their neighbours with more pain than pleasure, scornful Marianne usually averting her eyes while Elinor struggles civilly to keep her countenance. Although Lady Middleton, 'because they were fond of reading, ... fancied them satirical', the Dashwood sisters are hardly that; only the narrator is satirical, observing that Lady Middleton used the word 'perhaps without exactly knowing what it was to be satirical; but *that* did not signify. It was censure in common use, and easily given' (246). *Sense and Sensibility* is as critical of literary and linguistic commonplaces as *Northanger Abbey* is, and its definitions of distinction are more discriminating. As Marilyn Butler observes, it resembles didactic novels by Mrs. West and Maria Edgeworth that were published around the time it was drafted, which compare and contrast 'the beliefs and conduct of two protagonists – with the object of finding one invariably right and the other invariably wrong'.[4] The presence of the third, youngest Dashwood sister, Margaret, hints at Austen's intention to diverge from this pattern. *Sense and Sensibility* corrects the typical didactic emphasis by refusing to choose between Marianne and Elinor. While the action of the novel is mediated by the consciousness of the prudent sister, the narrative rewards both equally.

Marianne and Elinor are more interestingly alike than they are different. The first chapter acknowledges that Marianne has sense as well as sensibility, and that Elinor has 'an excellent heart' (6), and strong feelings as well as prudence. The opposing values of romance and practical realism are debated as each sister takes issue with the conduct and the 'doctrine' of the other. Marianne loves the poetry of Cowper and Scott, and picturesque landscapes; she believes in first and passionate love, a meeting of tastes and minds; she trusts her feelings to guide her conduct. Elinor is more circumspect, more aware of how the self interacts with others; in her view, conventions are necessary and even useful. The sisters are devoted to one another, but they can be cutting in debate, as when Marianne pretends to think Elinor believes that 'our judgments were given us merely to be subservient to those of our neighbours' (94). Each exaggerates and observes and indeed seems deliberately to fashion herself as her sister's opposite. Marianne depends for her identity on Elinor's watchful judgments of her; Elinor fears the force of Marianne's sympathy.

Elinor's view of the self as social, not isolated, is also the narrator's. When Marianne's lover inexplicably leaves town, the characterization of her as a would-be romantic heroine is reminiscent of *Northanger Abbey*'s satire; the difference is made by the emphasis on the feelings of others:

> Marianne would have thought herself very inexcusable had she been able to sleep at all the first night after parting from Willoughby. She would have been ashamed to look her family in the face the next morning, had she not risen

from her bed in more need of repose than when she lay down in it. But the feelings which made such composure a disgrace, left her in no danger of incurring it. She was awake the whole night, and she wept the greatest part of it. She got up with an headache, was unable to talk, and unwilling to take any nourishment; giving pain every moment to her mother and sisters, and forbidding all attempt at consolation from either. Her sensibility was potent enough!

(83)

Later, the social and psychological dangers of showing feeling are excruciatingly dramatized as Marianne insists on claiming intimacy with Willoughby in a crowded ballroom. In contrast, prudent Elinor painfully hears out Lucy Steele's story of Edward Ferrars' secret engagement to her under cover of the noise and music in Lady Middleton's drawing room. Then, heartbroken by the revelation of what she constrains herself to think of, conventionally, as Lucy's secret, she says nothing about it to her mother and sisters, who have assumed, with her, that Edward's mother is the only impediment to her marrying him:

> It was a relief to her, to be spared the communication of what would give such affliction to them, and to be saved likewise from hearing that condemnation of Edward, which would probably flow from the excess of their partial affection for herself, and which was more than she felt equal to support.
>
> From their counsel, or their conversation she knew she could receive no assistance, their tenderness and sorrow must add to her distress, while her self-command would neither receive encouragement from their example nor from their praise. She was stronger alone, and her own good sense so well supported her, that her firmness was as unshaken, her appearance of cheerfulness as invariable, as with regrets so poignant and so fresh, it was possible for them to be.
>
> (141)

Elinor's self-control is contingent, dependent on her control of others. The difference between her chilling chat with Lucy and Catherine Morland's sincere exchange of commonplaces with Eleanor Tilney in the Pump-room at Bath suggests the difference between the views of human nature and human relations in *Sense and Sensibility* and *Northanger Abbey*. As Lucy 'confesses' so as to steer Elinor away from Edward, in an effort to get him back, and Elinor seeks to find out the hurtful truth while convincing Lucy of her perfect serenity and propriety, the young women use what looks like an intimate exchange to strengthen the facades that conceal and serve their opposing purposes.

The world is wider in *Sense and Sensibility* than it is in *Northanger Abbey*: Colonel Brandon has been in the East Indies, and he could talk, were he only lively enough, about 'nabobs, gold mohrs, and palanquins'

(51); the heroines move around England, shuttled by their shifting fortunes from Sussex to Devonshire to London to Somerset. But as other people's lives and histories impinge on theirs, Marianne's and Elinor's moves (to a small cottage, suffocating crowded rooms, and finally adjoining properties, at the very end) seem constricting. While the cultivated Dashwood sisters argue about right conduct and the picturesque, instead of hunting for men, contrasting pairs of sisters underscore or undercut their superiority and gentility, and perhaps even the importance of the contrast between them: big-mouthed Nancy and small-eyed Lucy Steele, who mean to marry as well as possible, and polite Lady Middleton and inappropriate Mrs. Palmer, who already have. Lucy's calculating approach to life and her prohibited love affair with Edward caricature Elinor's, and the passionate love that nearly destroys Marianne is elaborately parodied by the story of the two Elizas that Colonel Brandon tells. The details of that story – a callous parent committed to primogeniture, brothers at odds with one another, two women's lives irrecoverably lost – echo the novel's plots, and its themes of selfishness and greed. Debates about taste seem a luxury, and true gentility a romantic dream, as a divorce and a couple of seductions, a fall into a life of sin and an illegitimate birth, a secret engagement and even a duel, touch the lives of scrupulous and sensitive Marianne and Elinor Dashwood.

Catherine Morland's adventures begin when she leaves her healthy, normal family; their climax comes when General Tilney forces her to leave his house. In contrast, Elinor and Marianne Dashwood are cast out of their home to begin with, by their own close relatives. A chronicle of deaths in the family begins their story. When his sister and housekeeper died, the owner of Norland Park, 'a single man', invited his nephew and heir Henry Dashwood, with his wife and three daughters, to live on the estate so as to care for him; the subsequent death of 'the old Gentleman' ensured the loss of their home, which he left to the father of the Dashwood girls, and then his son by a former marriage and that son's son, a child whose ordinary infantile charms made the old man forget 'all the attention which, for years, he had received from his niece and her daughters'. The death of Henry Dashwood and the occupation of Norland by the greedy John Dashwoods initiate the action. The narrator's even tone implies it is as certain as death that men merely use dependent women, that virtue goes unrewarded, that ingratitude, caprice, and selfishness prevail, that people do active harm and yet remain respectable. The Dashwood family had lived for generations 'in so respectable a manner, as to engage the general good opinion of their surrounding acquaintance' (3); and John Dashwood will clearly not lose the good opinion of his neighbours by leaving his dependent female relatives penniless. He is sketched in three long acidulous sentences:

He was not an ill-disposed young man, unless to be rather cold hearted, and rather selfish, is to be ill-disposed: but he was, in general, well respected; for he conducted himself with propriety in the discharge of his ordinary duties. Had he married a more amiable woman, he might have been made still more respectable than he was: – he might even have been made amiable himself; for he was very young when he married, and very fond of his wife. But Mrs. John Dashwood was a strong caricature of himself; – more narrow-minded and selfish. (5)

Beginning with a polite double negative and quickly modifying it, reiterating 'rather' to make it almost an intensifier, shifting the blame from the man to his wife – as people do – and sympathetically acknowledging John Dashwood's good points, or seeming to, before reverting in a damningly short, emphatic sentence to his character's fixed flaws, the narrator makes it clear that his respectability reflects badly on his neighbours. Towards the end of the novel, when Elinor meditates as generously as she can on the character of her sister's deceiver, she condemns Willoughby in the words used here of John Dashwood: 'Extravagance and vanity had made him cold-hearted and selfish' (331). A world where young men have these vices is a harsh one for young women.

Like all Jane Austen's novels, *Sense and Sensibility* is a comedy that ends in marriages, which traditionally affirm the connections between sexes and families, and between desire and public ritual or social convention. Its portraits of marriages already made are clear signs of the novel's darkness. As John and Fanny Dashwood, in the extraordinary dialogue in chapter 2, talk themselves, like King Lear's evil daughters, into ever less fairness and generosity to John's half-sisters, their marriage is revealed as effectively an anti-social relationship. The marriage of the less well-matched Sir John and Lady Middleton falls short of doing active social ill, but it also unpleasantly illustrates how both individual character and the wider society are affected by the most intimate of chosen social relations. The desperate hospitality of the Middletons is

necessary to the happiness of both; for however dissimilar in temper and outward behaviour, they strongly resembled each other in that total want of talent and taste which confined their employments, unconnected with such as society produced, within a very narrow compass. Sir John was a sportsman, Lady Middleton a mother. He hunted and shot, and she humoured her children; and these were their only resources. Lady Middleton had the advantage of being able to spoil her children all the year round, while Sir John's independent employments were in existence only half the time. Continual engagements at home and abroad, however, supplied all the deficiencies of nature and education; supported the good spirits of Sir John, and gave exercise to the good-breeding of his wife. (32)

The doubling that marriage effects can be negative when two minds move as one, as in the Dashwood dialogue, or, as here, when opposition and balance and antithesis uncomfortably prevail. In both unpleasant families, the fruits of marriage – the undeserving scion of the John Dashwoods, the spoiled and noisy children of the Middletons – are unappetizing. Lady Middleton's empty politeness, especially in view of her mother's and sister's vulgarity, can be called 'good-breeding' only ironically (and punningly) here. The Middletons' relatives, the even more badly matched Palmers, produce a child in the middle of the novel: they also provoke Elinor to reflect on 'the strange unsuitableness which often existed between husband and wife' (118).

Further dimming the view of romantic love is the depressing similarity among the three men who court the Dashwood sisters, repeating one another's moves and mistakes. Each one has had an earlier attachment to another woman; each one, beginning with Colonel Brandon, leaves the Dashwoods abruptly, for unexplained reasons. The suggestion that people may be substituted for one another is developed in a series of misrecognition scenes: Marianne, in her passionate eagerness to see her beloved Willoughby, twice mistakes another man for him, first as Edward Ferrars approaches on horseback, and then when Brandon arrives at the door of Mrs. Jennings' house in London (86, 161); Elinor, trembling with eagerness to see Edward but unwilling to hope, wrongly identifies him as Brandon (358); earlier, waiting for her mother to arrive at Marianne's bedside, she goes to the door to welcome her and finds 'only Willoughby', instead (316). Elinor sees on Edward's finger a ring that contains a lock of hair, supposes it is his sister Fanny Dashwood's, then decides it must be her own; it turns out – dramatically, at the end of volume 1 – to be Lucy's. When considered as candidates for marriage and possible sole heirs of their mother's fortune, sober Edward Ferrars and his silly brother Robert become indistinguishable; as she disowns one and then the other, their own mother can barely tell the difference between them:

> Her family had of late been exceedingly fluctuating. For many years of her life she had had two sons; but the crime and annihilation of Edward a few weeks ago, had robbed her of one; the similar annihilation of Robert had left her for a fortnight without any; and now, by the resuscitation of Edward, she had one again. (373)

In this world where sons and lovers seem interchangeable, where people affect by watching one another, and individuals seem neither integral nor unique, Marianne Dashwood romantically insists on an ideal of perfect self-fulfilment in a love based on mutual feeling and shared tastes, and hence on the impossibility of second attachments; it is one of 'her most favourite maxims' (366). A conversation between Elinor and Brandon, early in the novel, raises the nice question of whether she thinks them unimaginable or immoral:

> 'Your sister, I understand, does not approve of second attachments.'
> 'No,' replied Elinor, 'her opinions are all romantic.'
> 'Or rather, as I believe, she considers them impossible to exist.'
> 'I believe she does. But how she contrives it without reflecting on the character of her own father, who had himself two wives, I know not.' (55–6)

That Mr. Henry Dashwood had two wives – a fact central to the predicament of his daughters – is a poignant context for Marianne's creed; equally poignant is Brandon's loving correction of Elinor's harshly judgmental emphasis, and his sympathetic emendation of his own remark. Second thoughts are characteristic of this revisionary lover, who loves Marianne because she reminds him of the woman he loved before; when in the end he attaches her to himself, he changes her mind.

As nearly everyone but Elinor comes to love more than once, *Sense and Sensibility* comes to a thoroughly unromantic resolution, coupling Marianne with the colonel in the flannel waistcoat, and Elinor – who does not, as we might, count his history and family against him – with the familiar, hapless Edward. The reader is urged to believe that 'Marianne could never love by halves; and her whole heart became, in time, as much devoted to her husband, as it had once been to Willoughby' (379). To balance this, we are assured that Willoughby, although 'he lived to exert, and frequently to enjoy himself', will remember her forever, and make 'her his secret standard of perfection in woman' (379). But the concluding paragraph brilliantly undoes the requisite romantic resolution, by startlingly giving Elinor's and Marianne's attachment to one another pride of place, so as to make their second attachments, to their husbands, seem merely secondary.

> Between Barton and Delaford, there was that constant communication which strong family affection would naturally dictate; – and among the merits and the happiness of Elinor and Marianne, let it not be ranked as the least considerable, that though sisters, and living almost within sight of each other, they could live without disagreement between themselves, or producing coolness between their husbands. (380)

By returning the focus, surprisingly, to the family of origin, by the superfluity of 'naturally' and the ambiguity of 'would dictate', Austen questions by affirming the strength and naturalness of family affection. The words 'though sisters' shifts the ground under the reader who, being assumed to understand that married sisters commonly disagree, is abruptly disengaged not only from the characters and the fiction but from the premise of sisterly affection that the novel never questioned as it detailed the arguments and differences between Elinor and Marianne. The salubrious little distance from one's own reality that fiction provides is suddenly doubled; the reader is placed in an uneasy position where it seems possible – or necessary – to laugh even at oneself.

PRIDE AND PREJUDICE

'I have for the first time looked into "Pride and Prejudice", and it is really a very pretty thing', one of his literary advisers wrote to the publisher John Murray in 1815, when he was considering the manuscript of *Emma*. 'No dark passages,' William Gifford continued approvingly; 'no secret chambers; no wind-howlings in long galleries; no drops of blood upon a rusty dagger – things that should now be left to ladies' maids and sentimental washerwomen'.[5] No one these days would condescend, with such evident class and gender bias, to Jane Austen's masterpiece – any more than they would think of comparing it to a gothic novel. Gifford's comment reminds us that for its first readers *Pride and Prejudice* was a notable departure from the romantic fictions that were still popular and still expected of women novelists. It also reminds us – by miming it – of the novel's own remarkable easy superiority, the confidence with which it makes its critical judgments.

On its title page, *Sense and Sensibility* is identified as a work by 'A Lady'; *Pride and Prejudice*, published two years later, was signed 'by the Author of "Sense and Sensibility"'. In 1813, the author was thirty-seven years old. *First Impressions*, the first version of *Pride and Prejudice*, had been rejected unseen when her father had offered it to a publisher fifteen years earlier, but Jane Austen had continued to believe in it, encouraged by the continuing admiration of her family circle. At twenty-four, she had written playfully to her sister from Bath, about a close friend, 'I would not let Martha read First Impressions again upon any account ... She is very cunning, but I see through her design; – she means to publish it from Memory, & one more perusal must enable her to do it' (*L* 44). Long anticipated and denied, the joy of publishing *Pride and Prejudice* was intense. The author and her family read it aloud, in the evenings, during the week after the book ('my own darling Child') came in the mail from London. Austen searched it for errors, found a few, decided that 'a "said he" or a "said she" would sometimes make the Dialogue more immediately clear', but also that for readers like hers that was unnecessary (L 201–2). Gleefully paraphrasing Sir Walter Scott, she wrote to her sister Cassandra, ' "I do not write for such Dull Elves" / "As have not a great deal of Ingenuity themselves" ' (202). In the mood to flatter her readers and herself, she did so characteristically by indirection, delighting in her own ingenuity, telling Cassandra perversely:

> The work is rather too light & bright & sparkling; – it wants shade; – it wants to be stretched out here & there with a long Chapter – of sense if it could be had, if not of solemn specious nonsense – about something unconnected with the story; an Essay on Writing, a critique on Walter Scott, or the history of Buonaparte – or anything that would form a contrast & bring the reader with increased delight to the playfulness & Epigrammatism of the general stile.
>
> (L 203)

Like anyone who has written in obscurity for years, she felt sure no one would like her work as much as she did; and at the same time she felt grandiosely akin to the most respected author of the day.

She knew that her book had the authority of magisterial discourse – literary criticism or history, the sort of serious, abstract, philosophical, pretentious writing she compared negatively in *Northanger Abbey* to women's novels about people. Its brilliant first sentence takes the tone of a Johnsonian essayist pronouncing on the nature of universals and truths: 'It is a truth universally acknowledged, that a single man in possession of a good fortune, must be in want of a wife.' Takes the tone, of course, so as to mock it. As critics have enjoyed pointing out, that sentence is full of logical holes: *a* truth universally *acknowledged* is probably less than true; and the real truth is not that single men want wives ('in want of' merely means they lack them) but that poor young women need husbands, 'their pleasantest preservative from want' (PP 122–3). Far from describing the state of affairs even around Meryton, that sonorous first sentence, taken at face value, expresses the gossip's fantasy that women exchange or traffic in men, and not vice versa. The novel takes off, in other words, from Mrs. Bennet's notion (or is it only what Mrs. Bennet pretends to believe?): that rich men exist for people to marry. Its irony further suggests that the universal acceptance of this idea may make it operatively true – that what authorities say, and most people acknowledge, matters.

The first sentence of *Pride and Prejudice* pretends to repeat something like a proverb, one of those epigrammatic sayings that Richardson's novels illustrate and debate, like 'A reformed rake makes the best husband', or 'Once subdued, always subdued'. The novel's house moralist, Mary Bennet, rattles off a jumble of similar sayings gleaned from her reading when her sister Lydia runs off with the rake George Wickham: 'loss of virtue in a female is irretrievable ... one false step involves her in endless ruin ... her reputation is no less brittle than it is beautiful' (289). When Lydia's life is successfully patched up, in the end, Mary's morals prove to be wrong. But disproving the truth of generally accepted notions is not the aim of *Pride and Prejudice*, any more than proving a universal truth is. The novel's playful 'Epigrammatism' counters the generalities of philosophers and theorists with the specificities of individual styles and stories, the province of gossips and novelists. Epigrammatism itself is laughed at, when Charlotte Lucas intones her credo that 'Happiness in marriage is entirely a matter of chance', and Elizabeth protests, 'You make me laugh, Charlotte; but it is not sound' (23). When Elizabeth, dancing with the silent, awkward Darcy, teases him in Henry Tilney's engaging, disengaged manner ('It is *your* turn to say something now, Mr. Darcy. – *I* talked about the dance, and *you* ought to make some kind of remark on the size of the room, or the number of couples'), she jokes that they are both 'unwilling to speak, unless we expect to say something that will amaze the whole room, and be handed down to posterity with all the eclat of a proverb' (91).

'Her liking Darcy & Elizth is enough', Jane Austen wrote of one of her early readers (*L* 205). Theirs is the most romantic of love stories, rivalled in Jane Austen's *oeuvre* only by *Persuasion*. In *Sense and Sensibility*, *Mansfield Park*, and *Emma*, the happy marriages of the heroines are not quite exogamous, but Darcy and Elizabeth are perfect strangers. Darcy prefers Elizabeth to his first cousin, Anne de Bourgh, and to Caroline Bingley, his friend's sister; Elizabeth chooses him over her relative, Mr. Collins, and Mr. Wickham, whose relation to her is that of 'brother and sister' (329) at the end. Young, handsome, and justifiably proud of his tastes, standards, wealth, and antecedents, Darcy is captivated against his will by the second of five daughters of a country gentleman whose estate is entailed on the male line. (That Mr. Bennet's legal plight is the fault of nobody in particular is among the many elements that make *Pride and Prejudice* lighter and brighter than *Sense and Sensibility*.) Darcy dismisses Elizabeth at first sight, but is soon enchanted by her 'fine eyes' and 'the liveliness of [her] mind' (27, 380). Conventional himself, he admires her for defying convention. The first volume dramatizes Elizabeth's impatient divergences from the stock heroine of romantic fiction and the proper young lady of moralizing novelists. When her sister Jane falls ill and has to extend her visit to the Bingleys at Netherfield Park, just as her mother hoped, Elizabeth walks to see her, 'crossing field after field at a quick pace, jumping over stiles and springing over puddles with impatient activity, and finding herself at last within a view of the house, with weary ancles, dirty stockings, and a face glowing with the warmth of exercise' (32) – and her petticoat deep in mud. At Netherfield, she takes issue with the company's conventional idea that refined young ladies are to be admired for their various trivial 'accomplishments'; while she agrees to join Caroline Bingley in walking up and down the room so that Darcy can assess (and compare) their beauty, she dares to make him the object of her gaze later, refusing to join him and the Bingley sisters in a walk. 'You are charmingly group'd, and appear to uncommon advantage', she says. 'The picturesque would be spoilt by admitting a fourth' (53). By keeping a critical distance from both the ideal of woman and Darcy himself, she enchants him.

For her part, Elizabeth is annoyed by overbearing Darcy's first, unkind remark about her appearance, and dislikes him more after hearing a story told her by another, engaging young man. George Wickham turns out to be a liar, whose entanglements with Darcy's sister in the past, and then with Lydia Bennet, contribute to bringing the lovers together. The beautiful intricacy of the plot echoes the intricacy of Elizabeth's and Darcy's characters; the novel itself is characterized by the interesting quality discussed in an important conversation in the first volume, when Elizabeth slyly praises Bingley for not having 'a deep, intricate character' (like Darcy's), then satirically concedes that 'intricate characters are the *most* amusing. They have at least that advantage.' That conversation, memorably cut short by Mrs. Bennet's uncomprehending 'I assure you there is quite as much of *that* going on in the country as in town' (42–3), is one of several veiled private exchanges in public that charge the relationship of Elizabeth and Darcy with erotic power. Their implication in the wider world enhances the lovers' intimacy. Contemplating the happy couple at Pemberley in the end, the reader doesn't have to be told that everyone – Mr. and Mrs. Bennet, Charlotte Lucas and Mr. Collins and Lady Catherine de Bourgh, Bingley and his sisters and Jane, Wickham and Georgiana Darcy and Lydia – has been, like Elizabeth's aunt and uncle, the Gardiners, 'the means of uniting them'. (There is surely a note of justifiable authorial complacency in the triumphant two words that end the book.)

As if to affirm the reality of romance, the plot moves from a dialogue between a long-married couple who cannot understand one another – the first scene – to a marriage that will ensure happiness, benevolence, and laughter, moving Elizabeth from the clamour of Meryton and the instability of her father's entailed house through the vexing discordance between great house and parsonage at Rosings, in volume II, to end in the settled grandeur of Pemberley, with its park and woods and river, its library and picture gallery. When she first sees it on the first page of volume III, Elizabeth feels 'that to be mistress of Pemberley might be something!' (245). To visit

Pemberley as she does, as a tourist, with her pleasant uncle and aunt, is to reverse the position of the heroine of gothic, who is overcome by the influence of a haunted house with secret chambers and mysterious corridors that confine her while they also, horrifyingly, mirror her, reflecting the unexplored recesses of her virgin body and her intricate psyche. Pemberley, a place where old and new don't clash, where 'natural beauty had been so little counteracted by an awkward taste' (245), is grand but not romantic, as Northanger Abbey – in spite of having been renovated – is. Exploring a house that is open to the public, Elizabeth discovers her lover's hidden dimensions rather than her own. Instead of a black veil concealing a terrifying picture or statue or skeleton, she comes across a portrait of Darcy which she examines at leisure from a position of strength, activating its gaze by her own as she 'fixed his eyes upon herself' (251). William Gifford must have relished the anti-gothicism of the heroine's decorous transit through the 'lofty and handsome' rooms of the house, where she takes in the 'real elegance' of the furnishings, and the 'respectable-looking, elderly woman, much less fine, and more civil, than [Elizabeth] had any notion of finding her' (246), who receives the party and tells them about the excellence of her master and his affability to the poor, and about the price of the furniture. And how he must have savoured the matter-of-fact materialism of the heroine, who unromantically sighs out her desire to have the place!

By the time she gets to Pemberley Elizabeth has turned down two proposals of marriage from men who expect her to accept them simply because she is a woman, and poor, and must want a husband and home of her own. The first proposal is from sanctimonious Mr. Collins, who means to please his patroness by marrying, and to indulge his own pomposity by choosing a daughter of the house he is to inherit. Elizabeth has barely persuaded him that she is not an 'elegant female' refusing him so as to whet his appetite, but – she echoes Mary Wollstonecraft – 'a rational creature speaking the truth from her heart' (108–9), when Charlotte Lucas accepts him. Rejecting Mr. Collins in the first volume, Elizabeth seems to be in her father's camp against her mother, the business of whose life is to get her daughters married: she seems, that is, to rebel against the lot of women and the courtship plot. Refusing Mr. Darcy's first proposal in the second volume, she seems to reaffirm that position. But the amusing parallel makes the important difference clear. Darcy's proposal is quite as arrogant and overbearing and uncomprehending of its object as the stout young clergyman's ('In vain have I struggled', he tactlessly begins. 'It will not do. My feelings will not be repressed. You must allow me to tell you how ardently I admire and love you' [189].) After Elizabeth turns him down, he explains his behaviour and clarifies his character and feelings in a letter, which she reads and rereads at the dead centre of the novel, until she exclaims, 'Till this moment, I never knew myself' (208). Darcy's letter tells her what her family looks like to others; it even persuades her to be critical of her father, preparing her to move away from him. Learning that her first impressions of Wickham, who flattered her, and Darcy, who did not, were both mistaken, Elizabeth begins to understand the extent to which her character and her actions are a function of her relation to her neighbours. Austen's critical distance from the idea of a romantic heroine, explicit in the narrator's condescension to the heroine of *Northanger Abbey* and dramatized in the double heroines of *Sense and Sensibility*, is located, in this novel, in the protagonist's self-consciousness.

Elizabeth's searching rereadings, first of Darcy's letter and then of letters from Jane, are matched by her close attention to her own thoughts, her own story and character. After she has come to admire Darcy and to despair of marrying him, she reflects ruefully, like a thwarted novelist, that 'no such happy marriage could now teach the admiring multitude what connubial felicity really was' (312). And at the very end, when her spirits rise 'to playfulness again', and she asks Darcy 'to account for his having ever fallen in love with her', she observes that her thanking him for his kindness to Lydia had perhaps too great an effect on her lover, 'for what becomes of the moral, if our comfort springs from a breach of promise, for I ought not to have mentioned the subject? This will never do.' Happy and amiable Mr. Darcy soothingly replies that 'the moral will be perfectly fair' (381). Readers have disagreed, and argued that Elizabeth is either a proto-feminist or a fairy-tale heroine. Jane Austen's irony allows her to be both at once.

Although Elizabeth's consciousness is at the centre of the novel, the narrative shrewdly makes us privy to Darcy's mind – as she is not. As early as chapter 6, we learn that 'no sooner had he made it clear to himself and his friends that she had hardly a good feature in her face, than he began to find it was rendered uncommonly intelligent by the beautiful expression of her dark eyes'. We know before she does that he is 'caught' by the 'easy playfulness' of her manners, being told explicitly that 'Of this she was perfectly unaware; – to her he was only the man who made himself agreeable no where, and who had not thought her handsome enough to dance with' (23). Elizabeth's blindness to Darcy's feelings and merits and many of his very frequent blushes engages the reader in the love story. On the other hand, Elizabeth engages us as a character because she resembles the witty narrator, who refers to Mr. Bingley's sisters' maids as 'the two elegant ladies who waited on' them (41), and describes the end of an evening at Rosings as follows: 'The party then gathered round the fire to hear Lady Catherine determine what weather they were to have on the morrow. From these instructions they were summoned by the arrival of the coach' (166). Tricks like the narrator's echo of the very words Elizabeth has used ('Mr. Collins was not a sensible man', chapter 15 begins) encourage the identification of the heroine with the novelist – and with the reader, also outside the frame of the fiction. Elizabeth's infectious laughter does too.

Mr. Bennet and his favourite daughter do not do all the laughing in this comic novel: disdainful Miss Bingley can 'hardly keep [her] countenance' (36) when Elizabeth turns up at Netherfield with muddy skirts, and Lydia Bennet laughs too loudly and loosely and talks too much about laughing: 'Lord! how I laughed! ... I thought I should have died' (221), is how she finishes a story about a vulgar prank, and in the letter announcing her deplorable elopement she claims she can 'hardly write for laughing' (291). To observe Elizabeth's similarity to catty Caroline Bingley and the sluttish younger sister who marries the man she herself once found attractive is to begin to understand the moral point of Austen's novels, that on the one hand we are not so very different from our neighbours, and that on the other we must tirelessly discriminate among our common traits in order to understand the extreme importance – and moral implications – of the differences. Unlike Miss Bingley and Lydia, Elizabeth is not moved to laughter by gross deviations from arbitrary standards or norms. 'Follies and nonsense, whims and inconsistencies' (57), are what delight her – character-istics like the ones Jane Austen, towards the end of her life, was delighted to observe in her niece Fanny Knight, to whom she wrote, 'You are so odd! – & all the time, so perfectly natural – so peculiar in yourself, & yet so like everybody else!' (L 329). Early in *Pride and Prejudice*, when Elizabeth professes to be startled by the notion that 'Mr. Darcy is not to be laughed at!' she says pointedly, 'That is an uncommon advantage, and uncommon I hope it will continue, for it would be a great loss to *me* to have many such acquaintance. I dearly love a laugh' (57). Many chapters later, when she agrees to marry him, we are assured that the marriage will be happy since he will continue to amuse her: on the verge of making a mocking observa-tion, 'she checked herself'. Eventually, married to Darcy, she will amaze her young sister-in-law by making him 'the object of open pleasantry' (388), but the clever bride-to-be bides her time and bites her tongue: 'She remembered that he had yet to learn to be laught at, and it was rather too early to begin' (371). In the act of getting what she deserves, fulfilling the comic heroine's destiny by making precisely the marriage that would 'teach the admiring multitude', Elizabeth remains sufficiently outside her situation to recognize her man's limitations, keeps her wits about her even in the clinch.

Her greatest charm, which the reader must take even more seriously than her care in rereading, is her gift of disengaging herself. The shifting back-

and-forth between the narrator's mind and hers identifies the heroine with the text. When she first tells her sister she is engaged to Darcy, Jane thinks she is joking; not only Mr. Bennet has been convinced of her dislike of the man. Elizabeth insists, urgently but comically, 'I must confess, that I love him better than I do Bingley', so sober Jane begins to doubt herself, and says, 'do be serious. I want to talk very seriously ... Will you tell me how long you have loved him?' When Elizabeth replies, 'I must date it from my first seeing his beautiful grounds at Pemberley', the admission, which the reader recognizes as witty but also perfectly serious, provokes another 'intreaty that she would be serious' from her serious sister (373). Courtesy and caution mar the intimacy of the Dashwood sisters; playful Elizabeth and candid Jane have an easier time. Elizabeth's joking is a habit of mind: on the parallel occasion of Jane's engagement, she carries on a similar dialogue all by herself, which the narrative modulates into free indirect speech to render: 'Not a word passed between the sisters concerning Bingley; but Elizabeth went to bed in the happy belief that all must speedily be concluded, unless Mr. Darcy returned within the stated time. Seriously, however, she felt tolerably persuaded that all this must have taken place with that gentleman's concurrence' (346). Unwilling to tease her sister, Elizabeth pleases by teasing herself, professing – silently, but as if to an audience – an opinion that is not seriously, not in fact, her own. Taking herself not quite seriously, she is making sport for herself quite as if she were one of her neighbours.

'I am happier even than Jane', she writes to Mrs. Gardiner, when she announces her engagement to Mr. Darcy; 'she only smiles, I laugh' (383). This is joyous, not satirical laughter; nevertheless, laughing a little at Jane, who smiles too much and doesn't get jokes, is part of the strenuous joy. Does Elizabeth laugh too much? She is punished, perhaps, for doing so, when Mr. Bennet mortifies her pride by assuring her of Darcy's indifference, and she finds it 'necessary to laugh, when she would rather have cried' (364). Her laughter is nervous; the moral is not quite fair; but neither is life, and substituting laughter for tears is no small part of Austen's wisdom.

A clear chronology of her early novels would generate one likely story or another, about Jane Austen – that she learned romance, or restraint, or prudence, as she grew older. But we lack the grounds for such a narrative of development, and Austen's consistent elasticity of mind is more striking, anyway, than any transformative change over time. From her youth Jane Austen was committed to a clear moral vision and a stern moral code; she was always concerned with the same themes and issues and variations on the same plot. And from the beginning she was able to seize and enjoy an astonishing freedom to move from one to another level of her fictions, shifting easily from the romantic point of view to a place where romance can only be viewed ironically. More than anything else, these shifts convey the contagious pleasures of a free play of mind – while they signal that the turns and tones and surprising conjunctions, the differences between ways of seeing, are what matter most.

NOTES

1 Charlotte Maria Beckford, quoted in William Austen-Leigh, Richard Arthur Austen-Leigh, and Deirdre Le Faye, *Jane Austen: A Family Record* (London: The British Library, 1989), p. 178.

2 Simone de Beauvoir, *The Second Sex*, trans. H. M. Parshley (New York: Vintage, 1974), p. 301.

3 See, on Henrys in fiction, J. M. S. Tompkins, *The Popular Novel in England 1770–1800* (Lincoln: University of Nebraska Press, 1961), pp. 57–8.

4 Marilyn Butler, *Jane Austen and the War of Ideas* (Oxford: Clarendon Press, 1975), p. 182.

5 Samuel Smiles, *A Publisher and his Friends: Memoir and Correspondence of the Late John Murray* (London: J. Murray, 1891), 1:282.

4

JOHN WILTSHIRE

Mansfield Park, Emma, Persuasion

When Jane Austen moved to Chawton cottage in 1809 she sent off a poem to her brother Francis that celebrates the occasion:

> Our Chawton home – how much we find
> Already in it, to our mind,
> And how convinced, that when complete,
> It will all other Houses beat,
> That ever have been made or mended,
> With rooms concise or rooms distended.[1]   (*L* 176)

It was at Chawton that Jane Austen, settled with her mother, sister, and friend, found the conditions that fostered the writing of three of her greatest novels. *Mansfield Park*, published in 1814, *Emma*, published in 1816, and *Persuasion*, published after Austen's death, in 1818, develop that complicating of a romantic narrative with social satire and psychological insight so characteristic of her earlier work. These novels also display a more intensified sense of the influence of place and environment on personality and action, a broader and more thoughtful social critique, and a much greater power of imagining her figures within the social and geographical spaces they inhabit. In the action of the novels that Jane Austen wrote at Chawton, communal, family, and physical settings – homes, houses, and, indeed, 'rooms concise or rooms distended' – play an important role.

When Anne Elliot, in the last completed book, moves from one house to another, she reflects that each is a 'little social commonwealth', that manners and topics vary with place, and this observation, too, is pertinent to a reading of these major texts. Anne comments to herself that it is incumbent on her to 'clothe her imagination' in her setting as much as possible (*P* 43). In this discussion of the three texts I shall take her lead and suggest how each of the novel's distinct physical and social worlds is a conceptual world too. I shall clothe my account as much as possible in each novel's particular qualities, and in discussing their distinctive worlds, I shall relate these to the specific narrative techniques through which Austen brings these 'social commonwealths' into being.

MANSFIELD PARK

Mansfield Park was published only a year after *Pride and Prejudice*, but moving from one novel to the other the reader is keenly aware of a change of tone and atmosphere. Partly it is that *Mansfield Park* is evidently the work of an older, maturer, woman. The narrator is not an intrusive presence, by any means, but one who, while an insider of the world she depicts, can also see beyond it. 'Poor woman! she probably thought change of air might agree with many of her children', she remarks of the beleaguered Mrs. Price at the conclusion of chapter 1 (*MP* 11). It is a voice with a range of sympathy beyond the social commonwealth of rich families that is the milieu of *Mansfield Park*.

Almost everyone in this novel is wealthy. Sir Thomas Bertram is a Member of Parliament with a large estate and property in the West Indies; Henry Crawford also has an estate, and enough income easily to afford to have it totally 'improved' as soon as he comes of age. His sister Mary has twenty thousand. Mr. Rushworth has a park five miles round and a Tudor mansion. Told that Henry Crawford has 'four thousand a year', Mrs. Rushworth senior seems to feel that this is just enough to get by: 'Very well. – Those who have not more, must be satisfied with what they have' (118). These are 'young people of fortune', far better off than those in any other Austen novel, and untroubled, despite Sir Thomas' need to see to his Antigua estates, by any sense of financial insecurity. Only Mrs. Norris is obsessed with saving, a neurotic compensation for her inferior family position whose other manifestation is her remorseless bullying of her even poorer niece, Fanny Price. In part the novel is a study in the assumptions and manners of the very rich, in the manners of 'society', as the initial conversation between the Crawfords and the Bertrams, about 'coming out' (48–51), indicates. Spoilt, full of self-consequence, good-looking, healthy, the Bertrams do not need to be proud like Lady Catherine de Bourgh or Sir Walter Elliot. Their vanity is in such good order that they can appear free of it. Lordly, careless, insouciant, and selfish, Tom Bertram at least has some sense of humour.

In *Pride and Prejudice*, the great estate of Pemberley is viewed by a visitor and outsider, and Elizabeth Bennet gives it all the awe and respect of one who can say only that she is 'a gentleman's daughter'. But in *Mansfield Park*, the reader is, so to speak, a resident, shown what it is like to live from day to day in such a place. The spaciousness of the house is an important factor in the lives and events that the novel traces, and much of Austen's narrational skill in the brilliant first volume consists in the manipulation and interweaving of a large number of characters and destinies within one locale that is also a group of distinct spaces. For Fanny, the novel's uprooted heroine, '[t]he grandeur of the house astonished, but could not console her. The rooms were too large for her to move in with ease. Whatever she touched she expected to injure, and she crept about in constant terror of something or other' (14–15). Just taken away from her mother and her family, Fanny projects onto the furniture her own sense of the potential injuriousness of this space, felt to be both empty and hostile. Mansfield is not, on the whole, a glamorous or idyllic home (until it becomes such in Fanny's eyes at the end of the novel). Harassed and disregarded, Fanny gradually constructs a substitutively maternal space where she can be happy; furnishing the East room with discarded bric-à-brac and carelessly donated gifts, she makes a fragile 'nest of comforts' that is an emotional as well as physical improvisation. But this room which Fanny thinks of as 'her own', that she has made her own, is always actually marked as the room of a dependent, a transient, by the absence of a fire in the grate.

Jane Austen's ability to make the setting integral to her development of character can be illustrated too, by the early scene where the youthful Fanny is waiting for Mary Crawford to return with the mare that she has borrowed. She is scolded out of the house by Mrs. Norris and discerns the party of Edmund, Mary, and the groomsmen across the valley. 'The sound of merriment ascended even to her' (67): the phrasing subtly makes Fanny's geographical distance from the group a simultaneous index of her emotional isolation. 'After a few minutes, they stopt entirely, Edmund was close to her, he was speaking to her, he was evidently directing her management of the bridle, he had hold of her hand; she saw it, or the imagination supplied what the eye could not reach' (67); and the rhythm supplies the undercurrent of Fanny's jealousy. Not 'see' but 'reach'. How that suggests the distance across which Fanny's eyes are straining!

From one point of view, Fanny Price is an interesting psychological study in the manners and attitudes of a radically insecure and traumatized personality. The impatience that one inevitably feels with some of her more censorious or prim judgments may be moderated by the careful history of displacement Austen has provided for her, her years of unremitting intimidation by Mrs. Norris, and her youthful dependence on an Edmund whose kindness comes along with a good deal of tutorly instruction. Her disapproving attitude towards Mary is always complicated by its jealous colouring as well as an even more disqualifying trait, envy. Fanny's moral attitudes in general are overdetermined – part the result of Edmund's coaching, part the result of her own nature and insecurities – and so it is a great simplification to see her as modelling a 'conduct book', a Christian, or an evangelical heroine. Does she refuse to act in *Lovers' Vows* out of fear of acting, or out of disapproval of the play? She certainly offers her timidity as her excuse, thereby displaying that timidity rather than moral righteousness.

Mansfield Park is a novel in the mode of the omniscient narrator, and for the first and only time in her novels, Jane Austen continuously allows the narrative to move freely in and out of the consciousnesses of a whole range of characters. In *Pride and Prejudice,* there are moments, especially early in the novel, when Darcy's and Charlotte Lucas' thoughts are presented. In *Persuasion,* the reader is shown at one crucial moment Captain Wentworth's still-burning anger against Anne. But in *Mansfield Park* the independence of the narrator from any one controlling consciousness is a structural principle. This text at various times represents the thinking processes or picks up the internal speech-cadences of Maria Bertram, Edmund Bertram, Sir Thomas, Mary Crawford, and several others, besides Fanny Price. When Sir Thomas overhears Mr. Yates in full ranting flight on the improvised stage at Mansfield the narrative borrows his point of view at the beginning of the paragraph, and, to heighten the comic effect, Tom Bertram's at the close (182–3).

Perhaps most significantly, this novel presents whole scenes and dialogues from which the heroine is absent. The scenes at the Parsonage between Mary and Henry Crawford (and sometimes with Mrs. Grant) are quite freestanding. They depict the relationship between the Crawfords at first without reference to Fanny. Thus the novel is structured with two different centres or foci of interest. In the mode of 'free indirect speech', Mary's thoughts about her prospects on entering a new place and about older brothers, for example, are allowed to enter the text without authorial commentary. Following from these gay and brilliant introductory scenes (volume 1, chapters 4 and 5) the narrator naturally keeps the reader in touch with Mary Crawford's private thoughts – she has been given the representational treatment of a major figure, and her projects accordingly draw from one a certain sympathetic attention. It is not the fact that Mary is vivacious, while the supposed heroine Fanny is timid and nervous, that makes for this novel's moral complications: it is that the rival figures are each accorded an almost equivalent narrative stature until Fanny's removal to Portsmouth in the last volume.

The reporting of Mary's thoughts moves fluidly between the medium of indirect speech, the dramatic representation of her behaviour, and direct commentary on both. Different modes, or rather dimensions or aspects, of presentation throughout the novel tend to suggest different moral agendas. When Sir Thomas Bertram interviews Maria and asks her whether she wants to press on with the engagement to Rushworth (200–1) his thoughts are outlined like an internal monologue without quotation marks. The reader is expected to see through the self-deceptions and convenient blindnesses of his reasonings, but to retain the vestigial sympathy one conventionally has for a figure whose thought-processes, whose capacity to reflect, one has intimately followed. (This is one of the reasons why Sir Thomas, for all his failures – and he never fails in his kindness to his wife – is a fundamentally respectable figure.) The caustic comments that follow – 'Such and such-like were the reasonings of Sir Thomas' – are an abrupt shift of address, and require a change of attitude from the reader from participatory leniency to dismissive contempt. These abutments of aspect (not always as abrupt as here) are one source of the novel's scintillating life, but they sometimes cause ethical anxiety in the reader that is not entirely resolved.

The presentation of Mary and Henry Crawford, freestanding, but doubled through the perspective of the heroine, is the major instance of this challenge. Mary has lived in London and has a range of social skills that are apparently worldly and sophisticated, but viewed from Fanny's position, she often seems sadly maladroit. One complication of her tone – her 'sweet peculiarity of manner' as Edmund describes it – is a tincture of disillusionment that is not quite as cynical as she imagines. The sketch of Mary's years at the Admiral's house that emerges from her allusions, however witty and professedly unconcerned, indicates a history that invites sympathy for a damaged life. When she is married, she tells Mrs. Grant, she will be a staunch defender of the marriage state, and adds 'I wish my friends in general would be so too. It would save me many a heart-ache' (47). Her disrespectful description of her uncle's household – 'of *Rears* and *Vices*, I saw enough' – is witty, but the crudity of the wit laughs off an enormity she feels but has no way of approaching directly. (Her assessment is not in doubt: the narrator has said previously that the Admiral was a man of 'vicious habits'.)

'In short, it is not a favourite profession of mine. It has never worn an amiable form to *me*' (60). The remarks scandalize Fanny and Edmund, but their intensity, which is replicated whenever Mary brings up the topic of life at the Admiral's, betrays an unhappy experience that is clearly formative. Mary's history, brought up in the charge of her aunt and uncle, mirrors Fanny's, and one might justly suppose that the traumatic effects of her adoptive home on one personality are as relevant to the author's purpose as they are on the other. In other words, though Mary's worldliness is viewed critically (through the eyes of Fanny and Edmund especially) it is also readable as a coping strategy, a sign of an insecurity much less manifest than Fanny's, but nonetheless, critical.

The complications of feeling and judgment these different dimensions of narration give rise to can be exemplified by the famous scene when Mrs. Norris turns on Fanny and accuses her of being 'a very obstinate, ungrateful girl ... very ungrateful indeed, considering who and what she is' (147). The setting is the drawing room, where Tom, Maria, Henry Crawford, and Mr. Yates are at a table with the play in front of them, while Lady Bertram on her sofa, Edmund, Fanny, and Mrs. Norris are grouped nearer the fire. The separation is political. Mary Crawford's predicament and nervousness (she wants Edmund to act the Anhalt role but does not know how to approach the question) is defined by her movement between one and the other set of people within the room. She shifts from group to group, in response to different promptings, her freedom a sign not of independence but of her need to attach herself, to find a centre for her emotional life – almost, one might say, to find a home. When Edmund snubs her, she 'was silenced; and with some feelings of resentment and mortification', the reader is told, 'moved her chair' towards Mrs. Norris at the tea-table.

The reader's main focus is on Fanny, who is the target of Tom's plans, so that the little drama of Mary's manoeuvres interweaves it only as a subsidary theme. The climax is Tom's repeated 'attack' on Fanny and Mrs. Norris' angry speech. Mary's immediate response is 'I do not like my situation; this *place* is too hot for me' and her moving of her chair once again to the opposite side of the table. Mary's action, the completion of her series of movements, is sympathetically described as she continues to talk to Fanny and to try 'to raise her spirits, in spite of being out of spirits herself'. But in a moment one's admiration for her courage and kindness becomes undermined: 'By a look to her brother, she prevented any farther entreaty from the theatrical board, and the really good feelings by which she was almost purely governed, were rapidly restoring her to all the little she had lost in Edmund's favour' (147). This odd sentence, beginning with Mary's (or the narrator's) point of view and ending with Edmund's, seems to attribute to him an unwarranted insight into Mary's motives, and the upshot is a carping note all-too-consonant with the suspiciousness of Fanny. The dramas of the two young women have been presented contrapuntally, but at this point where their projects actually clash the task of keeping sympathy for both figures alive in the narrative proves just too much. This episode presents a miniature version of the narrative knot that Austen cuts in the last section of the novel by removing Fanny to Portsmouth and allowing only her consciousness to preside.

'By a look to her brother': the reader's responses to Mary Crawford are also complicated by the fact that the dialogues between Mary and Henry emphasize their mutual rapport. They seem to have a family style, teasing, humorous, generous, that contrasts with the absence of anything like wit or style among the Bertrams. One never sees Julia and Maria, who are said to get on well, for example, in conversation, and Tom only speaks to Edmund in order crudely to make clear who is boss. Henry, as Mary declares, 'loves me, consults me, confides in me' (59). Henry's regard for Mary invites the reader to see his flirtations with Maria and Julia in a light that is perhaps a shade different from the youthful Fanny's abhorrence. (Mary's resolve to keep her affections under control also cannot but make one despise Maria's sulky disregard of consequences.) Thus the Crawfords' worldliness is accompanied by a complicating un-Bertramesque mutuality, kindness, and adulthood. They exemplify that 'fraternal' tie (235) the narrator celebrates explicitly in reference to Fanny and William.

Henry Crawford is as marked as his sister by the arrangements in his uncle's household. Fatherless and allowed a free rein by the Admiral, Henry does not require the approval of others to feel justified in what he does: in fact he rather relishes opposition than the reverse, which perhaps explains his persistence in the courtship of the anything but graciously reluctant Fanny. Henry's pursuit of his sexual objects, in this instance Maria, is accompanied by contempt for those objects. Austen implies that he has picked up such attitudes from his uncle. But she also succeeds in suggesting how his spoilt and liberal upbringing can result in fascination when the beloved offers the challenge, but also the comfort, of inflexible resistance. ' "I could so wholly and absolutely confide in her," said he; "and *that* is what I want" ' (294).

Henry's courtship of Fanny is accompanied by conversations in which he discusses it with Mary, and his love for Fanny by her endorsement, or, perhaps, collusion. The dual focus is most brilliantly exploited in chapters 11 and 12 of the second volume. For many chapters, the novel has seen events mainly from the standpoint of Fanny Price. It is her view of Henry's flirtations that has been given, her mistrust, resentment, and reluctance have been highlighted, even while it is counterpointed and ironically at odds with the excitements and delights of the Crawfords. After the ball, which Sir Thomas has organized from the hardly conscious wish to promote Fanny's chances with Henry, Edmund goes away to be ordained. In chapter 11, Fanny's state of mind is described, but then the narrative shifts its focus on to Mary at the Parsonage. It is now she whose thoughts are filled with anxiety and self-mistrust, and who now contends 'with one disagreeable emotion entirely new to her – jealousy' (286). The positions of the two young women have been reversed as Mary tries to extract some reassurance of her power over Edmund from the unbending Miss Price.

In chapter 12, Henry returns and announces, to Mary's astonishment, that he intends to marry Fanny Price. The genius of this almost entirely dramatic scene is that it gives full recognition to the excitement, gaiety, and exhilaration of the two figures who challenge the narrative and moral status of the hero and heroine. The reader's responses are not inhibited by reservations from the narrator. What also makes it so telling is that it is not merely a scene of mutual delight and congratulation, but that it touches once more on the painful family history that has made these two, and their needs, what they are. Henry, even while he acknowledges the grossness of his uncle, says of him 'Few fathers would have let me have my way half so much.' In the midst of her delight, with her mind racing ahead to what this means for her own prospects, Mary is stopped and sounds a sombre note: 'Henry, I think so highly of Fanny Price, that if I could suppose the next Mrs. Crawford would have half the reason which my poor ill used aunt had to abhor the very name, I would prevent the marriage, if possible' (296). The gravity of this declaration suggests once again the unhappy psychological background that leads Mary, in this very dialogue, to fantasize a reconstituted family – cousins and brother and sister – together in Northamptonshire, a fantasy that ironically duplicates some of Fanny's own longings.

It is not only psychological depth and narrative orchestration that make *Mansfield Park* a milestone in the English novel. The novelist imagines the physical world in which her figures move to have a palpable presence, an effective bearing on their lives. At one point in *Pride and Prejudice*, the narrator remarks casually on 'the shrubbery where this conversation passed' (*PP* 86). Settings are never neutral backgrounds in *Mansfield Park*, and the gardens at Sotherton, famously, are made to play an integral, even determinative part in the action. It is not only that one can read them in allegorical terms, as the punning exchange of Henry and Maria about her 'prospects' invites one to do. It is rather as if emotional pressures and urgencies were felt, and conveyed to the reader, in spatial terms, as when Maria declares so intensely 'I cannot get out, as the starling said' (*MP* 99). As the figures move, disperse, and reassemble within the various venues Sotherton and Mansfield and Portsmouth offer them, one is made vividly conscious not only of the opportunities and inhibitions of these spaces, but of their being at issue – contested over, claimed, and owned. Maria's disregard of the locked gate is to be echoed in Tom's overturning the arrangements of his father's rooms: both express their egotistical drives as the usurpation of territory. Fanny seeks to keep Edmund at the window looking at the stars, Mary lures him indoors with her music. Characters and their bodies are imagined precisely within settings that are drawn into the narrative and act as provocations to conversation and action.

This capacity to dramatize space and to make the human drama inseparable from its physical location reaches its peak in the scenes at Portsmouth. As Edward Said observes, for example, the 'solitary candle' that Fanny's father holds 'between himself and the paper, without any reference to her possible convenience' (382) 'renders very precisely the dangers of unsociability, of lonely insularity, of diminished awareness that are rectified in larger and better administered spaces'.[2] It is this evening that Fanny remembers three months later when her depression is deepened by the sun that brings its glare to illuminate the dirt and disorder of her parents' parlour. When she returns to Mansfield with Edmund in early spring an affiliation between emotional state, narrative purpose, and landscape setting – the trees in 'that delightful state ... while much is actually given to the sight, more yet remains for the imagination' (446–7) – suggests the possibilities that are to be explored further in *Emma* and *Persuasion*.

EMMA

Emma is a novel with a quite different social setting and conceptual structure. From the vigorously trochaic rhythm of the opening words – 'Emma Woodhouse, handsome, clever and rich ...' – a confident, energetic, and commanding voice carries this narrative forwards. This is an optimistic book, coloured by Emma's 'eager laughing warmth', very much conceived of as a comedy, with the cross-purposes, misunderstandings, mistaken identities, tricking, and teasing that are definitive of comedy as a genre. In the vicinity of Emma, the narrative picks up her tone, her expressions, her phrasing, even when it is not formally committed to rendering her speech or thought-patterns. Occasionally, there is a note that does not belong to her, as in the description of Mrs. Weston's thoughts on her marriage: 'She felt herself a most fortunate woman; and she had lived long enough to know how fortunate she might well be thought, where the only regret was for a partial separation from friends, whose friendship for her had never cooled, and who could ill bear to part with her!' (*E* 18) – the voice of an older, sadder woman than Emma, that might not be out of place in *Mansfield Park* or *Persuasion*.

But for the most part the narrative voice of *Emma*, while flexible, and capable even of picking up Mr. Elton's vulgarisms when in his vicinity, is overwhelmingly the style of Emma, youthful, confident, presumptive, witty, dogmatic, commanding, assured. 'Harriet was to sit again the next day; and Mr. Elton, just as he ought, entreated for the permission of attending and reading to them again' (47): though this is formally information given by the narrator, the phrase 'just as he ought' construes his motives according to

Emma's point of view. Sometimes one can catch the narrator assuming Emma's viewpoint deliberately to trick the reader. A few moments later Mrs. Weston is said to talk to Mr. Elton of Miss Smith 'not in the least suspecting she was addressing a lover'; Frank Churchill, pressed to visit the Bates', is said to consent only 'with the hope of Hartfield to reward him' (235). In each of these cases, Emma's view of motives is allowed to tease the reader, to appear as if it is the book's.

So everything – more or less – is shown through Emma Woodhouse's eyes. Charged with her own spirits and energy and self-consequence, she shapes the narrated world according to her presumptions, preconceptions, and demands. The structural principle of the novel, this is formally broken with only twice. The scene in chapter 5, volume I, in which Mr. Knightley and Mrs. Weston discuss Emma in her absence, is matched by chapter 5 in volume III, in which Mr. Knightley's suspicions of a liaison between Jane Fairfax and Frank Churchill seem to be confirmed by their behaviour over the word game. As Mr. Knightley watches them in the gathering darkness of the room, he questions his observations – as Emma never does. Later a looser style of narrative takes over, but in the first two volumes the tunnelling of vision produces some of its most amusing and delicious effects.

But if the novel is bounded by this rule (a flexible rule) it is also bounded spatially. *Emma* is a novel in which circumscribed settings, limited spaces, and confinement (comforting and enabling, but at the same time imprisoning and suffocating) are crucially important. Highbury, the country village almost the size of a town, in which the novel is set, is conceptually, if not geographically, isolated from the rest of the world. Augusta Elton lets it be known that Mr. Elton has expressed fears 'lest the retirement' of Highbury be disagreeable to his bride (276), and, recommending Bath to Emma, comments that 'it would be a charming introduction for you, who have lived so secluded a life'. She also thinks that Jane Fairfax is wasting her sweetness on the desert air. Highbury is provincial and confined – a city-state, a commonwealth, that Frank Churchill takes out his freedom in by purchasing gloves at Ford's and declaring his *amor patriae* (200). (The true freedom of Highbury, of course, is won by the hard work of parish meetings and neighbourly concern that Mr. Knightley puts in.)

Yet to speak of Highbury's isolation and limitedness is to put the emphasis mistakenly. ' "Our lot is cast in a goodly heritage" ', effuses Miss Bates, and Highbury is depicted as a cheerfully functioning community (it is 'reckoned a particularly healthy spot'). For despite Emma's wariness – her wish not quite to define her identity in terms of the place – Highbury is not seen from the position of an amused or superior outside observer (as Elizabeth Gaskell's Cranford is). Though the reader sees from one point of view, and that rather one given to snobbery, the novel generates, especially in volume II, a sense of busy interplay between characters and between social classes, a network of visiting, gossip, charitable acts, and neighbourly concern.

One of the achievements of the novel is to populate 'the Highbury world' (352) and give it apparent depth. The loose ends and superfluous names that figure so much in Miss Bates' gossip do not just serve to camouflage the essential bits of information that she is feeding into the plot, they are a technically adroit means of conveying – especially in the Highbury ball scene – this sense of a social commonwealth. It is not only in Miss Bates' speeches that characters are spoken of familiarly who are never formally presented. Mr. Perry, the doctor who may or may not be setting up his carriage, is only the most frequently mentioned of a host of figures who pass in and out of the narrative and acquire a kind of familiarity by proxy. It is as if by having William Larkins, Robert Martin, Mrs. Goddard, and many others – Mrs. Hodges, John Abdy, Patty, James, the Coxes, even the Coles – partially within our field of vision, the novel persuades us of their richly extended existence beyond it.

The novelist makes sure that the reader grasps that the curtailment of space – this drawing of strict boundaries – has social and ethical dimensions too. She introduces a scene in which Emma and Harriet visit a poor cottage (volume I, chapter 10). The walk on the way offers opportunity for some of Emma's more preposterous pronouncements about herself but it also serves to define the parameters of the novel's scheme. This is a part of Highbury that is not part of Emma's Highbury, and Emma's words on surveying the cottage define the limitations of the conceptual world of the novel (not to be confused with the historical social world of Regency England). Emma and Harriet cross 'the low hedge, and tottering footstep which ended the narrow, slippery path through the cottage garden, and brought them into the lane again'. Emma tells Harriet that her impression of the misery in the cottage will not soon be over. 'I do not think it will', she says, 'stopping to look once more at all the outward wretchedness of the place, and recal the still greater within' (87). Then, 'the lane made a slight bend; and when that bend was passed, Mr. Elton was immediately in sight' and the novel resumes its comic intrigue: an elegant way for the novelist to put out of sight, out of the novel's focus, a whole aspect of Highbury life. The episode is relevant to the novel's concern with charity in all its forms, but what it also does is persuade the reader to see how geographical space, moral focus, and conceptual scheme can be identified.

Emma and Harriet's walk is an interruption to the sequence of Hartfield scenes in the first volume of *Emma*. Women in this novel are more or less limited to drawing rooms, but men can walk in at all hours, and even go off to London for a haircut. Jane Fairfax is subject to a neighbourly inquisition when she is caught walking in the rain to the local post office on the chance of hearing from her beloved, but Mr. Knightley is free to ride through the rain all the way from London to attend to the needs of his. Space is thus gendered: and the various dimensions of confinement interrelated: confinement to the indoors, to a restricted sphere of influence, to a small community; and on the other hand, freedom to enjoy the outdoors, freedom to exercise choice, to travel. The reader is asked to see a correlation, or correspondence, between being shut in and the possibilities of the moral life, as when Emma, pronouncing with ineffable complacency to Harriet that she will never get married, says 'those who live perforce in a very small, and generally very inferior, society, may well be illiberal and cross' (85).

In *Emma* women's imprisonment is associated with deprivation, with energies and powers perverted in their application, and events, balls, and outings are linked with the arousal and satisfaction of desire. But the presentation is not black and white: structure is perceived to be essential to the fulfilment of desire, and the freedom of the outdoors is depicted as potentially treacherous or empty. The novel's own momentum harnesses Emma's and the reader's desire for expansion and the release of energies. Confined to Hartfield for most of the first volume, the narrative then gradually expands its horizons with an increasingly far-flung series of outings, visits, and the ball at the Crown, until it climaxes in the two excursions, one a day after the other, a chapter after the other, to Donwell and to Box Hill. Then, when Emma learns of Harriet's great expectations of Mr. Knightley, there is a scene set in her father's drawing room in which the term 'prospect' (422), as in *Mansfield Park*, requires us to read the confined room, the miserable weather outside included, as both the material condition of Emma's melancholy, and a metaphor.

But Emma, like other ladies, does make visits. One particularly skilful exploitation of her point of view is the passage (literally) between chapter 9 and chapter 10 of volume II in which the reader, accompanying Emma and pursued 'by the sounds of [Miss Bates'] desultory good will' climbs the stairs to the Bates' apartment and (over the page, opening the next chapter) sees the room as if the curtain has gone up on a stage set: 'The appearance of the little sitting-room as they entered, was tranquillity itself; Mrs. Bates, deprived of her usual employment, slumbering on one side of the fire, Frank Churchill, at a table near her, most deedily occupied about her spectacles, and Jane Fairfax, standing with her back to them, intent on her pianoforté' (240). This is what Emma sees, and the following sequence in which Frank encourages her suspicions of Jane while at the same time speaking otherwise to his fiancée is a particularly delicious example of his skill, or damning evidence of his duplicity (depending on how one's sympathies lie). While we read the following scene from Emma's point of view, and are involved in Emma's responses – among them that characteristic shading of her hostility to Jane into pity and back again – the novelist is inviting the reader to step beyond her and to see it quite differently. That 'deedily occupied' raises the suspicion that the young occupants have just sprung into these innocent positions. Poor old Mrs. Bates has been as effectually blinded as Emma.[3]

Because of the confinement of focus to Emma, Frank Churchill is presented entirely dramatically and therefore enigmatically: is he appeasing or teasing Emma when he professes to take up all her suspicions regarding Jane Fairfax? How much is he being ironic at her expense when he says 'but I, simple I, saw nothing but the fact ... I do not mean to say, however, that you might not have made discoveries' (218)? When he murmurs about 'conjecture' – 'aye, sometimes one conjectures right and sometimes one conjectures wrong' – what kind of adroit act is he performing? In retrospect, one might be sure that he's slyly implying the same criticisms of Emma that Mr. Knightley makes so forthrightly, but the reader, listening with Emma's ears, laps up the flattery that his words appear to proffer. Frank is not merely a manipulator: Austen's presentation allows one to detect his moments of bad conscience, of uneasiness at the game he is forced into, as well as his enjoyment of the game itself – 'Then I will speak the truth, and nothing suits me so well' (200). The reader is free to imagine that Frank is both sly and impetuous – that he is always straining against the restrictions of secrecy and at the same time enjoying the opportunities for mischief it presents. The enigmatic and mercurial nature of the character is a product of the technique of presentation adopted. For reasons best known to himself, Mr. Knightley does not think much of him.

Neither does Mr. Woodhouse. 'That young man is not quite the thing' (or: 'not what he ought to be'). Frank dares to break the Highbury habit of deference to Mr. Perry, and, even more scandalously, provokes Mr. Wood-house into panic over open windows at the ball. 'Open the windows! ... Nobody could be so imprudent! I never heard of such a thing. Dancing with open windows! I am sure neither your father nor Mrs Weston (poor Miss Taylor that was) would suffer it.' And Frank replies, 'Ah! sir – but a thoughtless young person will sometimes step behind a window-curtain, and throw up a sash without its being suspected. I have often known it done myself' (251–2). The reader may well enjoy this teasing, as with Mr. John Knightley's earlier and much less good-tempered taunts about the snow thick on the ground at Randalls.

Frank throws open windows in the novel in a more modern sense – the opportunity of viewing the characters and events within a different ethic. If we laugh with him, we enjoy a temporary truancy from the official morality of the novel's conceptual world. Frank presents the possibility of seeing things another way – one that allows much more to impetuosity and surprise, to passion and risk-taking. In this view Mr. Woodhouse would be seen as blocking the way, a man whose depressive fussiness inhibits and shuts down opportunities and possibilities of life, and Mr. Knightley's masculine rationality and rule-giving an attempt to contain and organize a world that is actually much more volatile. Yet since Emma's perspective is so much the novel's, the reader who takes out his or her freedom in Highbury undertakes to accept its consensus and thus declines to pursue these options or doubts.

Emma, of course, is completely unaware of the relationship between Frank and Jane. But her misunderstanding is deeper than this. What she misses in Frank and Jane's situation is a romantic element that simply is foreign to her sensibility. For Emma the arrival of the piano is simply a stimulus for further speculation about Mr. Dixon: the gift might have been a piece of jewellery (an amber cross?) for all the difference it makes. But the choice of the piano as a gift is not accidental. It becomes clear that Jane and Frank fell in love over music, and that music is important to Jane in a way that Emma cannot fully conceive. In this very scene Frank manages to say to Jane:

> 'I believe you were glad we danced no longer; but I would have given worlds – all the worlds one ever has to give – for another half hour.'
> She played. (242)

Jane speaks, in effect, through the piano. Her eloquence passes unheard by Emma. Later, preoccupied by thoughts about Mr. Knightley, she scarcely notices 'the sweet sounds of the united voices' of Frank and Jane singing in the background. Only through music does the community unwittingly sanction their intimacy. One is left to speculate that perhaps it is an insight into her confined circumstances and the need for an outlet that has motivated the gift of the piano, a gift 'thoroughly from the heart', attuned to the needs of the beloved, as Frank contrives to declare. Moreover, a piano is a symbol of culture and gentility – as the discussion at Mrs. Cole's brings out – and the present is a pledge on Frank's part of a future larger, more comprehensive in its cultural horizons, than the Bates' two rooms. When the engagement is broken off, and Jane faces a future as governess, Miss Bates reports her addressing the piano directly: 'Poor dear Jane was talking of it just now. "You must go", said she. "You and I must part. You will have no business here"' (384).

Frank's gift of the piano is therefore loaded with implications – cultural, social, and erotic – that Emma cannot see. But mostly it is that the piano signifies passion. So that while Emma is busily constructing a tawdry romantic narrative around Jane, and taking Frank to be confirming her speculations, the reader is at the same time being given the material to substantiate a conception of love that is, indeed, romantic – a love that seems to have been more or less at first sight, that is expressed by both in passionate terms, and that is carried on in defiance of social proprieties. 'Had she refused', to become engaged, Frank later writes, 'I should have gone mad' (437). This intensity – Jane herself, not given to gush, speaks of Frank's 'bewitching' qualities – is all the more remarkable because it conflicts with, or is set up in opposition to, the notion of companionate love that is developed through the novel's focus on Emma. For *Emma*, which celebrates rational marriage, also offers credence to passionate and reckless love.

Austen's interweaving of the suggestions of a deeply romantic narrative within the novel is the more telling because its 'love story' is such a fundamental revision of the convention. Though superficially the relationship of Emma Woodhouse and Mr. Knightley resembles the pupil/tutor pattern that is discernible in Catherine Morland and Henry Tilney, Fanny and Edmund, and even Elizabeth and Darcy – he is so much older than she, for example – it is far more than these a relationship of equals, even though Emma is a woman and thus severely restricted in the ways she can exercise power, and in the forms her intelligence can take. Theirs are contests between equals in confidence, wit, and capacity for strong and sympathetic feeling. Both love everything that is decided and open. When they fight over Harriet Smith and Robert Martin, Emma may 'abuse her reason' but it is as if, underlying the real anger and indignation on both sides, there is a reciprocation of energy, a love of the other's strength of mind. The real identity of Emma and Knightley's views is defined in their next quarrel when Emma 'to her great amusement, perceived that she was taking the other side of the question from her real opinion' (145): the underlying and unconscious motive is clearly pleasure in crossing swords with Mr. Knightley.

Emma finds Mr. Knightley such a stimulus to her ingenuity that the reader may well feel swayed by her arguments. 'You are very fond of bending little minds; but when little minds belong to rich people in authority, I think they have a knack of swelling out, till they are quite as unmaneageable as great ones' (147). Like so much of what Emma says, this has the ring of intuitive truth. Some readers think that Mr. Knightley is never wrong, and, in the sense that the outcomes of Emma's meddling with Harriet's life are much as he predicts, they are correct: but dramatically,

Emma's ideas – just because they capture something of a world that is less tractable, more random and ungovernable than Mr. Knightley's own good sense and rationality allow – have a good deal of value, and what the reader watches, as a spectacle, is Emma's wit and fire in Mr. Knightley's presence. And in a later dispute, when Mr. Knightley says that Mrs. Elton would be subdued by Miss Fairfax into deference, and Emma doubts it, her more open sense of unpredictability and volatility in human relations certainly scores over him.

This is a relation in which, then, the erotic content is always implicit, always transmuted or sublimated. Mr. Knightley only learns how he feels about Emma from his own homosocial jealousy of Frank. Emma's desire for Mr. Knightley (as distinct from her admiration and regard for him) is out of her own awareness – impeded by her devotion to her father. So the novel needs to find ways to convey to the reader that the marriage with which it will inevitably close is plausible – has to make the reader desire Emma's union with Mr. Knightley, has to find ways of conveying her unconscious erotic or desiring attachment to him. 'She always declares she will never marry, which, of course, means just nothing at all' (41), Mr. Knightley has said: Emma declares as much to Harriet, and a good deal of the comedy of the novel concerns, of course, Emma's own pursuit of romantic matters by proxy. Austen shows, too, that Knightley is constantly in Emma's thoughts, but cumulatively these, and even the telling moment at the ball when she registers his 'tall, firm, upright figure' (326), do not quite amount convincingly to a demonstration of hidden desire. But perhaps the most effective technique for persuading the reader of the necessity of the marriage is the interlude of description of Donwell Abbey.

In this, as in so much else, *Emma* is a rewriting of *Pride and Prejudice*. The crucial point in the evolution of Elizabeth's feelings towards Mr. Darcy is her visit to Pemberley, where she sees him at home, at ease in his own setting, and given a glowing personal reference by his own housekeeper. It is evident that Pemberley, the estate, has a metonymic relation to its owner: it not only symbolizes or represents his social and financial status, but gives material presence to less definable qualities like his taste and his judgment. Even more than this: the stream abounds with fish, and the table, when Elizabeth visits Miss Darcy, is piled with 'beautiful pyramids of grapes, nectarines and peaches' (*PP* 268).

Donwell Abbey is introduced into the narrative at about the same point, and is a set-piece of a similiar kind. Both houses represent, or figure forth, their owners. Pemberley is manifestly an image of social power and wealth. Donwell Abbey is more complex; less idealized, less in the image of houses and their grounds 'improved' by Repton or Capability Brown. 'It was just what it ought to be, and it looked what it was' (*E* 358): Donwell Abbey, as Emma views it, has its limitations – the disputable taste of the walk, its neglect of prospect – it is without fashionable smoothness and thus presents or incarnates the blunt honesty, the moral integrity, even what Austen presents as the characteristic Englishness, of its owner. 'Eager to refresh and correct her memory with more particular observation, more exact understanding' Emma seizes the chance to explore alone (her father being temporarily taken care of) and look about her. She warms to 'its suitable, becoming, characteristic situation, low and sheltered – its ample gardens stretching down to meadows washed by a stream ... its abundance of timber in rows and avenues' (357–8). Emma feels a sense of propriety, of possession and affiliation. This is a spectacle of plenitude and comfort, richness, prosperity, and containment. Viewing it – and Emma slips off once again 'for a few moments' free observation of the entrance and ground-plot of the house' (362) – gives her peculiar relish.

One difference between Donwell and Pemberley is that Elizabeth Bennet is perfectly conscious that in seeing over it she is revising her view of Darcy. Emma is unconscious of the fact that the place is identified for her with its proprietor, that in being there – indeed in luxuriating in it – she is unconsciously imagining union with Mr. Knightley. She never thinks: 'To be mistress of Donwell might be something!' Yet the warmth of her response (here indistinguishable from the narrator's) is important for moving the narrative impetus forward. It suggests that Donwell is a place that, while realistic on the surface – the planning of its gardens is almost as awkward as Sotherton – offers a resting place for dreams. The house and its surroundings – the farm, the orchard, even the abundance of strawberries – augur satisfaction, fulfilment, amplitude. Seeing Harriet and Mr. Knightley admiring the view of the farm, Emma's description warms to 'all its appendages of prosperity and beauty, its rich pastures, spreading flocks, orchard in blossom, and light column of smoke ascending' (360).

In his notes to *Emma*, R. W. Chapman points out that 'the orchard in blossom' when the season is said to be 'about Midsummer' is 'one of Miss Austen's very rare mistakes of this kind' (493). The 'light column of smoke ascending' is also oddly unseasonal. But perhaps 'mistake' is too simple an explanation for these effects: what is being presented here is not a place but an idyll, the fantasy of the pastoral paradise. There is an enthusiasm that seeks to represent Donwell and its estate, not just as admirable and august, but as having *everything* – strawberries at their peak of ripeness, sunshine, 'spreading flocks', 'ample gardens washed by a stream', prosperous farmland, and the domestic hearth: a rich constatation of all that desire encompasses.

But by representing Emma's desire in the image of, as contained by, the house, garden, and estate, Jane Austen performs a narrative and ideological hat-trick. Erotic longing is united with a conservative political and social agenda. Emma's desire is not to possess the house, but rather the house is made an eloquent embodiment or vessel for that desire, which is thenceforth seen to be inseparable from the social institutions that may contain it. It is Donwell, thus, that persuades the reader that Emma's destiny is to be with Mr. Knightley – persuades one both of the social propriety (in the largest sense of fitness and likelihood of happiness) of the union, but also, more subtly, that Mr. Knightley will answer to Emma's needs just as much as to her desires: permanence, strength, and that stability that is also 'abundance', and growth which is an implicit warranty of sexual amplitude.

All this can be accomplished because Donwell is 'low and sheltered': this is an outdoor scene in which freedom is liberty, structured within an ordered, established, social world. At Box Hill, in the next chapter, the open air is an empty space, people wander off in all directions, social relations are unstructured, and the limitations of innovation and freedom are manifest. Soon follows the scene where Emma, confined to the Hartfield drawing room and with nothing to look forward to but a string of similiar evenings with her father, revisits the past: an indoors that encapsulates boredom and deprivation. When, next day, the proposal takes place, it is in the garden. Here, in this wonderful proposal scene, two intelligent people, each fearing that the other is devoted to another person, try their best to hold back their own emotions, and to give all their energy, their attention, their care, to further the other's happiness.

What Emma learns in this novel is not to think like Mr. Knightley, but that she has always, in fact, thought like him. There is no element of capitulation in the novel's ending, rather one of celebratory recognition. Their reconciliation would be the conclusion of a conventional romantic narrative, but Emma and Mr. Knightley converse a good deal after their private engagement. Unlike Elizabeth and Darcy who, in a similiar situation, educate each other into the intimacy of equals, Emma and Mr. Knightley enjoy already their reciprocal knowledge. They chafe and tease each other, working through the past, replaying their relationship in different terms: it is almost as if Austen were presenting Emma and Mr. Knightley as an already married couple. These scenes are by no means simply occasions for Emma to confess to being 'wrong'. 'What had she to wish for? Nothing, but to grow more worthy of him, whose intentions and judgment had been ever so superior to her own. Nothing, but that the lessons of her past folly might teach her humility and circumspection in future' (475). This is Emma thinking – vivaciously, but also extravagantly – as usual.

PERSUASION

Emma occupies her world so vividly that its sparseness – that there has been no ball at the Crown for many years – is hardly noticed. Anne Elliot is mentioned very early in *Persuasion*, but several chapters pass before this possible or potential heroine comes into her own in its pages. Instead this novel foregrounds the unnourishing world of her father and sister and those people, Lady Russell and Mr. Shepherd, who do duty as their 'friends'. Elizabeth 'did not quite equal her father in personal contentment', the narrator comments dryly:

> For thirteen years had she been doing the honours, and laying down the domestic law at home, and leading the way to the chaise and four, and walking immediately after Lady Russell out of all the drawing-rooms and dining rooms in the country. Thirteen winters' revolving frosts had seen her opening every ball of credit which a scanty neighbourhood afforded; and thirteen springs shewn their blossoms, as she travelled up to London for a few weeks annual enjoyment of the great world. (P 6–7)

Elizabeth 'would have rejoiced to be certain of being properly solicited by baronet-blood within the next twelvemonth or two'. This is Emma's 'what ought to be' seen as self-destructive presumption, pride now examined as self-immolation. While Elizabeth insists on her prerogatives and rights, the seasons perform in mechanical rotation about her, and springs only return to suggest a formal parody of renewed and replenished life. 'Fulfilment' is a Romantic word, but such a term is needed to suggest how Jane Austen associates Elizabeth's spiritual impoverishment, what the narrator calls later 'the sameness ... and the nothingness' (9) of her life, with the absence of love and erotic satisfaction. Instead she clutches, as does her sister Mary, at every sign of precedence the social world hands her.

Persuasion is, then, a novel about the inner and the outer life. This evocation of the sterility of Elizabeth's social space is a preface to its concern with the outward capability and inner turbulence of the quiet, recessive, and only gradually introduced heroine. Anne is without power in her family circle as she is at first without dramatic prominence in the text, but the narrative becomes gradually suffused with her presence, idioms, and approach. Yet it is through negatives, absences, understatements, merely the cadences and phrasing that shape her introspections, not through an assertive or dramatic voice, that Anne Elliot becomes for the reader a presence in her world.

'Nobody' in her immediate family, she is at least 'useful' in the neighbouring Musgrove circle. There, others talk while she plays the piano.

'She knew that when she played she was giving pleasure only to herself; but this was no new sensation: excepting one short period of her life, she had never, since the age of fourteen, never since the loss of her dear mother, known the happiness of being listened to, or encouraged by any just appreciation or real taste' (47). Such sentences exemplify the way Anne's consciousness is represented in this novel. Defining her solitariness, the sentence, by mentioning the death of her mother, and alluding more indistinctly to the forfeit of Wentworth, manages to suggest the enduring painfulness of both, and how that second loss inscribed the first yet more deeply. The plangent chords of these losses are dwelt on momentarily, but by enclosing, and holding, them within an assertion of Anne's competence, the phrasing also suggests how she has proceeded to a mature, if tenuous, accommodation. Anne's inner life is rendered in touches like this, which open brief perspectives on her emotional and psychological history, on the painful underpinnings of her present condition, but which never dwell on them. Anne's consciousness is imbued with memory and reflection, and the style which evokes it is at once suggestive and understated.

When Captain Wentworth once again enters Anne's life, he thus broaches a tentatively achieved stability. Anne's struggles to come to terms with the momentary encounters and challenges of his presence are represented as moral or ethical struggles to be 'rational' or 'sensible' but also as 'nervous' excitements, physiological responses of energies half repressed but now aroused and heightened, in blushes and agitations. Anne Elliot is thus a kind of moral-physiological entity, and the account of her 'reasonings' is accompanied by the continuous registration of a physical state, captured in a freer, more agitated prose than Austen has previously developed. Anne's thoughts after their first encounter are presented as a battle, as in a Shakespearian soliloquy, between the countervailing forces of desire and self-command, with desire repeatedly infiltrating the pitiful strategems of the stoic will that are marshalled to quell it (60–1). But since Anne's emotional needs are legitimate, the effect of her struggles is to produce a kind of ironic pathos, and the desire of the reader can only be to await their expression and fulfilment.

This sense of the intricacy of Anne's psychology – the pull of emotion imperfectly coinciding with conduct; the body, so to speak, having a will of its own (unexpectedly discerning Wentworth walking down the street 'She now felt a great inclination to go to the outer door; she wanted to see if it rained' (175), is one of Austen's main achievements. Capabilities, action, social life: these are only partially adequate vessels for, or expressions of, inner life, and Anne's various roles, until the novel's close, are never quite congruent with her nature. Wentworth's will is largely exercised in the domain of conduct, but just as much as Anne's, which addresses her emotions, it is out of harmony with desire.

The depth of Anne's solitary consciousness is contrasted with the absence of reflection (for Sir Walter picks up no books but the Baronetage) in the life of the surrounding small-time country gentry. The Musgroves are warm-hearted and unaffected, unlike the Elliots, but the whole family share an unreflecting philistinism. Finding Charles Hayter with books before him the Musgroves 'were sure all could not be right, and talked, with grave faces, of his studying himself to death' (82). They inhabit a taken-for-granted world, without an inkling that people are not entirely to be known by their appearances, without a glimpse of the pain behind Anne's apparent capability, and quite without insight into their own motives, as for example when Henrietta expresses so much concern for Dr. Shirley's health (102–3). When a man she likes talks to her about the value of firmness Louisa Musgrove takes him with her family's literal-mindedness and is resolute at every opportunity, becoming impulsive by rule.

Not even Wentworth and Lady Russell check their own feelings, or distance themselves from them. There is no hint that Lady Russell has felt guilt about the persuasion exerted over Anne in the past – indeed 'her heart revelled in angry pleasure, in pleased contempt' (125) when it appears that her original prejudice is being confirmed – for all the sadness of its consequences. The vehemence of Wentworth's protestation to himself that Anne's 'power with him was gone for ever' (61) suggests, of course, the opposite. But he does not consider this. He is a man of action and energy, trenchant convictions, strong and impulsive feelings that often take him to the verge of tactlessness, but little self-questioning or self-doubt.

Anne Elliot, then, is initially the only reflective consciousness of the novel. (The late-introduced invalid Mrs. Smith is perhaps a second.) Isolated within her family, she naturally takes the position of silent observer and is often privately amused at what she sees. Her own perception that she must accommodate to whatever social commonwealth she inhabits sets her always at a slight distance. Like the narrator whose interpretive role she gradually takes over, she is acutely alive to others' self-deceptions, but unlike the narrator – in this book a notably impatient voice – her response is usually kindly. Thus when she plays the piano for the Musgroves she is presented as being happy in their partiality for their daughters' performance over her own, while the writer, on the other hand, caustically suggests that they are 'fond parents' who only 'fancy themselves delighted' (47).

Anne's key interpretive role in the narrative is in sharp contrast to what is at first her peripheral place in her social circle. The novel is shaped, indeed, by the way this marginal observer gradually comes to take up a more central position, till in the climactic scene she is the focus of attention in the room. This is paralleled by the way Anne's inner life gradually comes to correspond to, make contact with, and be declared through, the outer life that surrounds her. These processes can be traced in her developing articulacy, for Anne is at first a notably silent observer. Only in chapter 4 does she become the subject of the narrative, and even then, she does not speak throughout. 'How eloquent could Anne Elliot have been ...!' declares the author, towards its close (30). But within the text, Anne is usually eloquent only by indirection or implication. It is with Anne's ears that the reader listens to the many monologues with which this novel defines characters – speeches from Elizabeth, Sir Walter, Mr. Shepherd, Mrs. Musgrove, Henrietta Musgrove, even Mrs. Clay – but what Anne herself says is often omitted. In dialogue, her responses tend to be absorbed into the meditative commentary of the text. In a powerful scene, Lady Russell tempts her with an eloquent vision of herself as Lady Elliot, 'presiding and blessing in the same spot' as her mother (160), and Anne is overcome with such emotion that she must rise and walk to a distant table. But there can be no words for the complexity of her recognition that what she valued in her family life cannot be restored.

Wentworth has made up his mind that he will not speak to Anne. The novel presents a carefully graduated sequence of incidents which bring the two into contact – an intimacy felt acutely in the first instance in bodily terms, as when 'they were actually on the same sofa' (68). Since words are not exchanged, the physical settings in which they meet play an important role. The episode in which her troublesome nephew climbs on Anne's back, for example, is constructed with Anne at the apex of lines of force – unspoken emotions – in the room, that run between herself and Wentworth, stationed at the window, between Wentworth and Hayter, jealously refusing to speak from behind his newspaper, and between herself and Hayter, who makes one perfunctory attempt to call off his little cousin. The setting is precisely imagined to focus these tensions and to increase them, give them material weight when the little boy hangs himself round Anne's neck (79–80). His unruliness is a metonym for the pressures that are present in the room. Anne has wanted to 'release' Wentworth and herself from embarrassment. Instead the release of the child's 'little sturdy hands' unlocks responses in Anne that are all the more intense for the embargo against their expression. And it is almost as if the boy's unruly attachment to her is an incarnation of Wentworth's still childish rage against, and therefore conflicted involvement with, Anne. His release of the boy thus figures as an initial movement towards his own relinquishment of a disabling psychological attitude.

Another moment of significant progress in their reconciliation occurs after the accident at Lyme. Anne, pausing at the parlour door, overhears Wentworth speaking of her directly. He ought to speak of her politely as 'Miss Anne Elliot', as he speaks of 'Mrs. Charles Musgrove', but instead he blurts out 'Anne': 'if Anne will stay, no one so proper, so capable as Anne!', for that is the name she goes by in his thoughts. After pausing, she enters the room. ' "You will stay, I am sure; you will stay and nurse her"; cried he, turning to her and speaking with a glow, and yet a gentleness, which seemed almost restoring the past' (114). He addresses her as if they were bound to concur – and she is consulted, not merely assumed to be useful. Anne's reply is to 'colour deeply' and her words of acquiescence are presented in indirect speech. Characteristically, physical or nervous responses are dramatized, verbal ones are recessed, and if Anne is often silent, her body language speaks volumes. When Wentworth turns to her in the carriage after their silent drive home and asks 'Do you think this a good plan?' Anne's reply is merely presented as 'She did' (117). One is reminded of similar moments of mutual consultation between Emma and Mr. Knightley, but here the traumatic presence of the past is felt, once again, in the inhibition of speech.

The accident at Lyme which concludes volume I is indeed the turning point both in the relationship of Anne and Wentworth, and in Anne's narrative position. Anne has responded with precisely similar authority to another fall, earlier in the tale (53), but the difference is now that her competence is dramatized and her performance seen by appreciative witnesses. Anne's becoming increasingly an object of regard in her circle is thus paralleled and matched by her increasing presence as a speaker and performer in the text. In volume II her responses are less elided in the narrative, and more and more fully represented within it. She is less and less confined to the responsive, reactive role (the glances and attentions of Mr. Elliot have at least this positive effect). 'My idea of good company, Mr. Elliot, is the company of clever, well-informed people, who have a great deal of conversation; that is what I call good company' (150): this assertiveness in his presence is a narrative as well as psychological development. Anne starts declaring her opinions to willing listeners, so that her private thoughts about the Musgrove sisters' impending marriages, for instance, are expressed fully and openly. ' "I am extremely glad, indeed", cried Anne' (217); she exclaims that Mr. and Mrs. Musgrove are excellent parents, she laughs out loud at Musgrove's sketch of Louisa and Benwick's courtship. This development culminates in dialogue with Harville at the White Hart – which is thus as much a formal as an emotional climax to the novel.

Perhaps the novel's greatest achievement is in the choreography of its public or 'crowd' scenes, for it is here that Austen threads her psychological theme through an active and almost picaresque setting, in which hidden motives are up against the exacting pressures of social business. In Bath there is a sense of personal communications having to be made within a crowded, complex world, in continual danger of being thwarted, interrupted or twisted by the projects and emotions of others. Three brilliant social chapters form the novel's climax, the concert in the octagon room (chapter 8 of volume II) and the gatherings at the Elliots' and Musgroves' apartments (10 and 11). In chapter 10 Austen succeeds in bringing together almost all of the personages of her novel, giving each of them a characteristic solo turn, and at the same time keeping up the psychological tension and emotional suspense of Anne and Wentworth's relationship. 'A large party in an hotel ensured a quick-changing, unsettled scene' (221). Serially, a set of incidents occurs which bear upon Anne and Wentworth indirectly: Mary's spying Mr. Elliot from the window, the squabble of Mary and Charles over the theatre tickets, the chilling visitation of Anne's father and sister to distribute their cards. Elizabeth Bennet had felt that her family conspired to disgrace her, but here the fear that one's projects are continually being trespassed upon, or contaminated, by one's relatives is felt even more acutely. Charles Musgrove's teasing of Mary about their social priorities is more good-natured than Mr. Bennet's taunting of his wife, but the significant difference is that the exchange is made to have bearing on the underlying (and quite distinct) drama of Anne and Wentworth's feelings, who extract from it meanings only for themselves.

It is not by chance that Austen sets the climactic scenes of her novel at an inn. This novel is concerned with that distinctively modern form of relation in which bonds are formed between people who are essentially transients. Elective affinities are seen to replace and even redeem the lost possibilities of Anne Elliot's emotionally sterile family. In chapter 11, again at the White Hart, Anne finds herself in the same room with Wentworth. His presence immediately causes a rise in her level of nervous tension. The exchanges of the two principals are once again mediated through a third party, here the overheard conversation of Mrs. Musgrove and Mrs. Croft, which modulates unexpectedly into a discussion of long engagements. Anne feels 'a nervous thrill all over her' (231). Captain Harville shows the miniature painting of Captain Benwick, once destined for the now dead Fanny Harville, to Anne. The themes of loss and mourning, fidelity and transience, that have occupied so much of Anne Elliot's consciousness in the novel are now resumed and played out dramatically in a conversation. The dialogue begins quietly but rises in seriousness and commitment, as Anne's responses become longer, more assertive, more eloquent. They are momentarily interrupted by a sound in Wentworth's 'hitherto perfectly quiet division of the room' (233), a sound that, punctuating the dialogue, makes one very aware of the spatial relations between the three.

The conversation with Harville resumes, with Anne's contributions once more increasing in length, till both are charged with intense personal feeling. Anne can now speak indirectly, but nonetheless eloquently and fervently, of her personal experience. 'She could not immediately have uttered another sentence; her heart was too full, her breath too much oppressed' (235). Their talk is about love and loyalties sustained over time; in its course Harville and she become friends, as his response indicates: 'You are a good soul', he says while 'putting his hand on her arm quite affectionately' – a wonderfully natural touch. The sequence is designed here to release, step by step, the energies of articulation that Anne has been forced to keep bound up, hemmed in, throughout so much of the novel. Thus this climactic scene resolves the tensions that have been built up in the course of this narrative. Jane Austen has found a way that gives her heroine the initiative, and gives her, finally, the heroine's place. Anne is now at once the woman through whose consciousness the world is seen and organized, and the speaking subject of the text. 'How eloquent could Anne Elliot have been ...!' Anne's yearning for fulfilment has been codified textually as a longing for expression. Her eloquence at last brings about the resolution of the romantic plot, and leads to the fulfilment of the hero and heroine's desires. At the same time Anne's expressive speech marries together those aspects of her nature that have been so unharmonized with each other throughout the text: feeling and moral action, the responsive body and the responsible self. The design of this novel, only sketched in parts, is effectively complete.

The three 'Chawton' novels are, then, incommensurate one with another. People are in the habit of speaking of 'Jane Austen's world', not perhaps separating the novels enough from the historical conditions in which their author wrote. But in truth there is no one, unified, homogeneous 'Jane Austen's world', but a number of different 'worlds', each defined and elaborated within the narrative frame that contains it. The wealthy and spoilt great upper gentry set of Mansfield and Sotherton is quite different from that local grouping of small gentry who form the comfortably enclosing – but also narrow, confining – community of Highbury. *Persuasion* takes different social groups again through which to pursue its concerns with emotional impoverishment and fulfilment. Jane Austen's creation of these distinct social and physical settings is inseparable, then, from her articulation of specific narrative designs. In *Sanditon*, imagination is even more specifically clothed in its setting, but this is the novel that Jane Austen did not live to complete at Chawton, that home so much 'to her mind'.[4]

NOTES

1   Letter to Francis Austen, July 26, 1809.
2   *Culture and Imperalism* (London: Vintage, 1994), p. 106.
3   I owe this point to Professor Joseph Wiesenfarth.
4   The author thanks Jo Barnes for her invaluable comments on an earlier draft of this paper.

5

MARGARET ANNE DOODY

The short fiction

In Jane Austen's unfinished *Catharine, or the Bower,* found in the notebook *Volume the Third,* we hear silly Camilla Stanley and her mother gushing over Camilla's correspondence with her friend Augusta:

> 'You received a Letter from Augusta Barlow to day, did not you, my Love?' said her Mother – . 'She writes remarkably well I know.'
>
> 'Oh! Yes Ma'am, the most delightful Letter you ever heard of. She sends me a long account of the new Regency walking dress Lady Susan has given her, and it is so beautiful that I am quite dieing with envy for it.'
>
> 'Well, I am prodigiously happy to hear such pleasing news of my young freind; I have a high regard for Augusta, and most sincerely partake in the general Joy on the occasion. But does she say nothing else? it seemed to be a long Letter – Are they to be at Scarborough?'
>
> 'Oh! Lord, she never once mentions it, now I recollect it; and I entirely forgot to ask her when I wrote last. She says nothing indeed except about the Regency.' 'She *must* write well' thought Kitty, 'to make a long Letter upon a Bonnet & Pelisse.' (*C&OW* 203)[1]

Austen's abortive novel can be heard here making fun of the epistolary mode, and of both the opposing views regarding female letter-writing. Mrs. Stanley approves of female correspondence: 'I have from Camilla's infancy taught her to think the same ... Nothing forms the taste more than sensible & Elegant Letters' (*C&OW* 202). This gush, like a pabulum concocted out of Hester Chapone's *Letters on the Improvement of the Mind* (1773), cannot quite conceal Mrs. Stanley's pride in having her daughter correspond with the daughter of Lady Halifax – a name amusingly reminiscent of Lord Halifax, author of a famous treatise *Advice to a Daughter,* a conduct book inhibiting to most female activity and feeling. Mrs. Percival, Catharine's aunt, takes the more traditional and sterner view, seeing 'a correspondence between Girls as productive of no good, and as the frequent origin of imprudence & Error by the effect of pernicious advice and bad Example' (202).

This mini-debate rages amusingly in this passage, as if there had been a revolution in manners. As debaters, the women manage to ignore the decorous insipidity and total triviality of their letters themselves, which reinforce a culturally desirable female vanity, empty-headedness, and fashion-conscious consumerism. In Richardson's *Clarissa*, or in Eliza Fenwick's *Secresy*, authority figures are not unreasonable in imagining that a female correspondence can change someone's mind and behaviour; correspondence can corrupt or encourage, and thus bring about some revolution in manners. It is more exciting to believe that than to think that false values merely repeat themselves – as seen in Mrs. Stanley's formal but hyperbolical expression – a hyperbole bought at the expense of realism. 'I ... most sincerely partake in the general Joy on the occasion' – as if Augusta had got engaged or had a baby, instead of acquiring her 'Regency walking dress'.

The phrase 'Regency walking dress' is itself my chief focus of interest. The manuscript of *Volume the Third* reveals, rather infuriatingly, that this phrase was substituted for another, but I have failed to decipher exactly the expression crossed out. It may well be 'Bonnet' with an underdeveloped 'B'. It looks a little like 'Panol', or 'Parrot' – or 'Parisol'. Whatever this reference to wearing apparel was (and it should match Bonnet and Pelisse) it has been excised in favour of another expression. Excised twice, for the same puzzling word was once there instead of 'Regency' in the sentence 'She says nothing indeed except about the Regency.'[2]

How and when did this change come about? I cannot accept George Holbert Tucker's suggestion that it indicates *Catharine* was written as early as 1788–9, when George III's first serious attack of deranging illness brought on agitation for a Regency.[3] *Volume the Third* was begun in May 1792 and the Regency crisis of the winter of 1788–9 was over by June 1789, when George III's return to health was celebrated.

I incline, rather, to accept Deirdre Le Faye's suggestion that Jane Austen rediscovered her earlier manuscript notebooks when she, her mother, and Cassandra at last came to roost in Chawton in July 1809.[4] 'Evelyn' is also added to in another hand, most likely by niece Anna Austen, though possibly by nephew Edward, and the last paragraph of *Catharine* is also the product of these other hands – and minds. The likeliest scenario is that on digging out her old notebooks Jane Austen shared her fiction with the nephew and niece, and allowed them to join her in her old game of writing. I believe their interest, perhaps even enthusiasm, inspired her to return to writing, and thus to undertake the serious and heavy work of finally revising *Sense and Sensibility*, the first of her novels to be published, in the very year of the Regency, 1811.

Catharine, or *Kitty, or the Bower*, that unfinished fiction, was probably begun in the mid-1790s, certainly not before the date at the top of the notebook volumes – May 6th, 1792; interior references to Charlotte Smith's novels accord well with the date 1792–3. The 'Regency walking dress' added to it indicates that Jane Austen turned back to this work at some point after – probably very soon after – the Regency Act was passed by Parliament on February 5, 1811. Fashion magazines were very quick to seize on the new era. The *Lady's Magazine* of 1811, along with the enticements of a running serial entitled *Sappho – An Historical Romance*, includes advertisements for, among other things, a plume of three feathers with silver and gold ornaments 'universally worn for the Regent's fête'; 'A new and elegant Pattern for Regency Borders' and a child's dress 'with the Regent hat of grey silk'. I have not yet found a 'Regency walking dress', but in picking up the comedy of such terms Austen was undoubtedly reflecting a trend of the time of 1811. Camilla's remark gains a new comedy: 'Augusta says nothing indeed except about the Regency', for Augusta is thus made to sound as if she had a political interest in current affairs, although her interest is entirely ladylike and fashionable.

In the period between 1809 and 1811 Jane Austen was working – and who can doubt *intently* working – on her own early writings. She was bringing what had been produced in the 1790s into line with current fashion. We have speculated about the 'Lost Novels' – lost to us in their old form. We know that *First Impressions* was the prototype of *Pride and Prejudice*; we believe that an *Elinor and Marianne*, perhaps epistolary, was the germ of *Sense and Sensibility*; and that *Susan*, which Jane Austen had tried to publish, and which had been once accepted (in 1803) but never brought out, was revised to make *Northanger Abbey* (published posthumously). Interestingly, 'Susan' was reclaimed from the publisher (Crosby) when the move to Chawton was an immediate prospect. Much of Jane Austen's writing career after the move to Chawton in 1809 consisted in revising or cannibalizing her own older works. But the revisions should be seen as a major matter.

In bringing her works into line with the new era – putting them into their Regency walking dress, as it were – Austen underwent a sort of personal and authorial revolution. That revolution made her publishable. It is startling to realize that Jane Austen might *never* have published. During the early years of the new century she had obviously begun to feel that her style of writing was not going to be acceptable to the press and the arbiters of taste. From her mid-twenties she had started to make some effort to reach a public, but had been severely balked by the lack of respect paid to the never-printed *Susan*. After the death of her father in 1805, Austen, now in her thirties, seems for a while to have given up writing, save for odd comic verses to friends. Removal to a real home in Chawton, and probably also the society of some young relatives interested in writing, helped to free Austen's mind and restore confidence. But it was not the same sort of confidence as that of the young woman who wrote the material in the notebook *Volumes*.

Jane Austen had to change, in short, from a 1790s writer to a 'Regency' writer. The term 'Regency', always loosely used (especially as an adjective), ought to refer to the period from 1811 (when the Prince of Wales, 'Prinny', was made Regent, as his father George III was unfit to govern by reason of insanity) to 1820 (when George III died and the Prince Regent became King George IV). In practice, the term in English usage has come to refer to the period from the onset of the nineteenth century through the 1820s. Jane Austen has really been recast in certain quarters as the first in line of the writers of 'Regency romances' – a fact underdiscussed in academic circles. I believe the appeal of the 'Regency romance' – for modern intents and purposes a genre invented by Georgette Heyer (1902–74) – lies in the combination of the traditional 'love story' with the idea of a charming and tastefully pert woman who is a *little* likely to question the *status quo,* but not too much. Of course, there is always the dashing lover – less likely to appear in Austen. Yet I think Jane Austen herself does bear some relation to this genre. Her kind of novel was achieved by a special mixture of eighteenth-century qualities of attitude and style combined with domestic seriousness and Romantic respect for both idealism and power. Georgette Heyer started by writing novels set in the eighteenth century (*The Black Moth*, 1921), but made her mark when she invented the story set in the Regency with *These Old Shades* (1926). Heyer, in the period from the 1920s through the 1950s, caught – and in her own way also parodied – the qualities in literature wanted by her audience. These were not at all dissimilar to some of the qualities desired by Jane Austen's public, though Heyer has the added element of a version of pastoral. Her 'Regency' is a happy abode of the past, a place to escape to. So Jane Austen's temporal setting has become idyllic – though it was a present-day setting for the author.

The desire for the combination of the flippant and the serious, the nostalgic and the entertaining, can be postulated in the readership (both male and female) of both writers. Heyer, like Austen, reached a public tired by a very difficult war which had brought not only painful loss but great upheaval. Some responses to the threat of change and some modified form of patriotism had to be incorporated in women's writing if it was to succeed – yet it could not be successful if it proposed itself as too critical a commentary. Fiction had to take the fundamental shape of things seriously, and to play by the rules.

I want to propose that Jane Austen's advance to the Long Novel acceptable to her contemporaries was a process of accommodation. It was a difficult and strenuous process – she had, as it were, to reinvent herself as a Regency figure. After all, the 'Regency' itself is a figure for substitution. We are so devoted to the six Austen novels, it is hard for us to think of them as substitutes for anything – but they may not really have been the works Jane Austen wanted to write.

Her comments on the process reach us filtered through irony – as in the famous remark in a letter of February, 1813, about the 'defects' of *Pride and Prejudice*:

> the work is rather too light & bright & sparkling; – it wants shade; – it wants to be stretched out here & there with a long Chapter – of sense if it could be had, if not of solemn specious nonsense – about something unconnected with the story; an Essay on Writing, a critique on Walter Scott, or the history of Buonaparte – or anything that would form a contrast & bring the reader with increased delight to the playfulness & Epigrammatism of the general stile.
>
> (L 203)

We take this simply as irony in self-praise, but there is more to it. 'Sparkle' was no longer in order – and particularly not in a woman. 'Sparkle' in general meant that old Augustan style, the taste for paradox and wit, for snip-snap antithesis – all things Jane Austen inherited. William Wordsworth, who had often praised the style of the poet Anne Finch, Countess of Winchilsea, was to say of Finch: 'her style in rhyme is often admirable, chaste, tender, and vigorous, and entirely free from sparkle, antithesis and ... over-culture'.[5] Lady Winchilsea's poetry is good because it is tender, and does *not* sparkle. Austen became increasingly aware, I think, that playfulness and epigrammatism had decided dangers. Regency readers wanted to be amused, but they liked to have a clear line drawn, the now-to-be-completely-serious line. An author like Maria Edgeworth met this demand through didacticism, and allowed herself some political leverage, though at the cost of suppressing a wit rarely allowed full emergence. Frances Burney, publishing *The Wanderer* (1814) in this new climate, got badly frozen by disapproval and some very negative reviews in reaction against her inclusive satire on England in the Revolutionary period. Burney wrote no more novels.

Jane Austen's relations to and with the 'Regency' are paradigmatically played out in the merry amusing comedy of relations between herself, the Prince Regent, and the Prince Regent's librarian, James Stanier Clarke. It was he who entertained Jane Austen at the library of Carlton House in November, 1815 – only a few months after Waterloo. Clarke told her that she was 'at liberty to dedicate any future work to H[is] R[oyal] H[ighness] the P[rince] R[egent]' (*L* 296). She tried to clarify whether this request amounted to a command, and Clarke's reiteration on paper that permission had been given showed Austen clearly that she was expected to dedicate her next work to the Prince. She was also told, flatteringly, 'The Regent has read & admired all your publications' (*L* 296). Though her opinion of the Regent himself, judging from comments in her other letters, was not high, Austen made the Prince Regent the lucky recipient of the dedication of *Emma*. The Regent undoubtedly intended to do good to Austen by getting her name more widely known; he supplied her thus with advertising that did have its effect on reviewers and readership (see the essay by Jan Fergus in this volume). Had Austen lived longer, she would have reaped the full benefit of this publicity. The Prince is to be congratulated on his taste. But James Stanier Clarke did go blethering on, suggesting that Austen write the life of a clergyman, modelled on his life, glorified. It was in evading this suggestion that Austen defiantly set herself down as 'the most unlearned, & uninformed Female who ever dared to be an Authoress' (*L* 306).

Unlike James Stanier Clarke, we have the benefit of Austen's parodic 'Plan of a Novel, according to hints from various quarters', which includes many phrases lifted straight from Clarke's letters, and applied to the father of the heroine:

> At last, hunted out of civilized Society, denied the poor Shelter of the humblest Cottage, they are compelled to retreat into Kamschatka where the poor Father, quite worn down, finding his end approaching, throws himself on the Ground, and after 4 or 5 hours of tender advice and parental Admonition to his miserable Child, expires in a fine burst of Literary Enthusiasm, intermingled with Invectives against Holder's of Tythes. – Heroine inconsolable for some time – but afterwards crawls back towards her former Country ...
>
> (*C&OW* 232)

This is great stuff, interwoven as it is with parodic references to other fictions, as well as with hidden references to the comments on Austen's novels passed by various acquaintances. The comedy, however, expresses irritation. In this 'Plan', novel-writing itself turns into a ridiculous ordeal. Dealing with James Stanier had been something of an ordeal. As the Regent's deputy, or the Regent's regent, as well as a clergyman, he is doubly a Father, and triply a substitute father. In the company of such mock fathers you get into the cold regions of Kamschatka, the extremity of Siberia.

Jane Austen's early writings, preserved for us in the three notebook Volumes, are short fictional pieces. It has been customary to imagine – unconsciously to imagine – that she always aspired to write three-volume novels, and that the early writings were mere apprenticeship or practice until she could arrive at that happier capacity for sustained work. But if we think of it, this may not be true. Short fiction has its place – and sometimes it is a very high place. The short fictional piece, the 'tale', had been used to good effect by earlier women writers like Aphra Behn and Eliza Haywood. Eliza Haywood, however, in mid-eighteenth century had to make a turn similar to Austen's. Her kind of short story and its longer sexy cousin the 'novel', or *novella*, had to be put aside for the sake of respectable long 'history' to match the works of Fielding and Richardson. So we move from stories like *Fantomina* to the full-length *Miss Betsy Thoughtless*. Yet it was certainly not female practitioners alone who had an allegiance to the short fiction.

Short fiction is a favourite Enlightenment mode, engaged in by Voltaire, for one notable example. It was explored by Diderot (e.g. *Ceci n'est pas un conte*) and more cautiously taken up by Marmontel in his *Contes moraux* (1789–92). Marmontel's *Contes* were appearing in France at about the time Austen began *Volume the Third*. She might have known that Horace Walpole had written his *Hieroglyphic Tales*, stories first printed in 1785 and later published by Mary Berry in Walpole's *Collected Works* (1798). Charles Burney, reviewing them, said they contained 'a great many *odd fancies*' and in their allusions were 'sarcastic, personal, and sometimes profane'.[6] Walpole in his Postscript to these *Tales* says they are 'an attempt to vary the stale and beaten class of stories and novels, which, though works of invention, are almost always devoid of imagination'. He professes himself surprised that fiction (especially current fiction) is so dull: 'that there should have been so little fancy, so little variety, and so little novelty, in writings in which the imagination is fettered by no rules' (*Oriental Tales*, ed. Mack 137). His tales play with the absurd, the disproportionate, the illicit; his characters are greedy bundles of expressionistic desire:

> [the princess] had purchased ninety-two dolls, seventeen baby houses, six cartloads of sugar plums, a thousand ells of gingerbread, eight dancing dogs, a bear and a monkey, four toyshops with all their contents, and seven dozen of bibs; and aprons of the newest fashion. They were jogging on with all this cargo over mount Caucasus ... (*Oriental Tales* 119)

Robert Mack points out that the tales 'reach into every conceivable area of narrative invention ... "An entire world of invention lies open for your use and enjoyment", Walpole seems to say, "why not take advantage of it?"' ('Introduction', xxvii). So too we might imagine Jane Austen saying – that is, the Austen of the early fiction. The characters are full of a fine excess, of energy impossible and disproportionate, of physicality unconcealed:

My mother rode upon our little poney and Fanny and I walked by her side or rather ran, for my Mother ... galloped all the way. You may be sure we were in a fine perspiration ... Fanny has taken a great many Drawings of the Country, which are very beautiful, tho' perhaps not such exact resemblances as might be wished, from their being taken as she ran along. It would astonish you to see all the Shoes we wore out in our Tour ... Mama was so kind as to lend us a pair of blue Sattin Slippers, of which we each took one and hopped home from Hereford delightfully – .   ('A Tour through Wales', *C&OW* 170)

Like Walpole's personages, Austen's are wonderfully greedy, illicit mental collectors of wealth:

'I shall expect a new saddle horse, a suit of fine lace, and an infinite number of the most valuable Jewels. Diamonds such as never were seen, Pearls as large as those of the Princess Badroulbadour ... and Rubies, Emeralds, Toppazes, Sapphires, Amythists, Turkey stones, Agate, Beads, Bugles & Garnets.'

('The Three Sisters', from MS version)

Much of the comedy of these early fantastic tales comes from the fantasticating capacity of the mind not only to desire, but to create wants. Narrative follows these jumps of desire. Those persons, such as parents or clergymen, who might represent law or sobriety have really only different forms of desire to offer.

Austen, like Cervantes, makes us see the organization of property and propriety from a comic underside:

Beloved by Lady Harcourt, adored by Sir George and admired by all the World, she lived in a continued course of uninterrupted Happiness, till she had attained her eighteenth year, when happening one day to be detected in stealing a banknote of 50 £, she was turned out of doors by her inhuman Benefactors. Such a transition to one who did not possess so noble and exalted a mind as Eliza, would have been Death, but she, happy in the conscious knowledge of her own Excellence, amused herself as she sate beneath a tree with making and singing the following Lines ...

('Henry and Eliza', *C&OW* 31)

In mocking depiction of the calm way in which the abnormal can be presented as normal, the criminal as the proper, the shameful as the excellent, Austen united with Cervantes and with others who target both individual lust and social assumptions.

Her stories explore irregular unions – hardly anybody is married, or married in a regular fashion. The heroine of 'Love and Freindship' is united to her true love shortly after he has wandered into their cottage. The young pair are married by the heroine's father: 'We were immediately united by my Father, who tho' he had never taken orders had been bred to the

Church' (C&OW 80). Austen's early fiction is a mock-pastoral world in which eviscerated institutions, or institutionalized ideas, though sometimes honoured in gesture, are unable to contain the characters' curiosity, animation, or general desire for self-gratification. The desire for self-gratification prevails everywhere – including in the heroine modelled on Jane's best friend and devoted sister. In 'The Beautifull Cassandra' the heroine goes out walking with a bonnet intended for a countess 'on her gentle Head'. 'She then proceeded to a Pastry-cooks where she devoured six ices, refused to pay for them, knocked down the Pastry Cook and walked away' (C&OW 42). This is not a moral world where punishment catches up with evil doers. At the end of her libidinous excursion Cassandra can whisper to herself, ' "This is a day well spent" ' (C&OW 43).

Jane Austen shares qualities with Rabelais – as G. K. Chesteron noticed.[7] She also has some of the cool wit of an eighteenth-century writer like Diderot or a twentieth-century one like Borges. Yet we have wanted to see these early works as chaotic and childish, mere 'prentice-hand attempts to perform what will be done properly in the six novels. For if the shorter works are not treated as childish effusions, they begin to loom very large indeed in Austen's oeuvre, pointing to the alternative Austen who might have been a different writer, who might have figured in our calendar more like Diderot or Borges. It is not enough to say she is a parodist – though that is much – or to say that she is a satirist – which is a great deal more. We have to acknowledge, I think, that she here creates in her short fiction a 'world of her own', as we say – or that such a world becomes adumbrated. The world she creates is a world of libidinous pressures only fictively constrained by conceptual structures imposed as order. English laws regarding marriage and property or the new laws of the English novel are alike revealed as pseudo-orderly and slightly crazed structures. Here, Austen's world is one where the law of the Father applies only nominally – or not even that. The law of the Father is a kind of gesture in the air.

Modes of defying the father in rebellion or *revolution*, which are likewise conventional ideas in themselves, especially between 1789 and 1800, come in for equally scornful treatment. This can be seen in Edward's stilted and conventional defiance of his father in 'Love and Freindship'. Love is refracted narcissism. Dislike of others is not only common but, as it were, decriminalized. In preposterous play with the idyll, the characters fare as they will without paying – money is everywhere, but it is always going missing, or becoming invalid. Austen proposes that libidinous desire is prior to the economic system, although constantly getting attached to it. Libidinous desire gets attached, for instance, to the feudal system of inheritance, creating a greed that cheerfully witnesses the removal of parents and siblings. Desire is officially attached to the system of monogamy. In attaching itself to any such systems, however, the libido proves itself capable of evading or transforming them – in Austen's world.

This is a very frightening philosophic production on the part of a young woman. The disconcerting elements in Austen's fiction (even in the six novels) are sometimes very palpable obstacles to our smooth approbation. But these elements in her early fiction can be redefined as lack of skill in doing the accepted thing. Doubtless Crosby, the publisher who got *Susan*, intuited that Austen's book didn't *feel* quite right, and put his response down to a sense that the author was amateurish, that she hadn't quite got the hang of writing novels. The obstreperous qualities that work well in short fiction were not highly valued in the novel. Short fiction was not as available to writers as it had been in the mid-eighteenth century as a vehicle for new and outrageous thought. The bright wit of the eighteenth century is felt to be political, and politically dangerous. The Regency is a tight time. Regency fashions may have been sexy – but they hampered women's movement in tight skirts, and left men strangulated in neckcloths.

We tend to confuse the 'Regency' manners of the Prince Regent and his circle with the tone of the period in general. In English culture in general, however, raffishness was out of favour, and morality – especially as that concerned the moral behaviour of young ladies – was steadily gaining ground. As Claudia Johnson has shown,[8] the era of the Napoleonic wars brings a backlash against cultural experiment, and particularly against experiment in the representation of women in fiction. The courtship novel is returned. It is softened, moralized, made safer.

Augustan wit in general is shunned. The early nineteenth century admires the serious. Byron had been serious and melancholy in *Childe Harold*. He returned in *Don Juan* to wit – with a vengeance. But Byron was already an established author, and there is an intermixture of the serious and the personal and the pathetic which saves his mock-epic from the accusation of total flippancy. One of Byron's strengths is that he (or his narrator) can give us the impression of being able to see through Culture – Culture not in the anthropological sense but in the modern urban sense, of an accumulation of knowledge about knowledge and artefacts that serves an individual's social turn and creates a unified dominant class. Jane Austen shares a doubt about the cultural – in part, such doubt is an inheritance of Enlightenment views that what is past is prologue, and that everything should be held up to question. The Romantic Age in its own way takes 'culture' very seriously. We are headed towards the world of Matthew Arnold where there is a plain distinction between 'Culture' and 'Anarchy'. To Jane Austen, culture often *is* anarchy.

I had for many years constantly hollowed whenever she played, *Bravo, Bravissimo, Encora, Da Capo, allegretto, con espressione,* and *Poco presto* with many other such outlandish words, all of them as Eloisa told me expressive of my Admiration; and so indeed I suppose they are, as I see some of them in every Page of every Music book, being the Sentiments I imagine of the Composer. ('Lesley Castle', *C&OW* 125–6)

Such a passage moves us from the simple satire (Charlotte's stupidity in not knowing musical terms) to a complex satire on cultural knowledge and its close relation to absurdity. Our thoughtful reaction is compounded by the culturally dense meanings of the two girls' names, 'Eloisa' and 'Charlotte'. 'Eloisa' refers us to the heroine of Rousseau's novel *Julie, ou la nouvelle Héloïse* (1761). Julie, the 'New Eloisa', is an emotionally complicated and doomed young woman who has sex before marriage and will meet a tragic fate. By contrast, 'Charlotte', the virtuous and practical beloved of the emotionally overwrought Werther in Goethe's *The Sorrows of Young Werther* (1774), involves herself in no illicit sex, and leaves the suffering to others. The names of Austen's characters in 'Lesley Castle' are thus complicated for any reader who has knowledge (guilty knowledge) of two famous but controversial novels about sex and suffering. To know such works is itself a cultural achievement, if one not without risk for women. Through such works women have access to philosophical ideas. Here, however, the reader's vision is beclouded by an excess of association. Reading Austen's 'Lesley Castle' one is apt to run into a new reading of Rousseau's 'Eloisa' as too limp and die-away, as well as into a parody of the bread-and-butter 'Charlotte' of *Werther*, who becomes that fiendish cook with a one-track mind, Charlotte Luttrell. Austen turns the culture into anarchy.

But the Novel itself – what of that? In England, in particular, the Novel had undergone many trials. The Renaissance and the seventeenth century had seen a great festival of fiction-reading, much amplified by new editions and translations of older novels from antiquity, such as the works of Helidorus, and from the Middle Ages, such as Boccaccio. The rage for fiction-reading gave rise to a certain nervousness. Sixteenth-century scholars and divines had begun to take a dim view of prose fiction. Yet, on the whole, it survived and prospered until that universal European post-war period of the later seventeenth century. After the abortive French revolution of the 1640s known as the 'Fronde', after the English Civil War and the Thirty Years War, European governments reformed themselves, more or less awkwardly, either into a more absolute monarchic form to achieve the status of nation state (like France, and later Germany, and Austria), or into a more republican form, allowing rule of an oligarchy. To both kinds of new politically adjusted power the tradition of prose fiction bore special dangers. The novel is critical of what is. It gives the younger generation a chance. Reading it can make women and boys think themselves too important. In France, the novel is represented as bourgeois – a brilliant stroke initiated by Boileau. In the plutocracies (England, Holland) the Novel under the label 'Romance' was attacked as too royalist, old-fashioned, and feudal. Prose fiction continued to be in a period of great experiment in the early eighteenth century, but the mid century saw more determined efforts to police it, not the least of these being novel reviewing. Whole tracts of the older fiction (and in Britain, practically all foreign fiction) were labelled off limits – a process of banning recorded in that ambiguous and clever novel that Jane Austen knew very well, Charlotte Lennox's *The Female Quixote*, in 1752. As Lennox shows us in that book, the Novel can be allowed to continue to exist – even the novel about a woman by a woman – but only if the terms are agreed to. Nothing outlandish or dangerous must be shown. The novel is to exhibit the taming of a girl as she dwindles into a wife – the story of a girl learning her place. This is the story that Rousseau adapts in creating Sophie in his *Emile* (1762).

The novel, then, is tamed. 'Realism' is the name that we give to an ideology of tameness and tightening applied to the novel. The novel in England – which defines itself as History or ultimately Novel as against *Romance* – is especially domesticated. The history of its domestication in relation to women has been traced by many other writers, including Vineta Colby, Sandra Gilbert and Susan Gubar, and Nancy Armstrong.[9] I see the point of this domestication in another sense. The new novel is *domestic* in that it deals with home, and with England. Foreigners don't count. If you meet a Muslim in a work of fiction, then it isn't a proper novel, but Romance. All sensation (this in an era of colonization, wars, battle, murder, and sudden death) is the baggage of the bad old 'Romance'. The Novel is to be allowed to exist, and to be read by women and the young, on condition that it always knows its own place in the Culture, which is a low place. It is 'only a novel!' (*NA* 38). This is a quiet, subservient, inferior form. Its best use and sole justification is that it can inform the young (especially women) of well-known truths, and teach them their place in the universe. Realism is valued because it resists thought-experiment. And if a woman writes only of what she strictly and severely knows then her fictional world – unlike that of, say, the seventeenth-century French novelist Madeleine de Scudéry – will be constricted indeed.

The courtship plot of the regular novel is always sneered at (women, bless their silly little hearts, like to read love stories). But courtship is of the essence, particularly if it ends in a synthesizing middle-class marriage. Jane

Austen's early works cannot be called courtship novels, though they show an exact knowledge of the formulas. In her six full novels, she had to adapt the courtship plot in good seriousness (or with some degree of seriousness). That she was not quite successful in her Regency disguise, perhaps, can be felt in the weight of Scott's complaint, in his cumulative review of *Emma*, that Austen does not pay enough attention to love. It may be because of that review that Austen discusses love, and male and female views of it, as thoroughly as she does in *Persuasion*.

Certainly, the novel as it was being shaped – the domestic novel, safe for women to write – and read – was not the appropriate home of social criticism or free aesthetic play – still less of moral questioning. Young people – especially but not only women – were to be instructed in their moral duties. So heavy did the weight of the real Regency formulations lie on the novel, one may feel, that the novel became flattened under the burden and passed out. How else can we explain the paucity of novels in the period between Jane Austen's death and Queen Victoria's ascent to the throne? The 1840s were to inaugurate a new era in fiction, but the preceding decades from a novel-lover's point of view are fairly dismal. There are few new writers in the 1820s and 1830s. Scott dominates the field, and he had developed in the historical novel a route out of the impasse offered by the domestic fiction. Maria Edgeworth did not die when Jane Austen did – she lived until 1849. But had she died in 1817 we should have lost but one important work by Edgeworth – the novel *Helen* (1834). Another novel, *Taken for Granted*, finished in 1838, was (interestingly) destroyed by its author. Frances Burney the novelist was apparently silenced by the reviews of *The Wanderer*. The author published a three-volume biography of her father in 1832, but wrote no more novels. Peacock's early spurt of novel-writing ceases with *Nightmare Abbey* (1818). There is one novel in the 1830s (*Crotchet Castle*, 1831); Peacock waited until the High Victorian Age to produce *Gryll Grange* (1860). Looking at such a record, one begins to think better of Catherine Gore, with her satiric 'silver fork' novels in the 1830s – but even Mrs. Gore turned to song-writing and drama as more profitable.

The challenge that Jane Austen offered to other writers of fiction was not then to be taken up, and by the time it was truly taken up she was burdened with a certain imposed quaintness never quite totally shaken off. She could also be smothered in Aunt Jane-ism.

The challenge that Austen offered contemporary fiction arose from the challenge she herself faced – how to sustain some of her own deeper interests while submitting to the restrictions of the domestic and moral courtship novel as the only truly available form. What she does, I want to suggest, is to tap into the deep roots of the Novel as a whole – the Big Novel, not in the sense of the *long* novel but of the larger traditions of prose fiction, going back to antiquity. If a novel is deep enough it can escape the shallowness of contemporary polite and prudential formulas. Austen's depths are very well hidden. She is strikingly unlike her contemporaries, female as well as male, in not overtly alluding to any of the heathen mythology in her novels. Indeed, the allusion to the fact of its existence comes in the form of mockery:

> 'How long ago it is, aunt, since we used to repeat the chronological order of the kings of England ...'
> 'Yes', added the other; 'and of the Roman emperors as low as Severus; besides a great deal of the Heathen Mythology, and all the Metals, Semi-Metals, Planets, and distinguished philosophers.' (*MP* 18–19)

Austen is not going to let us catch her making her novels mythical. She customarily shies away even from explicit allegory of names of the type familiar enough in Fielding (with his 'Squire Western' and 'Mr. Allworthy'). We can catch her – just barely – in a name like Mr. Knightley. But she uses to a considerable degree and in a very fascinating way what I call the 'tropes of the Novel'.

One of these important tropes is the image of *mud*, the mixture of earth and water, usually combined with a margin, threshold, or no-man's land of in-between. *Mud* is earthy and mobile, the deep primal slime from which things grow, the union of male and female, the party of *hylé*, the celebration of life on earth. Mud is thus exactly what is banned from drawing rooms and has no place in the transcendent. To name mud is to name what is *not* transcendent – it goes with the flesh, the muddy vesture of decay. Mr. Knightley has to display his shoes to Mr. Woodhouse to reassure him that he has no mud or dirt on them. This dry beginning of *Emma* tells us that relationships are baulked, that this is something of a waste land of sterility – the sterility arising from propriety. When the hero and the heroine at last come together, they are outdoors after a shower. Earth and water have reunited, there is plenty of dirt around, and fertility is possible. To use the image thus is to join in the great Novel-work of celebrating the physical, of resisting the transcendent insofar as that does not honour the world of matter and flesh. Elizabeth Bennet gets mud on her petticoats racing over the fields and leaping over stiles on a rainy day. Her muddy vesture scandalizes the Bingley sisters – but not Mr. Darcy or ourselves. The beginning of *The Watsons* shows the sisters 'As they splashed along the dirty Lane' (*MW* 315). Life offers a new beginning.

It is this sense of vitality that offers the deepest pleasure in Austen's work.

With this her truest 'religious feeling' (as we sometimes term it) is conjoined. We recognize in her mature novels the places of deception, the arid places where hypocrisy reigns, where the spiritless meets the spiritless. The truly spiritual in Austen is spirited.

In her early fiction, Jane Austen could write with zest and confidence. She had inherited a taste for irony, paradox, and 'sparkle' from the eighteenth century. Her early writing is rough, violent, sexy, joky. It sparkles with knowingness. It attacks whole structures, including cultural structures that had made a regularized and constricted place for the Novel, as well as the very workings (in stylized plot and character) of the English novel itself.

The ordeal of creating her own novel, I would suggest, was an ordeal painful for Jane Austen, a retreat to Kamschatka and a crawling back. The elements that we find in Austen's early short fiction are what kept her later works from dwindling into comfortable prosy little comedies of upper middle-class courtship, with didactic elements carefully inserted. Yet, to a certain extent and not in trifling ways, Austen had to pretend – in order to get published at all – that her mature novels were such innocuous and didactic things. At the beginning of the nineteenth century, Austen had, in effect, been warned that she would have to 'chill out' to match the chillier decorum that constituted the conventions of fiction allowed into public discourse. The original 'Siberia' to which she had been sent was the Siberia of rejection by publishers. She escaped, but at the price of subscribing to conformity, of adapting to the confinements of propriety. Her movements became constricted and she spoke in an altered tone. The early fictions tell us what Austen might have sounded like without such domestication. She had to go a very long way round to get back into fiction – wearing her Regency walking dress, which must have been uncomfortable to walk in, and coming from Kamschatka.

NOTES

1 My quotations for this essay are from Jane Austen's *Catharine and Other Writings*, ed. Margaret Anne Doody and Douglas Murray (Oxford: Oxford University Press, 1993), which more closely represents the manuscript than R. W. Chapman's edition of the *Minor Works*. A version of this essay appeared in the annual journal of the Jane Austen Society of North America, *Persuasions*, 16 (1994), 69–84.

2 See *Volume the Third* MS, p. 67.

3 George Holbert Tucker, *Jane Austen: The Woman* (New York: St. Martin's Press, 1994), p. 114.

4 Deirdre Le Faye, *Jane Austen: A Family Record* (London: The British Library, 1989), p. xxii.

5   Quoted in Roger Lonsdale, *Eighteenth-Century Women Poets: An Oxford Anthology* (New York: Oxford University Press, 1990), p. 6.

6   Robert Mack, Introduction to Horace Walpole's *Oriental Tales*, ed. Robert Mack (Oxford: Oxford University Press, 1992).

7   G. K. Chesterton, ed., *Love and Freindship and Other Early Works* (New York: Fredrick A. Stokes, 1922), p. xv.

8   Claudia L. Johnson, *Jane Austen: Women, Politics, and the Novel* (Chicago: Chicago University Press, 1988), 'Introduction'.

9   Vineta Colby, *The Singular Anomaly: Women Novelists of the Nineteenth Century* (New York: New York University Press, 1970); Sandra M. Gilbert and Susan Gubar, *The Madwoman in the Attic: The Woman Writer and the Nineteenth-Century Literary Imagination* (New Haven: Yale University Press, 1979); Nancy Armstrong, *Desire and Domestic Fiction: A Political History of the Novel* (New York: Oxford University Press, 1987).

6

CAROL HOULIHAN FLYNN

The letters

As she recalls her own memories of Aunt Jane to help brother James-Edward Austen-Leigh construct his *Memoir of Jane Austen*, Caroline Austen questions the possibility of ever representing a 'life' that already seems too obscure to recover. 'I am sure you will do justice to what there *is* – but I feel that it must be a difficult task to dig up the *materials*, so carefully have they been buried out of our sight by the past generation.'[1] She dismisses the more obvious 'materials' at hand: 'There is nothing in those letters which *I* have seen that would be acceptable to the public – They were very well expressed, and they must have been very interesting to those who received them – but they detailed chiefly home and family events: and she seldom committed herself *even* to an opinion – so that to strangers they could be *no* transcript of her mind – they would not feel that they knew her any the better for having read them – '[2]

What I find so compelling about Caroline Austen's scepticism is its applicability to Austen studies in every generation. Readers coming to her letters usually find something 'missing' that vexes them. In his introduction to the first edition of the letters, R. W. Chapman recites what will continue to be 'a familiar defence' of the letters. They have been 'robbed of their general interest by Cassandra Austen's pious destruction of all that she supposed might possibly excite general curiosity'.[3] By blaming Cassandra for keeping us from the 'real' Jane Austen, we are able to sustain an idea of the writer regardless of materials, or lack of materials, that occlude the portrait of the artist. We look to the letters for deep feeling, but are kept relegated to the surface of things, rewarded with 'small matters' and 'momentous minutiae'.

Caroline Austen rejects what is *in* Austen's letters, not what is left *out*. Not the mysteriously buried materials, but those mundanely visible above ground, the letters preserved by Cassandra, disappoint her for failing to provide 'a transcript' of the writer's mind. Her concern reveals the investment that readers looking for a transparent relationship between 'mind' and 'art' bring to the letters, an investment her brother seems to share. Like Caroline, he is disappointed by his aunt's epistolary productions, and he warns the reader of his *Memoirs* 'not to expect too much' from his aunt's letters. Their 'materials', he explains, 'may be thought inferior', treating only 'the details of domestic life ... They resemble the nest which some little bird builds of the materials nearest at hand.'[4] It is only recently that the domestic nature of the letters has been freed from such a condescending interpretation. Jo Modert suggests that the very banal domestic surface of the letters offers us a tool for understanding the foundations of Austen's creative production,[5] while Deborah Kaplan and Susan Whealler read Austen's depictions of self-denial and housewifery as subtle productions emerging from a feminine culture which supports the self-expression of women who are conscious of dual allegiances to claims of social class and gender.[6] We are learning to look more carefully at the coded interpretations that Austen and her female correspondents make of their positions of relative powerlessness in their class and gender systems, and to look for their painfully calibrated understanding of the disappointments and adjustments which mark the feminine experience. It is Austen's awareness of the texture of domestic life that generates her densely realized novels.

In the novels, Austen is careful to make certain that her understanding of the 'dual cultures' which claim her allegiance not be made entirely transparent. Her sensitivity to the privileged obligations of class and gender encourages her to disguise her representations of the desire for power and its disappointments, and to frame such situations with ironic pronouncements which undercut desire while they pretend detachment. The very style of her novels, tersely and laconically epigrammatic, insists upon a graceful inevitability of social forms that must triumph over individual acts of rebellion and desire. Nothing is ever so inevitable in Austen's own letters, however, which awkwardly disclose disjointed fragments of everyday social exchange. 'I wonder whether the Ink bottle has been filled', she writes. 'Does Butcher's meat keep up at the same price? & is not Bread lower than 2/6. – Mary's blue gown! – My Mother must be in agonies' (L 239). Seldom moderated, extreme positions are more often than not enumerated, blandly, in jarring catalogues of 'little matters' that unsettle a reader looking for coherence.

It is this incoherence that so alarms Caroline Austen, who is looking for a proper 'transcript' of an elegant, composed mind. In her letters, Austen employs a jolting, frustrating style which disallows for subordination. Dashes casually break up endless paragraphs to signal fresh 'matters' inappropriately joined, subjects as momentous as 'a dead Baronet' and as mundane as a dose of rhubarb (320–1). Alternately 'ringing the Changes of the Glads & Sorrys' (118), she seems to be exploring the limits of a stream of consciousness located somewhere between Sterne and Samuel Beckett, one that represents her own awareness of the endless nature of her domestic tasks. Since 'correspondence' becomes one of these tasks,[7] she must always be in search of a subject. In fact, it is the search itself which ties her to a constant reading of the vicissitudes of her own mind, the one that Caroline doesn't like to see transcribed.

'THERE IS NO REASON TO SUPPOSE THAT MISS MORGAN IS DEAD AFTER ALL'

In a letter to Fanny Knight, Jane Austen apologises for the polarities of her state of mind: 'I am feeling differently every moment, & shall not be able to suggest a single thing that can assist your Mind. – I could lament in one sentence & laugh in the next ...' (279). Although Austen presents her state as both extreme and unsuitable, it actually underlies much of her more familiar epistolary discourse. Mocking her domestic duties, she produces a typical 'not ... quite so triumphant ... account' of daily life:

> We met with no adventures ... except that our Trunk had once nearly slipt off, & we were obliged to stop at Hartley to have our wheels greazed. – While my Mother and Mr Lyford were together, I went to Mrs Ryders, and bought what I intended to buy, but not in much perfection. – There were no narrow Braces for Children, & scarcely any netting silk; but Miss Wood as usual is going to Town very soon, and will lay in a fresh stock. – I gave 2s/3d a yard for my flannel, & fancy it is not very good; but it is so disgraceful & contemptible an article in itself, that its' being comparatively good or bad is of little importance. I bought some Japan Ink likewise, & next week shall begin my operations on my hat, on which You know my principal hopes of happiness depend. – I am very grand indeed; I had the dignity of dripping out my mother's Laudanum last night, I carry about the keys of the Wine & Closet; & twice since I began this letter, have had orders to give in the Kitchen: Our dinner was very good yesterday, & the Chicken boiled perfectly tender; therefore I shall not be obliged to dismiss Nanny on that account.
>
> (16–17)

What is characteristic about this excerpt, a small piece from a large letter filled with dashes and memoranda and tidily expressed laments ('I am quite angry with myself for not writing closer; why is my alphabet so much more sprawly than Yours? Dame Tilbury's daughter has lain-in – '), is its low level of affect. Adventures sink into obligatory stops where one's wheels are greazed. Purchases are either 'disgraceful & contemptible' or sublime, like

Japan Ink elevated ironically into the means to perform an operation upon which 'my principal hopes of happiness depend'.

The grandeur of Jane Austen's 'lesser duties' is undercut by the level of 'obligation' which motivates her actions. 'Twice since I began this letter, I have had orders to give in the Kitchen.' While she is the one giving the orders, she 'has to' give them. Such momentous small matters force writer and reader alike to attend to the domestic duties, even while the writing itself becomes an obligation that she often chafes against ('why is my alphabet so much more sprawly than Yours?'). This particular letter holds within itself the famous, still shocking report that 'Mrs Hall of Sherbourn was brought to bed yesterday of a dead child, some weeks before she expected oweing to a fright. – I suppose she happened unawares to look at her husband' (17). What is most notable about this statement is not so much its heartless wit, but its context. It becomes in this long and rambling letter just one of many careless-seeming remarks squeezed in between reports about the uncommon largeness of Mary, about to give birth, the lying in of Dame Tilbury's daughter, and the dirtiness of Steventon's lanes.

Austen the novelist addresses the stylistic problem that the oddly juxta-posed detail presents in *Persuasion* when her narrator, quite unexpectedly, exposes the 'large fat sighings' that Mrs. Musgrove is guilty of displaying: 'Personal size and mental sorrow have certainly no necessary proportions. A large bulky figure has as good a right to be in deep affliction, as the most graceful set of limbs in the world. But, fair or not fair, there are unbecoming conjunctions, which reason will patronize in vain, – which taste cannot tolerate, – which ridicule will seize' (*P* 68). The narrator's horror of the 'unbecoming conjunction' establishes a canon of taste and decorum that Austen violates frequently and eagerly in her own domestic letters. The Austen that we think we 'know', that writer whose mind could be transcribed, stands as an arbiter of taste, a modest tyrant who insists upon the appropriate forms of discourse. Her letters, however, repeatedly embar-rass her own standards in transgressions, which, unlike Mrs. Musgrove's, appear to be deliberate and self-conscious.

When she chronicles her 'little matters', Austen exploits with mundane precision the sheer tedium not only of committing oneself to practising 'the civilities, the lesser duties of life, with gentleness and forbearance',[8] but of being obliged to record them in closely written letters for the inspection of others: 'There is no reason to suppose that Miss Morgan is dead after all. Mr Lyford gratified us very much yesterday by his praises of my father's mutton, which they all think the finest that was ever ate' (*L* 24). 'There is no reason to suppose that Miss Morgan is dead after all.' Samuel Beckett could have written such a line. Or Swift. Or closer to home, Austen's own parasyntactic, always obliging Miss Bates, who sees and reports *every thing* with a flat, undistinguished, decidedly unbecoming zeal.

'FLY[ING] OFF, THROUGH HALF A SENTENCE, TO HER MOTHER'S OLD PETTICOAT'

Miss Bates is first introduced to the reader as 'great talker on little matters' (*E* 21). Her aimless, convoluted accounts invest her character with great significance as one who sees and tells the plot of *Emma* as it unfolds. But her conversation also serves as an oddly perverse model for Austen's own epistolary production. Miss Bates' monologues, stuffed with roast pork and baked apples, chimneys that want sweeping, spectacles that need mending, sound suspiciously like her creator's own prosey, rambling letters. Miss Bates is, of course, designed to be exasperating enough to excuse Emma's dread of engaging her in conversation. We are even allowed to laugh at Emma's imitation of Miss Bates, when she imagines the 'evils' of a marriage between Mr. Knightley and Jane Fairfax:

> How would he bear to have Miss Bates belonging to him? – To have her haunting the Abbey, and thanking him all day long for his great kindness in marrying Jane? – 'So very kind and obliging! – But he always had been such a very kind neighbour!' And then fly off, through half a sentence, to her mother's old petticoat. 'Not that it was such a very old petticoat either – for still it would last a great while – and, indeed, she must thankfully say that their petticoats were all very strong'. (*E* 225)

But when Emma mimics Miss Bates' 'fly[ing] off, through half a sentence, to her mother's old petticoat', she reproduces Austen's own epistolary use of the trusty dash that she applies in any direction to link together matters great and small:

> I am full of Joy at much of your information; that you should have been to a Ball, & have danced at it, & supped with the Prince, & that you should meditate the purchase of a new muslin Gown are delightful circumstances. – *I* am determined to buy a handsome one whenever I can, & I am so tired and ashamed of half my present stock that I even blush at the sight of the wardrobe which contains them. – But I will not be much longer libelled by the possession of my coarse spot, I shall turn it into a petticoat very soon. – I wish you a merry Christmas, but *no* compliments of the Season. – Poor Edward! It is a very hard that he who has everything else in the World that he can wish for, should not have good health too. – But I hope with the assistance of Bowel complaints, Faintnesses & Sicknesses, he will soon be restored to that Blessing like-wise. (*L* 30)

I chose this particular excerpt because of its conveniently invoked petticoat, but its structure as well as its content connects this very typical mixture of romance, practicality, sentiment, and passive aggression to Miss Bates' meditations on rivets, baked apples, civility, and the consumption of bread (*E* 236–7). Both speakers excel at filling empty space with sentiments, 'I am full of joy … Poor Edward', that jostle against each other inconsequentially, suggesting the relative meaninglessness of what is being set down. As Miss Bates would say, 'One takes up a notion, and runs away with it' (176).

When Austen seems to mimic a character that she might have been able to love, but could never admire, her letters reveal a profound consciousness of the artificial and vacant nature of most discourse, which flies off through half sentences because there is nothing substantial to hold it down. 'Do not be angry with me for beginning another Letter to you', she writes to Cassandra from Henrietta Street. 'I have read the Corsair, mended my petticoat, & have nothing else to do. – ' (*L* 257). Employing another petticoat, Austen exploits a comically painful awareness that any discourse will serve to fill up the time and space facing the most adept conversationalists and correspondents, particularly if they are women.

In her letters, the absence of the subject often motivates the writing itself: 'Expect a most agreable Letter; for not being overburdened with subject – (having nothing at all to say) – I shall have no check to my Genius from beginning to end. – Well- & so …' (74–5). Six years later, writing from Southampton, cut off from country life and still unpublished, she sounds less eager to write about 'nothing'.

> My expectation of having nothing to say to you after the conclusion of my last, seems nearer Truth than I thought it would be, for I feel to have but little. I need not therefore be above acknowledging the receipt of yours this morning; or of replying to every part of it which is capable of an answer; & you may accordingly prepare for my ringing the Changes of the Glads & Sorrys for the rest of the page. (118)

'We are all sorry, & now that subject is exhausted', Austen reports, but continues to write doggedly on, vexed over disappointments in getting fish, charmed by a 'little Visitor' who makes her wonder 'What is become of all the Shyness in the World?' With 'nothing to say', Austen uses up all of her writing paper, squeezing in references to sofa-covers and carpets below the address panel, and crossing over a rather snide reference to brother James' impending visit. Straining to fit him onto her filled up page, she complains about the way he takes up too much room, 'walking about the house & banging the Doors, or ringing the Bell for a glass of Water'. She writes here as the recessive, dutiful sister, one who hardly takes up any room at all, observing with careful, painstaking acuity the cost of daily life, as she compares the bumptious excess of her brother's presence to her own relatively empty and tidy surface. The act of writing becomes here a necessary weapon in the domestic war waged against tedium, emptiness, and occasional despair.

In closing, Austen reminds Cassandra that she has 'constructed ... a Smartish Letter, considering my want of Materials. But like my dear Dr Johnson I beleive I have dealt more in Notions than Facts. – ' (118–21). While she looks to Johnson as her model, she sounds more like Swift and Sterne, writers making their subject the task of writing upon nothing at all. Her choice of materials, however, radically separates her from more self-consciously literary productions – Johnson's Idler, Swift's Hack, Sterne's White Bear – that depend upon the generative power of the literary market-place. Swift and Sterne and Johnson pretend that they write upon nothing because they are being paid to do so. Austen claims that she is writing upon no subject because she is obliged to do so; epistolary production is one of her domestic duties, what women do for free.

Austen's praise of her sister's epistolary skill ('you write so even, so clear both in style & Penmanship' [229]) is complicated by the way that letter-writing is judged in Austen's novels. The greatest admirer of close writing is Miss Bates, who stupefies Emma with her proud reports of Jane Fairfax's literary productions: 'in general she fills the whole paper and crosses half. My mother often wonders that I can make it out so well. She often says, when the letter is first opened, "Well, Hetty, now I think you will be put to it to make out all that chequer-work."' When Emma says 'something very civil about the excellence of Miss Fairfax's handwriting', and is rewarded with 'hearing her own silly compliment repeated twice over' (E 157–8) it is clear that Austen has little patience for the fetishizing of the letter. Miss Bingley, fawning over Darcy's talent for writing long letters (PP 47–8), Harriet, betraying her 'bad taste' by judging Robert Martin's proposal of marriage to be 'too short' (E 51–4), and Lady Bertram, who shines in the epistolary line, all expose their foolish satisfaction with the form of the letter and their dissociation from its substance.[9]

While Austen the novelist can satirize misplaced, self-important dedication to the fine art of letter-writing, Austen the sister, engaged in friendly rivalry, determined to exhibit her social skills, gets 'sick' (L 131) and 'hates' herself when she writes ill (13). Her doubled consciousness sets her against cultural productions that she herself pursues with great interest. Chafing against the demands of her position, for 'I assure you I am as tired of writing long letters as you can be', she corrects herself, holding tenaciously onto her appreciation of the necessity for the letters that take up so much of her energy: 'What a pity that one should still be so fond of receiving them', she reminds them both (137). The commitment wavers, however, when the writer faces the well worn terra cognita of her epistolary landscape: 'I am not surprised my dear Cassandra, that you did not find my last Letter very full of matter, & I wish this may not have the same deficiency; – but we are doing nothing ourselves to write about, & I am therefore quite dependant upon the Communications of our friends, or my own Wit' (162). It is, after all, Austen's awareness of such dependency that motivates her most moving characters, unaccommodated women like Miss Bates, *Persuasion*'s Mrs. Smith, and perhaps most poignantly, Miss Jane Fairfax, another great letter-writer, 'dependant upon the communication of [her] friends', quite literally tied to the post.[10]

DETERMINED TO HAZARD NOTHING

It is in *Emma* that Austen explores the problem of feminine dependence most thoroughly, splitting the source of her anxiety, the unaccommodated woman squeezed by circumstance, into Miss Bates and Miss Jane Fairfax. Miss Bates stands for the exposed, needy, woman 'so very obliged' to the support of *every body*. Her 'simplicity and cheerfulness' might recommend her to her neighbours, but they do not command respect. She deserves rather 'compassion', for sinking 'from the comforts she was born to' (E 375). Austen's more admirable, elegant creation, Miss Fairfax, is never entirely forgiven for her egregious acts of secrecy. Emma might recognize that 'If a woman can ever be excused for thinking only of herself, it is in a situation like Jane Fairfax's. – Of such, one may almost say, that "the world is not their's, nor the world's law"' (400). But somehow, in spite of the sympathy that her circumstances awaken in the reader, we are always kept on the outside of Jane Fairfax's character, looking in, and irresistibly judging her reserve.

Yet, it is in this oddly faulty Jane Fairfax that we can discover Austen's own elegant, secretive sensibility. To understand Jane Fairfax's clandestine habits of mind is to enter into the hidden world of Jane Austen's own epistolary production. For like her character, Austen, always eschewing both the sentimental response and the angry complaint, aims for, and most often succeeds at, impenetrability. Waiting for the carefully regulated deliveries of clandestine letters from Frank Churchill, Jane Fairfax presents an elegant, invulnerable exterior. But in her necessary reserve, Jane Fairfax, however repulsive she seems to bossy, powerful Emma, resembles most poignantly the Jane Austen, reported by one Miss Hinton to have 'stiffened into the most perpendicular, precise, taciturn piece of "single blessedness"', known for being 'no more regarded in society than a poker or a fire screen, or any other thin, upright piece of wood or iron that fills its corner in peace and quiet', the sort of maiden aunt who at least in her letters 'seldom committed herself *even* to an opinion' for public consumption.[11]

The secret integrity which depends upon silent self-censorship protects Jane Fairfax's and Jane Austen's position of relative powerlessness in a culture which privileges the communications of those rich enough to afford them. Truly marginal characters like Miss Bates are allowed to talk because they don't matter. 'I do not think', Mrs. Weston tells Emma, 'Mr. Knightley would be much disturbed by Miss Bates. Little things do not irritate him. She might talk on; and if he wanted to say any thing himself, he would only talk louder, and drown her voice' (226). The stakes are higher for the less pathetic figures, like Jane Fairfax, looking for more out of life than roast pork and baked apples.

The stakes require silence and cunning, producing a reserve which is often strategic. We can see Austen managing the secrets that are passing between her and her niece Fanny. 'Your sending the Music was an admirable device', she reports; 'it made everything easy, & I do not know how I could have accounted for the parcel otherwise' (*L* 281). In another letter dedicated to the interesting private discussion they are conducting over the merits of Fanny's ultimately unsuccessful suitor, Austen advises her to send her next letter by Saturday, 'as we shall be off on Monday long before the Letters are delivered – and write *something* that may do to be read or told' to the other members of the household (286–7).

Epistolary reserve can also be political, designed to maintain peace in the family commonwealth. It is remarkable how few times Jane Austen complains about her mother in her correspondence, although we sense an implicit criticism in the daughter's veiled references to her hypochondriacal presence. Since explicit remarks made against the mother would unsettle the pretence of harmony, Austen seems to speak most loudly in her silence: 'It began to occur to me before you mentioned it that I had been somewhat silent as to my mother's health for some time, but I thought you could have no difficulty in divining its exact state – you, who have guessed so much stranger things' (38). Cassandra presides over the letter as its most adroit reader, providing the hidden knowledge that is not allowed into the text.

Reserve and indirection is most valued as a weapon against the condescending outside world. It protects the powerless woman from being taken over by the active 'interest' of patrons looking to engage in what Sterne called 'sentimental commerce'.[12] Austen's opposition to sentimentality can be detected in her depiction of Jane Fairfax's struggle to remain free from the power of Emma's sympathy: 'I do pity you', Emma says to herself. 'And the more sensibility you betray of their just horrors, the more I shall like you' (*E* 363). To be in want is to be open and vulnerable.

Jane Fairfax's struggle to resist Emma's patronizing sympathy makes me wonder just how often Jane Austen herself needed to defend herself against interested, patronizing parties? So many friends and relations must have displayed interest in the trials of poor Cassandra in 1797, the year in which Thomas Fowle died of yellow fever in San Domingo in the West Indies, just weeks before he was to return to his fiancée in England. How did she protect herself from solicitous friends who heard reports of her distress when she learned she would be moving to Bath? Austen knew too well how eagerly the friend, the patron, indeed the reader, looks to dig out evidences of 'sensibility'. Austen herself doesn't want to be 'liked' for sentimental reasons, the sort that motivate Emma to grow fonder of poor, dear Jane. She would rather be taken for a poker or a fire screen, silent, superior, guarded.

In her letters Austen fiercely defends herself against the powers of sympathy. Disgusted by 'fat sighings' seeping from a soft heart, she resists pity, the taking in of it or the giving out of it, in edgy displays of an uncertain, sometimes awkward wit. Her irony contains the most mortal implications, as in the case of Mary Lloyd Austen, ready to deliver her first child, James Edward (who will be his aunt's biographer):

> I am ... to tell you that one of [my Father's] Leicestershire sheep, sold to the butcher last week, weighed 27 lb and 1/4 per quarter. I went to Deane with my father two days ago to see Mary, who is still plagued with the rheumatism, which she would be very glad to get rid of, and still more glad to get rid of her child, of whom she is heartily tired. Her nurse is come, and has no particular charm either of person or manner; but as all the Hurstbourne world pronounce her to be the best nurse that ever was, Mary expects her attachment to increase. What fine weather this is! Not very becoming perhaps early in the morning, but very pleasant out of doors at noon, and very wholesome – at least everybody fancies so, and imagination is everything. To Edward, however, I really think dry weather of importance. I have not taken to fires yet. I believe I never told you that Mrs Coulthard and Anne, late of Many-down, are both dead, and both died in childbed. We have not regaled Mary with this news ... *Sunday.* – I have just received a note from James to say that Mary was brought to bed last night, at eleven o'clock, of a fine little boy, and that everything is going on very well. My mother had desired to know nothing of it before it should be all over, and we were clever enough to prevent her having any suspicion of it, though Jenny who had been left here by her mistress was sent for home. (*L* 20–1)

Leicestershire sheep, a nurse of no particular charm, an irritating sister-in law plagued with rheumatism and unborn children, fine weather, breeding women, two of them, both dead in childbed. My mother displays some degree of sensibility, not wanting to know anything about 'it' until 'it' should be over. There is no getting into this letter. The imagination revealed here is a particularly fortressed one, expressed laboriously, without one dash, staving off the enormity of moments of emotional vulnerability. But then, Austen is always uneasy when she writes about childbirth. Her own darling children, her novels, provide her with a more dependable source of reproductive pleasure. Breeding, which turns women into 'animals',[13] too often leads to death.

POLICING THE PARAPHERNALIA

Virginia Woolf imagines the strains of being under Jane Austen's surveillance: 'A sense of meaning withheld, a smile at something unseen, an atmosphere of perfect control and courtesy mixed with something finely satirical, which, were it not directed against things in general rather than against individuals, would be almost malicious, would, so I feel, make it alarming to find her at home.'[14] Is it the natural squalor of domestic life that makes the act of observation so threatening, or the hidden squalor of the observed herself? There is a straightness, a 'perpendicular' penchant for order that accompanies strict observation, an intolerance for looseness. Miss Hinton, who emphasized this quality of stiff uprightness when she reported that Austen had been 'no more regarded ... than a poker', immediately corrected such a representation, adding that once understood to be the author of *Pride and Prejudice*, Austen became regarded as 'a poker of whom every one is afraid. It must be confessed that this silent observation from such an observer is rather formidable ... a wit, a delineator of character, who does not talk, is terrific indeed.'[15]

Letters provide an excellent vehicle for such formidable observation. Silent and reserved, the correspondent can record household faults with impunity. It is, in fact, the letter-writer's duty to describe the 'minute' details of everyday life before her, however offensive they might appear. Thus we find that James' Mary, for one, lying in, 'does not manage matters in such a way as to make me want to lay in myself. She is not tidy enough in her appearance; she has no dressing-gown to sit up in; her curtains are all too thin, and things are not in that comfort and style about her which are necessary to make such a situation an enviable one' (24).

Offences can also be less personal, shards lodged painfully in the observer's penetrating (and penetrated) eye. In a tartly critical letter, written with a shaking hand ('I beleive I drank too much wine last night'), Austen describes the belle of last night's ball, one Mrs. Blount, 'the only one much admired', as having 'the same broad face, diamond bandeau, white shoes, pink husband, & fat neck' that she possessed in September, while the daughter of Sir Thomas Champneys appeared to be 'a queer animal with a white neck'. In a postscript, determined to apprehend that which offends, she adds that she 'had the comfort of finding out the other evening who all the fat girls with short noses were that disturbed me at the 1st H. Ball. They all prove to be Miss Atkinsons of Enham' (60–3). This surreal account collapses the bland, broad glittering wealth of the Blounts into characteristics that merge together. Which one has the fat neck; and what is it about 'necks' that particular evening that so irked our commentator? By joining a 'white neck', traditionally a body part held in some degree of esteem, to the figure of a 'queer animal', Austen creates a minor monster shocking in her catachrestic singularity. The Miss Atkinsons, more traditionally unappealing, become bizarre in their multitudinous potential to disturb the observer. How many could 'all' be?

The desire to catalogue offences makes Austen a most daunting enforcer of 'straight' conduct. Acting as one long accustomed to repressing her own considerable powers, Austen expected no less from those who looked to her as their monitor. We can see her establishing standards of conduct in a letter to Fanny Knight, reporting on her visit to another niece, Anna Austen Lefroy, newly married.

> Our visit to Hendon will interest you I am sure, but I need not enter into the particulars of it, as your Papa will be able to answer *almost* every question. I certainly could describe her bed-room, & her Drawers & her Closet better than he can, but I do not feel that I can stop to do it ... Her purple Pelisse rather surprised me. – I thought we had known all Paraphernalia of that sort. I do not mean to blame her, it looked very well & I dare say she wanted it. I suspect nothing worse than its' being got in secret, & not owned to anybody. – She is capable of that you know. – (285)

John Halperin finds this to be 'perhaps' the 'worst moment' in Austen's correspondence.[16] But it is also rather funny to watch Jane Austen poking into her niece's closet, searching for secrets. This letter supposes a public awareness of the private paraphernalia of life while it makes particular claims for Austen's expertise in discovery and disclosure. When she takes on the role of monitor to police the pelisse, she is acting out a cultural obligation, one that she has inherited from her novelistic models, and one that she will pass on to her heirs. For if one thing is constant in the domestic novel, it is the exposure of the female, who is always subject to the watchful eyes of others. Richardson might have started this tradition, placing Pamela

CAROL HOULIHAN FLYNN

under Mr. B.'s covert gaze, subjecting Clarissa to Lovelace's careful surveillance, but it is in *Sir Charles Grandison*, one of Austen's favourite novels, that we are introduced to the benevolent male monitor, one who will be reproduced in Burney's *Evelina* and *Camilla*, in Austen's own *Emma, Mansfield Park*, and *Northanger Abbey*, and later in Eliot's *Daniel Deronda*. Austen's talent for surveillance locates her at the centre of a tradition both literary and domestic which requires that the female figure be always ready for inspection.

The familiar letter allowed the powerless to criticize the powerful, but as an instrument serving two cultures, it also served to maintain powerful systems of social control. Austen's position here as critic of Anna's desire, for 'I dare say she wanted it', places her in the service of a larger system of conduct, one that she is in this epistolary moment nurturing. For the codification of manners and the pressures of surveillance will develop into such a carefully policed system that even Jane Austen, however careful she might have been to protect herself from the judgment of others, will be found wanting by her own heirs, by her own Fanny Knight Knatchbull, who will make her infamous remarks about her aunt's lack of refinement. 'Yes my love,' she will write to her sister many years later, 'it is very true that Aunt Jane from various circumstances was not so *refined* as she ought to have been from her *talent*, & if she had lived 50 years later she would have been in many respects more suitable to *our* more refined tastes.'[17]

The letters of Jane Austen reveal the difficulties that she faced under a system of checks and repressions that needed to be negotiated. Since Austen keeps reminding us of the challenge of finding 'subject' and 'matter' full enough and proper enough to motivate writing at all, it is particularly appropriate that the last letter we have written by Austen is one heavily edited by her brother Henry. As the original letter is missing, we are left only with his edited version which he published in his 'Biographical Notice'. Austen's brother enters her text to suppress dangerous material:

> She next touches with just and gentle animadversion on a subject of domestic disappointment. Of this the particulars do not concern the public. Yet in justice to her characteristic sweetness and resignation, the concluding observation of our authoress thereon must not be suppressed.

The watchful brother returns us, quite briefly, to Austen herself, who seems herself to regret 'getting too near complaint', but then interrupts her last words once more:

> The following and final extract will prove the facility with which she could correct every impatient thought, and turn from complaint to cheerfulness.

(NA, P 9)

112

What follows should not surprise us. By now we should be used to oddly placed domestic and social details – the price of meat, Mary's blue gown, my mother's agonies. Austen appears to be taking up the most mundane social task, recommending one Captain — (the name has been excised by brother Henry), 'a very respectable, well-meaning man, without much manner, his wife and sister all good humour and obligingness, and I hope (since the fashion allows it) with rather longer petticoats than last year' (*L* 343). Petticoats, more petticoats, fly off 'through half a sentence'. If she knew these were to be her last known written words, would Jane Austen, remembering Miss Bates, laugh or lament?

NOTES

1 Deirdre Le Faye, *Jane Austen: A Family Record* (London, 1989: The British Library), p. 249.

2 Le Faye, p. 249.

3 'Introduction' to the first edition (1932), *Jane Austen's Letters*, ed. Deirdre Le Faye (Oxford and New York: Oxford University Press, 1995), p. ix. Jo Modert argues that Cassandra appears to have taken 'better care of the letters than most of the recipients', and made few incisions in the letters that 'had nothing to do with Jane Austen's emotional expressions or secrets', *Jane Austen's Manuscript Letters in Facsimile* (Carbondale and Edwardsville: Southern Illinois University Press, 1990), pp. xx–xxii. Susan C. Whealler discusses the Cassandra controversy in 'Prose and Power in Two Letters by Jane Austen', *Sent as a Gift: Eight Correspondences from the Eighteenth Century*, ed. Alan T. McKenzie (Athens, Georgia, and London: University of Georgia Press, 1993), pp. 180–4. Most recently, Terry Castle, in 'Sister–Sister', *London Review of Books* (3 August, 1995), attributes Cassandra's 'high-handed' editing of Austen's letters to a (passionately) 'jealous winnowing down of her brilliant younger sister's personality in the name of a judicious decorum' (3). Castle's suggestions of Austen's 'homophilic fascination' with women and the 'primordial bond' between the sisters (5) provoked outraged letters which sometimes revealed a homophobic fetishization of 'Jane' that inspired misreadings of the review itself.

4 *Memoir of Jane Austen*, ed. R. W. Chapman (Oxford: Clarendon Press, 1926), pp. 59–60.

5 'Letters/Correspondence', *The Jane Austen Handbook*, ed. J. David Grey (London: Athlone Press, 1986), p. 277.

6 Kaplan argues in 'Representing Two Cultures: Jane Austen's Letters', *The Private Self: Theory and Practice of Women's Autobiographical Writings*, ed. Shari Benstock (Chapel Hill: University of North Carolina Press, 1988), pp. 211–19, and more fully in *Jane Austen among Women* (Baltimore and London: Johns Hopkins Press, 1992), that Austen created within a framework of both 'gentry' and 'women's cultures'. Chapter 3, 'The Women's Culture', locates Austen's epistolary habits firmly within a feminine context. Whealler argues that it is in the collection and dissemination of 'the minute details of domestic life' that Austen finds the source of 'private power', p. 195.

7 Kaplan, *Jane Austen among Women*, pp. 47–50.

8 I am citing Marianne Dashwood's resolution, one which Austen certainly shows signs of taking to heart (*SS* 347).

9 In 'Jane Austen and the Look of Letters', *Romantic Correspondence: Women, Politics and the Fiction of Letters* (Cambridge: Cambridge University Press, 1993), Mary Favret argues for the importance of 'even lines' and 'close writing'. Since the recipients of a letter were usually required to pay postage upon delivery, letters needed to 'look as if they were worth the cost of postage', pp. 136–7.

10 See Favret on the importance of the post office for Jane Fairfax, pp. 158–62.

11 Le Faye, *Jane Austen: A Family Record*, pp. 198, 249.

12 'Preface in the Desobligeant', *Sentimental Journey*.

13 'I want to tell you that I have got my own darling Child from London', she reports after receiving her first copy of *Pride and Prejudice* (*L* 201). Real babies do not inspire such rejoicing. Austen complains to Fanny Knight that Anna Austen Lefroy, pregnant again, 'has not a chance of escape ... Poor Animal, she will be worn out before she is thirty. – I am very sorry for her. – Mrs Clement too is in that way again. I am quite tired of so many children' (336).

14 Quoted in John Halperin, *The Life of Jane Austen* (Baltimore: Johns Hopkins University Press, 1986), p. 186.

15 Le Faye, *Jane Austen: A Family Record*, p. 199.

16 John Halperin, *The Life of Jane Austen*, p. 265.

17 Quoted in Le Faye, *Jane Austen: A Family Record*, pp. 252–3.

7

JULIET McMASTER

Class

We hear of Lady Catherine de Bourgh, one of the most memorable and least likeable characters in Jane Austen's novels, that 'she likes to have the distinction of rank preserved' (*PP* 161). The obsequious Mr. Collins enjoins her guest Elizabeth Bennet to dress simply, and not to emulate the elegant apparel of her high-ranking hostess: the differences in station are not only present, but must be *seen* to be present.

Class difference was of course a fact of life for Austen, and an acute observation of the fine distinctions between one social level and another was a necessary part of her business as a writer of realistic fiction. Nor would she have wished it away, although at the time of writing her novels, she herself – as the unmarried daughter of a deceased country clergyman, like Miss Bates – knew what it was to suffer from the class system. Her favourite niece, Fanny Knight, 'whom she had seen grow up from a period when her notice was an honour' (*E* 375), was shamelessly patronizing after she married a lord, and said her aunt, but for the advantages she gained at Godmersham, would have been 'very much below par as to good Society and its ways'.[1] In certain ways Austen was ideally placed to observe the finely nuanced social distinctions around her. As an unmarried woman she was to some extent outside the game (since women were assumed to take their status from their husbands) and hence could see the more of it. Moreover, she had different vantage points: she could alternate between her relatively humble position of living with her widowed mother and unmarried sister in the Chawton house by the grace and favour of her landlord brother, and visiting that brother's family at his country estate of Godmersham, and drinking French wine (a rare treat) with the opulent (*L* 139).

'There are far finer and more numerous grades of dignity in this country than in any other', claimed Edward Lytton Bulwer, who was growing up in England while Austen was writing her novels.[2] He and other Victorians like Carlyle and Thackeray became excellent and explicit analysts of class and class difference in England; but Austen had already specialized in the dramatizing of the nuances and intricacies of the subject. My procedure in this essay will be first to turn snob myself, and erect a social ladder as she represents it, with the personnel of her novels arranged on its rungs in order of precedence; then to try to extract Austen's own attitude to class distinction, and the immense importance that some of her characters assign to it.

Although in her own life Austen did have some dealings with royalty, however mediated, when she was graciously invited to dedicate *Emma* to the Prince Regent, she never presents royalty in her fiction, nor any of the great aristocrats who still owned great tracts of the country, and were prominent in its government. So we must start several rungs down the ladder. Among the onstage characters (as opposed to those who are merely mentioned), Lord Osborne in the fragment *The Watsons* is probably the one with the highest rank in her fiction, and he is not much better than a fool. The indications are that he will be sufficiently educated by the heroine to learn to value her and to propose to her; but that she will turn him down (*MW* 363). So much suggests that for Austen there is nothing divine about royalty, and not much that is special about peers. In fact characters with titles – or 'handles to their names', as the Victorians used to say – are seldom admirable in the novels. Sir Thomas Bertram, a baronet, is the best of them, but even he overestimates his own and his family's importance. Sir Walter Elliot's obsession with his status and the Baronetage in which it is published is made not only comic but contemptible. (In Sir Walter, Austen anticipates the Victorian social criticism of Carlyle, who characterized the aristocrat as 'The Dandy', obsessed with appearances, and sick with self-love.[3]) Sir John Middleton, who is also presumably a baronet, is well-meaning but vacuous, with a 'total want of talent and taste' (*SS* 32). A servant's rendering of the title as 'a baronight' suggests that being a baronet can be a somewhat benighted condition (*P* 106).

A baronetcy is an inherited title, passed down from father to son; a knighthood, also signalled by the title 'Sir' attached to the first name, is awarded for a particular service; since it is not hereditary, it carries less prestige. Even a Mr. Lucas, 'formerly in trade in Meryton' (*PP* 18), can become a 'Sir William Lucas' of Lucas Lodge, and introduce 'St. James's', the palace where he received his knighthood, into every conversation. 'The distinction [of being knighted] had perhaps been felt too strongly', notes the narrator drily (*PP* 18). A title, it seems, is sometimes almost a guarantee of fatuousness in Austen's fiction. 'The Dowager Viscountess Dalrymple, and her daughter, the Honourable Miss Carteret', merely from the stately parade of their names, are almost bound to be the kind whose status is their only attraction (*P* 148). So too with the Honourable John Yates, who spends his time in solitary declamation as he rehearses the role of a baron (*MP* 169). ('Honourable' is a courtesy title given to younger sons and daughters of peers below the rank of Marquess.)

Women too sometimes have handles to their names, although they could not inherit a peerage or a baronetcy. Lady Catherine de Bourgh would not want us to miss the fine shades in the title 'Lady'. When it comes attached to the first name – as with Lady Catherine, her sister Lady Anne Darcy, and the unscrupulous Lady Susan Vernon – it signifies that the lady in question has the title 'in her own right', as the daughter of an earl; she is thus 'to the manner born', as the expression goes, and she retains her title irrespective of her husband's status. Lady Bertram of *Mansfield Park*, however, along with Lady Middleton, Lady Russell of *Persuasion*, and Lady Denham of *Sanditon*, whose titles are attached only to the last name, hold them only by virtue of being married to a baronet or knight; and the lady would lose it if she were remarried to a plain 'Mr.' In such circles, such things matter.

Lady Anne Darcy is married to plain Mr. Darcy, and Lady Catherine makes a point of Darcy's family as being 'untitled'. It is nevertheless 'respectable, honorable, and ancient', and Darcy's fortune, at £10,000 a year, is 'splendid' (*PP* 356). The long-established but untitled landowning family does seem to gather Austen's deep respect, especially if its income comes from land and a rent-roll; and her two most eligible heroes, Mr. Darcy of Pemberley and Mr. Knightley of Donwell Abbey, come from this class, the landed gentry. So does Mr. Rushworth of Sotherton, however, who despite his long rent-roll is morally and intellectually not worth much more than his name signifies.

Austen is often happy to follow the Cinderella plot, and to make a happy ending out of marrying her heroine to a man notably above her in income and social prestige. The landowning country gentleman is as close to a prince as her heroines approach. As to income, they usually follow, in effect if not in intention, the prudent advice of Tennyson's 'Northern Farmer': 'Doänt thou marry for munny, but goä wheer munny is!' Elizabeth's initial rejection of Darcy usefully assures us that she is not marrying him for his £10,000 a year. But she half-jokingly admits that her love has been influenced by 'his beautiful grounds at Pemberley' (373). Money is only one of a number of factors that count, however.

Elizabeth's marriage to Darcy is the greatest 'match' in the novels, and Mrs. Bennet has every right to rejoice in it. But we have different views on the extent of the social disparity between them. In Lady Catherine's eyes Elizabeth is a nobody, with 'upstart pretensions', a woman shrewdly on the make, who will pollute 'the shades of Pemberley' (356–7). Elizabeth herself, however, is not overwhelmed by the social difference. 'He is a gentleman; I am a gentleman's daughter; so far we are equal', she claims calmly (356). Austen seems to approve of this relative flattening of the degrees of distinction above the country gentry. But she notes too, with irony, the tendency to be acutely aware of the degrees of distinction in the scale below. Emma Woodhouse is enraged that Mr. Elton should 'look down upon her friend, so well understanding the gradations of rank below him, and so blind to what rose above, as to fancy himself showing no presumption in addressing her!' (E 136). Emma too has a vivid sense of the gradations below.

The country gentleman, who leads a leisured existence and who subsists on income from land and inheritance, is at his best the moral and social ideal as a partner for a heroine. But the condition takes some living up to: Austen, like other social commentators, insists that with the privileges go extensive responsibilities. Elizabeth freezes Darcy off when he is proud and pretentious; but she warms to him when she discovers how as master of Pemberley he uses his extensive power for the good of those around him.

> The commendation bestowed on him by Mrs. Reynolds was of no trifling nature. What praise is more valuable than the praise of an intelligent servant? As a brother, a landlord, a master, she considered how many people's happiness were in his guardianship! – How much of pleasure or pain it was in his power to bestow! – ... Every idea that had been brought forward by the housekeeper was favourable to his character.   (PP 250–1)

Emma strikes us as a glowing and optimistic comedy partly because the hero Mr. Knightley stands highest in the moral as well as the social scale: he lives, after all, at 'Donwell' Abbey.

The Highbury of Emma is close to presenting a microcosm of Austen's social world. Here, from Mr. Knightley (whose knightly moral status is expressed in his name rather than a literal title) to the poor family to which Emma dispenses charity, we have assembled nearly all the levels of society that Austen presents. Moreover, the novel's heroine is one who specializes in social discrimination, and makes prompt though often inaccurate judgments about the social station of the people around her. I will use Emma, therefore, to provide the main example of the levels of the social ladder, while drawing freely on examples from the other novels as well.

Highest in the Highbury circle, then, is Mr. Knightley of Donwell Abbey, the first in virtue as in place. Austen insists that part of his virtue is that he refuses to trade on his rank. He walks, when status-conscious people like the Osbornes in The Watsons would make a point of riding in a carriage. When he does get out his carriage, it is to transport Miss Bates and Jane Fairfax, not himself. Though he could leave the management of his estate to an employee, he takes an active interest, is often in conference with his steward William Larkins, and is warmly interested in the domestic affairs of his tenant farmer, Robert Martin. In *Persuasion*, by contrast, we are invited to consider the derogation of such duties by the bad landlord, Sir Walter Elliot, who is consequently exiled from his estate, and even leaves the farewells to his daughter (*P* 39). Sir Walter is enraptured by the prestige of his position, but neglects the responsibilities.

Next in status in Highbury is Mr. Woodhouse of Hartfield. Hartfield is a gentleman's residence, and it has a farm attached; but Mr. Woodhouse clearly has nothing to do with its management, and we hear of no tenants. The fact that Emma has a fortune of £30,000 suggests that much of his income comes from investment rather than from land: hence his status is relatively lower than Knightley's. Mr. Bennet of Longbourn in *Pride and Prejudice* and old Mr. Dashwood in *Sense and Sensibility* also belong in this category. Though gentlemen of property, and owners of estates, they lack the long-term commitment to the land that makes good stewards and moral aristocrats of Darcy and Knightley.

One might suppose that the siblings in a single family would be almost by definition of the same rank. But even here there are marked differences in status, not only between sons and daughters, but also between one son and another. The aristocracy and the inheritance of land depended heavily on the system of primogeniture. Just as only the eldest son can inherit a peerage, so the bulk of land would normally descend by the same system. The entail, so prominent in *Pride and Prejudice*, legally formalizes this customary practice of inheritance. If an estate were divided equally between all siblings, as our understanding of equitable practice would suggest today, the estate would be dispersed, and would ultimately cease to exist. The system of primogeniture, which unfairly privileges one family member by accumulating all property in his hands, was developed as an arrangement for the preservation of the family name and the family estate through the generations. Austen highlights the injustices of this system of inheritance. At the beginning of *Sense and Sensibility* the narrator informs us how a rich old gentleman, Mr. Dashwood, so ties up both his money and his estate that it must stay in the male line, and may not be alienated to the girls of the family, even though the son is already amply provided for. 'Wife and daughters' are deprived; and the estate and the money as well must descend 'to his son, and his son's son' (*SS* 4).

Hence there is a considerable difference in prestige and expectation between elder sons and younger sons, as between sons and daughters. Austen notices this, and dramatizes it; but not without conveying a strong sense of the inequity of such arrangements. The five Bennet girls are to be turned out of Longbourn when their father dies, since the estate is entailed on a distant male cousin, Mr. Collins, who shows precious little sign of being morally worthy of it. Even among these five girls, too, there are notable shades of difference in prestige. Jane, the eldest, is called 'Miss Bennet', while her younger sisters are referred to as 'Miss Eliza', 'Miss Mary', and so on. The elder may be 'out' in society before the younger, and *should* be, according to Lady Catherine; but in this matter, in this family, equity prevails. 'I think it would be very hard upon younger sisters', says Elizabeth, 'that they should not have their share of society and amusement because the elder may not have the means or inclination to marry early. – The last born has as good a right to the pleasures of youth, as the first' (*PP* 165). Once married, a sister gains prestige over a sister, whatever her place in the age sequence. 'Lord! how I should like to be married before any of you', Lydia tells her elder sisters ingenuously; 'and then I would chaperone you about to all the balls' (221). And presently – though not without some moral sacrifice – she gains her wish, and takes pride of place at table at her mother's right hand, saying to her eldest sister, 'Ah! Jane, I take your place now, and you must go lower, because I am a married woman' (317).

Among the brothers at this level of society the difference is even greater. The eldest, who can expect to inherit the estate and the income that goes with it, if not a title as well, is often bred to idleness; and Austen shows how such expectations can make him spoilt and frivolous, like Frederick Tilney in *Northanger Abbey* and Tom Bertram in *Mansfield Park*. A younger son, like Henry Tilney or Edmund Bertram, who has his living to earn, is sympathetically treated, and becomes a suitable mate for the heroine. Mary Crawford has every intention of marrying an *elder* brother, and is so discontented with herself for falling in love with Edmund by mistake that she wishes his elder brother dead (*MP* 434). Edward Ferrars, who is an elder son by birth but not by temperament, chafes at the idleness expected of him. 'Instead of having anything to do, instead of having any profession chosen for me, or being allowed to chuse any myself, I returned home to be completely idle' (*SS* 362). His mother, the rich and powerful Mrs. Ferrars (one wishes Austen would sometimes show a powerful woman in a favourable light!) in effect turns him into a younger son (at least economically speaking), by transferring all her money to his younger brother Robert, who relishes idleness. Edward turns to making his living as a country parson.

So much suggests that Austen's best sympathies rest with the professional class – her own, that is. Although her most vivacious heroines (Marianne, Elizabeth, and Emma) marry upwards into the landowning gentry, Catherine, Elinor, Fanny, and (probably) Emma Watson marry clergymen; clergymen, moreover, who are usually younger brothers. Austen represents the sterling virtues of the profession to which her father and two of her brothers belonged, although she doesn't dwell on their duties or their status within their profession, as Trollope was to do a generation later. In novels where the heroine marries into the gentry, however, Austen permits herself some satire of the ministry. Mr. Collins and Mr. Elton are parsons on their preferment, servile towards a 'patron', and eager to marry money. Even the highly principled Edmund Bertram, after he has 'been married long enough to begin to want an increase of income', submits to taking a second living, and so becomes a pluralist (*MP* 473).

A gentleman's son who must earn his living has still rather limited choices in Austen's world: the church, the army, the navy, the law, and medicine (and the last was still of dubious gentility). The army was a doubtful proposition as a living, since an officer's commission had to be purchased. / Captain Tilney, an eldest son, can expect patronage, as he is following his father's profession. (General Tilney must have inherited his estate, as his army pay would not suffice to buy an abbey.) Colonel Brandon was originally a younger son, but inherits his estate on the early death of his elder brother. Wickham, a lieutenant in the militia, is chronically short of funds. Mr. Weston, as a Captain in the army, was considered beneath the gentry family of the Churchills; and before he can buy himself into Randalls and gentlemanhood he must make his money in trade (*E* 16). The army, that is, though it has prestige, is not a reliable source of income. But Emma, snob as she is, would probably not have taken so kindly to Mr. Weston as the husband of her friend if he had not once been 'Captain' Weston.

The navy, of course, is the profession Austen favours next after the clergy. In *Persuasion* she uses it as the model of a system of promotion by merit, to contrast with the old-world system of heredity that Sir Walter Elliot considers sacred.[4] He objects to the navy 'as being the means of bringing persons of obscure birth into undue distinction, and raising men to honours which their fathers and grandfathers never dreamt of' (*P* 19). Sir Walter's disapproval signals Austen's approval. In her last novel she famously demotes the landed gentry and replaces them by the navy, substituting Admiral Croft for Sir Walter as the proprietor of Kellynch Hall, and allowing her heroine to reject William Elliot, heir to the estate, in favour of a relatively self-made man, the gallant Captain Wentworth. Wentworth, moreover, has made money by his profession. Since England was at war with France and its allies, and moreover dominant at sea, a Captain and his crew (whose shares of profits were minutely discriminated) could take 'prizes', capturing enemy ships at sea and realizing huge profits. 'Ah! those were pleasant days when I had the Laconia', muses Captain Wentworth. 'How fast I made money in her' (67). The woman author's sharp recognition of the economic motive for warfare is implicit in Admiral Croft's bluff hopes for 'the good luck to live to another war' (70).

Austen shows herself quite knowledgeable not only about prizes and money-making in the navy, but about its internal hierarchy and systems of promotion. It was next to impossible to be genuinely 'self-made': in the absence of money, a man on his promotion would need 'interest', and/or luck. Wentworth's first command, the Asp, is pronounced unfit for overseas service; but Admiral Croft insists, 'Lucky fellow to get any thing so soon, with no more interest than his' (65). We see some of this 'interest' at work when Henry Crawford procures William Price's lieutenancy by using his influence with his uncle the Admiral (*MP* 298–9).

Austen's preference for the navy over the army is signalled by the notice she takes of their uniforms. The susceptibility of young Kitty and Lydia Bennet to 'the regimentals of an ensign' marks them as 'two of the silliest girls in the country', in their father's opinion; and their foolish mother's wistful fondness for 'a red coat' puts her in the same company (*PP* 29). (There is often a sense of sexual threat attached to army characters, as to the seducers Wickham and Captain Tilney.) On the other hand, we are invited to participate in Fanny Price's association of the naval profession with pride and virtue when she looks on her brother, 'complete in his Lieutenant's uniform, looking and moving all the taller, firmer, and more graceful for it, and with the happiest smile over his face' (*MP* 384). As usual, however, Austen provides a qualification. Lest she be thought to generalize in her approval of the navy, she provides us with a negative example in Admiral Crawford, who has considerable power and wit, but who keeps a mistress. He is considered partly responsible for the vitiated morality of his niece and nephew, Mary and Henry Crawford.

For representatives of the other professions we have to turn to relatively minor characters. The law is represented in *Emma* by Mr. Knightley's younger brother, John Knightley, who is a respectable attorney in London. Country attornies, such as Mr. Phillips in *Pride and Prejudice*, Robert Watson in *The Watsons*, or the Coxes, father and son, in *Emma*, are seen as verging on the vulgar. When Mary Crawford urges Edmund to 'go into the law', she probably hopes he would become a London barrister, the more distinguished branch of the legal profession, and one that was frequently a route to political office. Austen's sympathies are clearly with Edmund in his defence of his choice to be a clergyman as the more honorable calling (*MP* 93).

Physicians and surgeons, too, are relegated to the sidelines, although Austen notes their rising social status in making a memorable incident out of Mr. Perry's changing decision about setting up a carriage in *Emma*. Like an expensive car today, carriages were status symbols. To maintain one's own carriage and horses was a considerable expense, and the decision to do so must be taken with care. For this time Perry postpones the purchase; but we are given reason to believe that in due course he will indeed rise to the carriage-owning class (*E* 344–6). Perhaps in the heroine's brother Sam, in *The Watsons*, 'only a Surgeon, you know' (*MW* 321), we would have had a sympathetic picture of a medical man; but in the fragment as we have it, he is in a fair way to being cut out in his courtship of the heiress by the 'Military Men' (328).

Austen locates few major characters in 'trade', and for many of her characters the word has a ring that seems to require apology. It is not surprising that the gentry and professional classes felt somewhat threatened by the large changes that were coming with the Industrial Revolution, and tended to close ranks against the newly powerful and the *nouveaux riches*. Trade represents new money, and money, like wine, isn't considered quite respectable until it has aged a little. Austen is clearly fascinated by this process: though she doesn't share the snobbish prejudice against trade, she pays close attention to the gradual assimilation of the trading classes into gentility. Emma Woodhouse again can represent the snobbish position, at least in her initial reaction, on the rise of the Cole family in Highbury. But it is important to notice that Emma's attitude evolves and changes. The Coles, as Emma places them, are 'of low origin, in trade, and only moderately genteel' (*E* 207). However, they have prospered financially, and they have 'added to their house, to their number of servants, to their expenses of every sort; and by this time were, in fortune and style of living, second only to the family at Hartfield' (207). (Mr. Knightley, strictly speaking, is from the nearby parish of Donwell.) Their place and their mobility in society are exactly rendered; Austen pays attention to the assault on gentility of the new mercantile middle class. Emma is stand-offish; she severely disapproves of Mr. Elton's 'propensity to dine with Mr. Cole' (213), and she looks forward to refusing any invitation they may have the presumption to address to her. However, she must learn to swallow her pride. By the time she knows that all the people she likes best are to be assembled at the Coles' dinner party, she is very glad to accept the invitation when it comes. But she is careful not to show any eagerness. 'She owned that, considering every thing, she was not absolutely without inclination for the party' (208): the sentence, with its careful qualifications and humorous double negative, signals the condescension of the *grande dame* of Highbury in thus confer-ring her stamp of approval on the parvenus. Hereafter, apparently, the Coles, for all their tincture of 'trade', will be on visiting terms even with the most exclusive families of Highbury; and perhaps the young Coles of the next generation may aspire to marry the Westons' daughter, or even the offspring of Mr. and Mrs. Knightley of Donwell Abbey.

Much has to do with manners and tact. However reluctantly, Emma accepts the Coles into the genteel society of Highbury, because they 'expressed themselves so properly', they show 'real attention' (208). The new Mrs. Elton, however, is another matter. Before meeting her Emma has ascertained that she is 'the youngest of the two daughters of a Bristol – merchant, of course, he must be called' (the dread word 'tradesman' may not be uttered) (183). But she conscientiously withholds judgment until she meets the bride in person. When she does appear, Mrs. Elton confirms Emma's worst prejudices: Emma can't stand her 'airs of pert pretension and under-bred finery' (279). Moreover, nor can most readers. It is a difficult exercise in discrimination to pick apart social standing, manners, and morals. But Austen enables us to distinguish between Emma's unapproved social snobbery and her proper moral aversion to Mrs. Elton's loud-mouthed self-approval. For instance, like Miss Bingley Mrs. Elton regularly uses her newly acquired status to put down others.

A later stage of this assimilation of one class into another is seen in the Bingleys of *Pride and Prejudice*. Young Charles Bingley is a gentleman of leisure, and already associates with such a prestigious member of the country gentry as Darcy. But his is new money, 'acquired by trade' in the industrial north of England (*PP* 15). We see him in the process of buying his way into the gentry. His father 'had intended to purchase an estate, but did not live to do it' (15). Bingley, then, in a leisurely manner, is shopping; by renting Netherfield manor, he is trying out country gentlemanhood. Once he marries Jane, he does buy an estate near Derbyshire (385); so the 'next generation' will be correspondingly a step upward in the social hierarchy. In Bingley we see the best of social mobility. He is good-humoured and charming, and he never stands on ceremony. Like Elizabeth when she moves into Pemberley, he will benefit his new social level by not trying to live up to it all the time. His sisters, however, show the aspect of social mobility that Austen distrusted. They are status-hungry, 'proud and con-ceited' (15), and Caroline Bingley is over-eager to ally herself and her brother with the prestige of the Darcy family. Conveniently forgetting that her own fortune was made in trade, she is spitefully scornful of Mr. Gardiner, the Bennet sisters' merchant uncle, 'who lives somewhere near Cheapside', she sneers. 'If they had uncles enough to fill *all* Cheapside', Bingley bursts out warmly, 'it would not make them a jot less agreeable' (36–7). Generously undiscriminating about shades of social distinction, he cares more about their manners, the amenable social conduct that makes them 'agreeable'. His is the approved attitude.

On this issue, however, Darcy realistically argues that the Bennet sisters' connection with trade 'must very materially lessen their chance of marrying men of any consideration in the world' (37). His qualification is presented as a point of fact, and he is not malicious, like Miss Bingley. But still, Darcy is to go through an evolution in his attitude, at last marrying, like Bingley, one of the Bennet girls, Cheapside uncle notwithstanding. Indeed, he comes to value the Gardiners, despite their connection with trade, more highly than his father-in-law the country gentleman. The quality of humanity is to be judged by moral and humane standards, Austen suggests, not by social status; but like her own temporary snobs, Darcy and Emma, she pays full attention to their social status first.

Since the union of the merchant's daughter with the earl's son depicted in Hogarth's 'Marriage à la Mode' (1745), England has been famous for its alliances between 'blood' and money, the bargain by which the aristocracy is enriched, and the merchant class can promote its grandchildren into rank and title. 'By this intermixture of the highest aristocracy with the more subaltern ranks of society', Bulwer explained, 'there are far finer and more numerous grades of dignity in this country than in any other' (Bulwer, *England and the English* 31). In exploring some of the finely nuanced distinctions that can arise from the subtle intermixture of birth and cash, he notes one marker of consequence that can easily be overlooked.

> You see two gentlemen of the same birth, fortune, and estates – they are not of the same rank, – by no means! – one looks down on the other as confessedly his inferior. Would you know why? His *connexions* are much higher!
> (Bulwer, *England and the English* 31)

Austen is alert to this distinction as to others. Emma Woodhouse is indignant that the clergyman, Mr. Elton, should dare to propose marriage to her, or to 'suppose himself her equal in connection or mind!' (*E* 136). 'Connection', like the 'interest' that Wentworth needs in order to get a good command in the navy, is a term fraught with significance. Bingley raises his status (though in his case it is unconsciously done) by being the friend of Darcy, as Harriet begins to be out of Robert Martin's reach when she becomes the friend of Miss Woodhouse.

If those involved in trade hover on the brink of gentility, there are many grades and degrees below them. Mrs. and Miss Bates in *Emma* are similarly poised, and a gulf of poverty yawns below them. They are of a class that was later to be called 'shabby-genteel', people who have come down in the world. Once prominent as the wife of the vicar, Mrs. Bates as a widow lives on slender means, in cramped quarters in an upstairs apartment, with only one servant, a maid-of-all-work. But though she and her daughter are short of money and can't entertain, they still have *connections*: they are on visiting terms with the best families of Highbury; and that's more than can be said, as we have seen, for the Coles, with all their money and servants.

Another kind of amphibian, one who can move upwards or sink downwards in society, is the governess. Jane Fairfax, for instance, is well bred and well educated, beautiful and talented. But because her relatives cannot support her, she must earn her living at one of the only professions available to women, as a governess. The novels of Charlotte and Anne Brontë amply dramatize the painful position of well-educated girls from the impoverished upper classes who become virtually the servants of families often much less well bred than themselves. Jane Fairfax speaks in poignant terms of employment agencies for governesses: 'offices for the sale – not quite of human flesh – but of human intellect' (*E* 300). The alignment with the slave trade is explicit; there is a passing hint, too, of prostitution. Jane Fairfax, like Jane Eyre, is one of those governesses who survive by marrying into the gentry. But her escape from a life of drudgery, looking after Mrs. Smallridge's three children for a pittance, is a narrow one.

The governess in the nineteenth-century novel becomes a culture heroine for the sad army of economically vulnerable single women, who had virtually no means of acquiring independence outside marriage, and little hope of independence within it either. 'You know we must marry', sighs Elizabeth Watson, one of four unmarried daughters of an impecunious clergyman. '... It is very bad to grow old & be poor & laughed at' (*MW* 317). Charlotte Lucas chooses to marry the pompous and inept Mr. Collins, not for love, but because her only alternative is to live as a spinster on the charity of her obnoxious younger brother. Herself a single woman of small means, Austen can represent the bleak existence of such women, as well as the happier fate of the heroine who finds fulfilment in marriage to the right man.

Those who make big money in 'trade' are the merchants and wholesalers. But their great houses are dependent on the small tradesmen, the retailers, who distribute the goods. There is a large social difference between the two. In Thackeray's *Vanity Fair*, a satirical panorama of the nineteenth-century class scene, the hero Dobbin is sneered at and called 'Figs' in school, because his father is a retail grocer, whereas the other boys are wholesalers' sons. 'My father's a gentleman, and keeps his carriage', boasts one young snob (chapter 5). The ladies and gentleman who are Austen's major characters exist in a commodity culture that depends on the retail trade for its luxuries, its status symbols, often its very food and drink. Mrs. Allen in *Northanger Abbey* can think of nothing but her clothes; Robert Ferrars in *Sense and Sensibility* brings his whole personality to bear in the choice of a toothpick-case; Sir Walter Elliot praises the efficacy of Gowland's lotion in removing freckles: such characters suggest an idle upper class obsessed with material luxuries, and ironically dependent on the very tradesmen they affect to despise. Austen sets some memorable scenes in shops: Harriet and Emma define themselves and their relationship in the matter of buying ribbons, feminine fripperies, in Ford's of Highbury. Anne Elliot has a nervous reunion with Wentworth at Molland's in Bath, where the crowds of the fashionable gather and assert their status: 'altogether there was a delay, and a bustle, and a talking, which must make all the little crowd in the shop understand that Lady Dalrymple was calling to convey Miss Elliot' (P 176). Mary Crawford in *Mansfield Park* humorously notices the elaborate lines of communication in a country community: she gets word of the harp, on its way to the country from London, only when 'it was seen by some farmer, and he told the miller, and the miller told the butcher, and the butcher's son-in-law left word at the shop' (MP 57–8). These retailers and small tradesmen do not figure prominently as characters, but their presence as part of the busy scene of life is carefully registered. There are many other relatively 'low' and minor characters who help to make society work smoothly in Austen's novels. Mrs. Smith's Nurse Rooke, in *Persuasion*, though not in genteel society, knows and transmits more of what goes on there than people who are.

Emma, which provides unobtrusive information on the whole community of Highbury, right down to the poor and the gypsy vagrants, has a number of minor characters who occupy places in the social hierarchy well beyond the gentry and professional classes where Austen's major characters are situated. She writes no explicit analysis, but by passing details, she fills in the large social picture and provides indirect commentary. We hear of Wallis the baker, who bakes Mrs. Bates' apples; of the village shop, Ford's; of Mr. Knightley's steward, William Larkins; his tenant farmer, Robert Martin, a sensitive young man who is bettering himself by reading; of Mrs. Goddard's school, an unpretentious establishment 'where girls might be sent to be out of the way and scramble themselves into a little education' (E 22).

The leisured and professional classes of Regency England were sustained by a great army of servants, an army which like the actual military had its own internal hierarchy and pecking order. Though Austen doesn't usually give servants speaking parts, she recognizes the unobtrusive influence they have on the lives of their masters.[5] It is a material convenience to Mr. Woodhouse of Hartfield, for instance, that his coachman's daughter is placed as housemaid at Randalls: James therefore never objects to harnessing the horses to the carriage, even though it is a very short drive (E 8–9). Such little negotiations between one social level and another are the stuff of life.

Beyond the servants comes the great mass of what was yet to be named the working class; but with them Austen's main characters have little to do. Like most 'ladies and gentlemen' of their day, their acquaintance with this huge section of the population would be only through their servants, who are not truly representative. However, we get glimpses. Mary Crawford learns of the 'sturdy independence' of rural labourers at hay harvest time (*MP* 58). Harriet Smith and a schoolfriend have a disturbing encounter with disreputable gypsies, but the 'whole gang' is swiftly dispersed when Frank Churchill arrives; and we hear that Mr. Knightley, as magistrate, is to be informed 'of there being such a set of people in the neighbourhood' (*E* 334). Dickens might give us scenes of the unleashed fury of the mob in the Gordon riots or the French Revolution; but in Austen's novels, by and large, law and order prevail.

'The poor' are seldom mentioned, but they are there, for Lady Catherine to 'scold ... into harmony and plenty' (*PP* 169) or for Anne Elliot and Emma to visit compassionately. Although Emma is aware she will probably soon forget the distress of the poor sick family she visits, she pays them full attention while she is with them, and she is neither arrogant nor sentimental: 'She understood their ways, could allow for their ignorance and their temptations, had no romantic expectations of extraordinary virtue from those, for whom education had done so little, ... and always gave her assistance with as much intelligence as good-will' (*E* 86). We have the sense of those 'two nations,' as Disraeli was later to characterize rich and poor in *Sybil*; but Austen allows for some humane contact between them, however minimal.

Lionel Trilling humorously quotes a reader exasperated by the obsessive attention paid to social class in the English novel: 'Who cares whether Pamela finally exasperates Mr. B. into marriage, whether Mr. Elton is more or less than moderately genteel, ... whether Lady Chatterley ought to be made love to by the game-keeper, even if he was an officer during the war? Who cares?'[6] The novelist, and especially Jane Austen, always cares, because it is the business of the novel to represent people – not exclusively, but prominently – in their social roles, and to be precise about the differences between them. It sometimes seems that if class difference did not exist, the novelist would have to invent it, because of the rich potential it provides for definition and fine distinction. Austen, as we have seen, goes in for fine distinctions, whether between the degrees of quality of mind in her characters or the fine shades of difference in their social standing. But to say so much is not to contend that she approved of the bastions of privilege in her very hierarchical society, or resisted the changes towards freer movement between the classes that she saw happening around her.[7] Nor did she subordinate moral and aesthetic judgments to issues of social rank. To use that term of later development that I have applied to Emma, Austen was no snob, though she knew all about snobbery.

According to Lionel Trilling's definition, 'Snobbery is pride in status without pride in function' (203). This applies perfectly to Sir Walter Elliot, who wants all the privilege and prestige belonging to his baronetcy, but none of the responsibilities. Thackeray, the most prominent of the many nineteenth-century commentators on class difference, supplies a definition that emphasizes the vitiated value system of the person who considers social station to be all-important: a *snob*, he says, is 'he who meanly admires mean things'.[8] To such a person social station is the defining condition that overrides all other categories of judgment, physical, intellectual, or moral.

In Jane Austen's world, human worth is to be judged by standards better and more enduring than social status; but social status is always relevant. With amused detachment, she registers exactly the social provenance of each of her characters, and judges them for the ways in which they judge each other. The importance assigned to class distinction is the source of much of her comedy and her irony, as of her social satire. In *Emma*, for instance, the snobbish heroine becomes both our guide as to where each character in the novel should be 'placed', and our negative example of one who assigns far too much importance to the matter of status. And the best treatment for her self-importance is laughter. 'Nonsensical girl!' laughs Mr. Knightley, when she has indulged in one of her elaborately class-conscious flights of fancy (*E* 214). But snobbery unchecked raises indignation too. Many of Austen's most contemptible characters are those who place undue emphasis on social station; and they come from all levels of the social ladder: Isabella Thorpe and General Tilney; Mr. and Mrs. John Dashwood; Lucy Steele and Mrs. Ferrars; Miss Bingley; Mrs. Norris; Mr. Collins and Lady Catherine de Bourgh. Those principal characters with an overdeveloped pride in their position, like Darcy and Emma, must learn the error of their ways.

Before Emma has met Mrs. Elton, she reflects that '*what* she was, must be uncertain; but *who* she was, might be found out' (183). It is the lady's social identity that can be discovered in advance: whose daughter she is, where she comes from, how much money she has, and how it was made. But *what* she is – that is, what sort of person, vivacious or reserved, kind or arrogant, intelligent or silly: all the things that really matter – is another issue altogether, and can be established only by personal contact. Austen brilliantly dramatizes these essential matters of personal identity in the personnel of her novels, and we come to know her people and the individual *feel* of them as intimately as we know any in fiction; but in this essay I have necessarily concentrated on *who* they are (in Emma's terms), rather than on *what* they are.

'Tinker, tailor, soldier, sailor,' goes the rhyme, as the child divines possibilities from the cherry-stones left on the plate; 'Rich man, poor man, beggar-man, thief.' The folk imagination, like the individual's, necessarily busies itself with such matters. Austen's heroines play the cherry-stone game too, and we learn to care whether they will come to reside in 'Big house, little house, pig-stye, barn,' and dress in 'Silk, satin, cotton, [or] rags.' Her novels are rich in detail of the status symbols and cultural markers of her society: the estates, lands, houses, cottages; the coaches, carriages, barouche-landaus, hatchments, lozenges, liveries; the silks, satins, muslins, pearls, amber crosses, rings, and beads. As a sensitive and informed commentator on class, that huge topic of the nineteenth century, Austen shows us amply how such things matter. She also shows us how they should not matter too much.

NOTES

1 Park Honan, *Jane Austen: Her Life* (London: Weidenfeld and Nicolson, 1987), p. 118.

2 Edward Lytton Bulwer, *England and the English* (1831), ed. Standish Meachum (Chicago and London: University of Chicago Press, 1970), p. 31.

3 Thomas Carlyle, *Sartor Resartus*, first edition 1833-4 (New York: Odyssey Press, 1937), p. 272.

4 '*Persuasion* ... [has] the distinction in Austen's novels of celebrating the professional ranks frankly and openly, of placing them above the aristocracy and gentry as responsible economists.' Edward Copeland, 'The Austens and the Elliots: A Consumer's Guide to *Persuasion*', in *Jane Austen's Business*, ed. Juliet McMaster and Bruce Stovel (London: Macmillan, 1995), p. 150.

5 For a study of the servant classes in Austen's novels, see Judith Terry's 'Seen but not heard: Servants in Jane Austen's England', *Persuasions*, 10 (1988), 104-16.

6 Quoted by Lionel Trilling, in 'Manners, Morals, and the Novel', in *The Liberal Imagination* (New York: Doubleday, 1953), p. 205.

7 Mark Parker, 'The End of Emma: Drawing the Boundaries of Class in Austen', *JEGP*, 91:3 (July 1, 1992), 34, notes, 'She produces a narrative voice at once ... inside and outside ideology: able to perceive bourgeois subjects (like herself) making decisions about class in ways that smack of false consciousness, yet arguing, subtly but firmly, for a maintenance of the system.' While I agree with much of what he says, I read Austen as much more critical of the operation of class ideology than Parker allows.

8 William Makepeace Thackeray, *A Book of Snobs, by One of Themselves* (1846), ch. 2.

8

EDWARD COPELAND

Money

Once upon a time, as the story goes, there lived a beautiful young woman of modest rank and excellent manners, but no significant income to speak of, and a handsome young man of great rank, haughty manners, and an estate 'ten miles round'. The beautiful young woman and the handsome young man meet, his haughty manners improve, they fall in love, he proposes marriage, and, in the concluding pages, her very modest means are joined to his very great estate in an event that surpasses even the wildest dreams of her ambitious mother.

It's an irresistible story, so irresistible, in fact, that garbled accounts from the popular press fluttered readers for three years and more with rumours that Jane Austen's text was not only being readied for television, but was going to feature a *nude* Mr. Darcy – as if Austen's economic romance were not more complex, shaded, and, well, more passionate, than mere flesh. If sex were all there were to it, we've seen it before. But when the BBC camera turns its yearning gaze on Britain's Historic Houses, Castles, and Gardens, their vast acres smiling in the sunshine, their sweeping Capability Brown parks, the splendid house presiding over it all, then the blood begins to pump in earnest.

For the BBC executives, of course, the yearning gaze of the camera and the rising heart of the viewer are little more than tokens in their own game of consumer desire. Industry moguls care nothing for Pemberley and its ten miles round except as it attracts the consumer eye. Paradoxically, Jane Austen's position as a 'viewer' of Pemberley is a consumer's point of view as well. If desire is most likely to afflict the viewer who is outside the gates, one who does not naturally belong within the charmed circumference of the Pemberley estate, that is to say, a person who could, if *tempted*, become an appreciator of such an estate, and who could, if *convinced*, contemplate becoming a consumer of it, then both Jane Austen and her readers qualify in *Pride and Prejudice*. In short, Pemberley exists as a consumer token in Austen's novels, even as it does for the BBC, but in a much deeper game of desire.

Throughout her career, would-be consumers, over-consumers, and wise consumers turn Austen's attention to the economy. From the focus of *Sense and Sensibility*, *Pride and Prejudice*, and *Northanger Abbey*, where the single most significant economic problem for women is the lack of a fortune, Austen's works steadily engage women in more and more complex relationships to the economy. *Mansfield Park*, *Emma*, and *Persuasion*, each in turn, move through an examination of the economy as measure of social morality, as agent of social disruption, as source of national identity, and, in the final fragment *Sanditon*, as 'Activity run mad!'

It may, in fact, surprise some readers to know that Jane Austen does not write as a member of the landed gentry, or as a representative of the proprietors of such piles as Pemberley, Netherfield, Rosings, Norwood, Mansfield Park, Sotherton, Donwell Abbey, Kellynch Hall, or any other of the imagined great houses of her novels, but as a member of a somewhat humbler rank that the historian David Spring calls the 'pseudo-gentry': that is, a group of upper professional families living in the country – clergymen or barristers, for example, or officers in the army and navy, retired *rentiers*, great merchants – allied by kinship and social ties, and by social aspirations as well, to their landed-gentry neighbours, but different in an essential economic condition: they do not themselves possess the power and wealth invested in the ownership of land, but depend upon earned incomes.[1] Nevertheless, they *are* gentry of a sort, Spring notes wryly, 'primarily because they sought strenuously to be taken for gentry', through the acquisition of the manners, the education, and the same markers of station as their landed-gentry neighbours (60). The consequence of such aspirations, however, presents this class with a two-fold economic burden: first, of course, the need to pay for the necessary markers of their genteel appearance; and, second, the need to soften the inherent weakness of their economic position: with the loss of the breadwinner, there is the loss of his income as well.[2] This essential economic fact attaches itself firmly to Jane Austen's fiction and to her life. Her father, a clergyman living in rural Hampshire, later retired to Bath, with a moderately good income, moderately poor health, and three dependent women (his wife and two spinster daughters), headed a family exposed to exactly the kind of sudden and irreversible fall in fortune implicit to their station in life.

As a consequence, *money*, especially money as spendable income, is the love-tipped arrow aimed at the hearts of Jane Austen's heroines and her readers: first of all, for its power to acquire the material goods that can support the all-important signs of her rank's claims to genteel station; second, as the prod of anxiety that focuses its own potential for loss. In her novels, Austen approaches the subject, money, from three different, but related, points of view. First, as a member of the pseudo-gentry, that is to say, the upper professional ranks of her rural society; second, as a woman in that society, severely handicapped by law and custom from possessing significant power over money; finally, as a novelist who joins other women novelists in a larger conversation about money.[3] And, as Jan Fergus reminds us in this volume, novel writing is itself an economic activity, with money the importunate force that moves this conversation along.

The heartbeat of romance lies in a good income. That is the universal truth about which there is no doubt in contemporary women's fiction. The Dashwood women, for example, Elinor and Marianne in *Sense and Sensibility*, name their hearts' desires: 'About eighteen hundred or two thousand a-year; not more than *that*', Marianne confides. '*Two* thousand a-year!' cries Elinor, shocked: '*One* is my wealth!' (*SS* 91). Marianne defends two thousand a year as she specifies the consumer expenses appropriate to it: 'I am sure I am not extravagant in my demands. A proper establishment of servants, a carriage, perhaps two, and hunters, cannot be supported on less.' Elinor smiles to hear her younger sister 'describing so accurately', and so transparently, the exact consumer expenses suited to the potential income of her lover, the soon-to-prove-faithless Willoughby. But in her own turn, Elinor's projection of 'one thousand pounds' is the income of the prosperous clergyman family that she longs to be mistress of. There is no room for error in this novel's system of accounting. In the concluding pages, Marianne gets her two thousand pounds a year, though from a different lover, and Elinor gets her one thousand a year, or suitably near it.

Incomes are openly discussed in all of Austen's novels, and, when the significant details are not given in the first pages of the novel, and they usually are, they follow when it is most useful for them to appear. *Pride and Prejudice*, for example, commences with the grand announcement of the arrival of Mr. Bingley with his fortune of £4,000 or £5,000 a year (*PP* 4). It is followed by the arrival of Mr. Darcy and the invigorating news of his £10,000 a year (10). Common conversation has it in *Sense and Sensibility* that Willoughby spends beyond his income of £600 or £700 a year (*SS* 71); that the Dashwood women have only £500 a year for the four of them (12); and that Colonel Brandon has £2,000 a year and a very nice estate to go with it (70). When incomes are *not* specifically named by Austen, then the signs of them are: the house, the furnishings, the garden, the park, the number of servants, the presence of a carriage.

Consumer markers of income and rank regularly pace the romances of Jane Austen's novels. In each novel, decisions of domestic economy define the heroine – and the hero – on a scale of expense familiar to contemporary readers. As distant from us as late eighteenth- and early nineteenth-century incomes and spending practices are, there is no real difficulty in learning the system.

Except for heiresses, almost all incomes in women's fiction are announced unambiguously as *yearly* incomes: 'two thousand a-year', or 'one thousand a-year', just as the Dashwood sisters refer to them.[4] Heiresses, however, have their fortunes reported in lump sums, like the 'proud and conceited' Miss Bingley in *Pride and Prejudice* who has a fortune of 'twenty thousand pounds' (*PP* 15), or Miss King, Elizabeth Bennet's richer rival for Wickham's attentions, with her 'ten thousand pounds' (149). But these heiresses' fortunes are understood immediately by contemporaries as *yearly* incomes through multiplying them by 5 per cent, a procedure that reveals their yearly income from investment in the 5 per cent government funds. Miss Bingley's yearly income from her £20,000 fortune is, thus, £1,000 a year; and Miss King's yearly income from £10,000, figuring it the same way, constitutes a lure of £500 a year for the impecunious Wickham. Elizabeth Bennet's pitifully small fortune of £1,000 is a minor exception, invested at a lower rate of 4 per cent (£40 a year), a fact Mr. Collins notes with some minuteness when he proposes to Elizabeth (106). With this formula for turning inherited money into yearly incomes (as investment at 5 per cent), heiress fortunes quickly come into focus as yearly income – the significant bottom line for romance.

For the present-day reader, however, there remains a problem in how to recognize with Austen's contemporaries the style of life attached to a specific income. Even though Austen herself generally explains each case as it arises, specific incomes also operate as shorthand in her fiction and in the rest of women's fiction – three hundred a year, four hundred a year, five hundred a year, and so on – to express rank, social aspirations, and consumer power. The telling range in women's fiction, however, is not large, being made up of those fine gradations of income that mark the aspirations of the middle ranks of society, each income bringing with it a set of specific consumer signs that reveal to the world both the income and the social level attached to its possessor.[5]

Numbers of servants mark incomes at the lower levels; the acquisition of a carriage does it for incomes that are a bit higher; and 'the house in town' certifies the presence of great incomes, usually those belonging to the prosperous landed gentry. Servants, an unfamiliar reckoning device these days, might be considered as the equivalent of modern household conveniences: add a servant, add a convenience – hot water, central heating, a washing machine, and so on.

£100 a year: this is the lowest income that can support the price of a ticket to a circulating library. It embraces poor curates, clerks in government office (both only marginally genteel), and moderately prosperous tradesmen. It could supply a family only with a young maid servant, and at a very low wage. When Edward Ferrars and Lucy Steele seem about to marry on an income of £100 a year, Mrs. Jennings' immediate reaction is to trim the number of servants she had imagined for them: 'Two maids and two men indeed! – as I talked of t'other day. – No, no, they must get a stout girl of all works. – Betty's sister would never do for them *now*' (*SS* 277). In *Emma*, the presence of Patty, Miss Bates' only servant, suggests the fragility of the Bates' present claims to genteel station.

£200 a year: Austen's father and mother married in 1764 on a church living of only £100 a year, plus the use of 200 acres of land as a second source of income, but found that even with an increase to £200 a year four years later, then £300 a year, their growing family made it difficult to maintain the appearance of genteel station. Mr. Austen was driven to take in students to increase the family's income.[6] Two hundred pounds makes a claim to gentility, but only with the narrowest style of life. The £200 a year income supplies a better servant, 'a Servant-Maid of all Work', at a higher salary.[7]

£300 a year: 'Comfortable as a bachelor', Colonel Brandon says of £300 a year for Edward Ferrars, but 'it cannot enable him to marry' (*SS* 284).[8] The income brings two servants. Austen's brother James married on this sum, but found it decidedly insufficient to maintain his elevated notions of consumer display: a carriage for his bride and a pack of harriers for himself.[9]

£400 a year: An income that approaches the comforts of genteel life, but not readily. It brings a cook, a house maid, and, perhaps, a boy. Isabella Thorpe turns up her nose at James Morland who is granted this income in *Northanger Abbey*. In *Mansfield Park*, Fanny Price's mother has just this amount per year for domestic expense and the requisite number of servants (two), but she manages very badly. Fanny's parsimonious Aunt Norris, Fanny notes, would have done better.

£500 a year: This sum, according to the domestic economists, fills the cup of human happiness. Jane Austen is not so confident. Five

hundred pounds a year is the very income that in *Sense and Sensibility* gives rise to such malicious gloating from the Dashwood women's prosperous sister-in-law, Fanny: 'and what on earth can four women want for more than that? – They will live so cheap! Their house-keeping will be nothing at all. They will have no carriage, no horses, and hardly any servants' (*SS* 12). Fanny is absolutely right on the first two counts (no carriage and no horses), and as for the third, the number of servants, she knows that her mother-in-law, the former mistress of Norland, and her sisters-in-law will now have only the three servants, two women and a man, prescribed by the professional economists for that income. Austen speaks from experience on this one: it is the sum, even a bit more, that she and her mother and her sister had to live on after Mr. Austen's death.[10]

£700 to £1000 a year: This higher range of upper professional incomes marks the most prosperous pseudo-gentry families, though Mary Crawford, the rich London heiress in *Mansfield Park*, doesn't think much of its potential: 'You would look rather blank, Henry,' she tells her brother, 'if your menus plaisirs were to be limited to seven hundred a year' (*MP* 226). Its most significant consumer marker becomes the ownership of a carriage. Jane Austen's father took a carriage when his income reached £700, though he found it too expensive to maintain on that income.[11] Mr. Perry, the local physician in *Emma*, lets his income be known to Highbury when Mrs. Perry begins to long for a carriage. The ambitious Mrs. Elton in *Emma* rubs everyone's nose in her ownership of a carriage: 'I believe we drive faster than anybody', she boasts (*E* 321).

£2,000 a year: At two thousand pounds a year (the landed-gentry income of Mr. Bennet in *Pride and Prejudice* and of Colonel Brandon in *Sense and Sensibility*), domestic economy must still hold a tight rein, especially in *Pride and Prejudice* where there are five daughters in need of dowries. Mrs. Bennet is noted as a poor economist; Mr. Bennet is better, though still inadequate considering his daughters' situation. Mrs. Jennings in *Sense and Sensibility* emphasizes the quiet, at-home pleasures of £2,000 a year when she describes Colonel Brandon's Delaford as 'without debt or drawback': 'every thing, in short, that one could wish for . . . Oh! 'tis a nice place!' (*SS* 196–7).

Above £4,000 a year: Incomes of £4,000 a year and above (Darcy's, Bingley's, Crawford's, Rushworth's) leave behind the cheese-paring cares of middle-class incomes – the problems of £100 to £1,000 a year, and even £2,000 a year – to enter a realm of unlimited genteel comforts. To spend more, according to contemporary wisdom, a man 'must go into horse-racing or illegitimate pleasures'.[12] In terms of consumer show, any income over £4,000 a year is characterized by its ability to provide a house in London for the social season, the beguiling consumer temptation that brings romantic disaster to both Mary Crawford and Maria Bertram.

The great incomes of this last category comprise those handsome land-based fortunes in Jane Austen's novels that could put to rout, if only they were managed by the prudent economic principles of Austen's own class, all economic anxieties for women. But in Austen, this almost never happens – and for good reason. As Gary Kelly notes, and others as well, the larger social picture tends to place Austen, along with other women novelists, in an advance guard of middle-class encroachers on the political and economic turf of the landed interest.[13] Mr. Darcy's and Mr. Knightley's great estates in *Pride and Prejudice* and in *Emma* are under the safe guidance of heroes who share the author's economic principles, but Northanger Abbey, Rosings, Norwood, Mansfield Park, Sotherton, and Kellynch are bywords for extravagance and/or faulty domestic economy. Representatives of this monied class show a regular pattern of catastrophe as they stumble without the aid of the economic principles of Austen's own more humble rank: What if Henry Crawford had remained at Everingham to manage his estate properly? What if Mary Crawford had given up her unreasonable demand for a house in town? What if Willoughby had kept out of debt? What if Sir Walter Elliot were not a fool?

In the more intimate, domestic negotiations of the novel, women's fiction turns to the particular relationship that women have with money – that is, no legal title to it for married women, and rights severely curtailed for unmarried women.[14] In a frustrating social irony, the pseudo-gentry woman finds herself responsible for the management of the household, but prevented by law and custom from exercising any significant control over the management of the family's income, a male prerogative. If money affairs go badly, as they certainly will with a feckless, foolish, improvident man like Willoughby, or with an out-and-out scoundrel like Wickham, the woman is still responsible for the economic consequences, a victim herself of course, but still responsible. Elinor Dashwood has no illusions about this harsh double bind when she consoles Marianne for the loss of Willoughby:

Had you married, you must have been always poor ... His demands and your inexperience together on a small, very small income, must have brought on distresses which would not be the *less* grievous to you, from having been entirely unknown and unthought of before. *Your* sense of honour and honesty would have led you, I know, when aware of your situation, to attempt all the economy that would appear to you possible; and perhaps, as long as your frugality retrenched only on your own comfort, you might have been suffered to practise it, but beyond that – and how little could the utmost of your single management do to stop the ruin which had begun before your marriage?

(*SS* 350–1)

'Just suppose it was your husband!' cries a character in Eudora Welty's Southern gothic tale, 'The Petrified Man' – a twentieth-century outcry, but one that names the same fear haunting most women's fiction conceived in the 1790s, including of course *Northanger Abbey*, *Sense and Sensibility*, and *Pride and Prejudice*. What is woman's defence? Principles of domestic economy offer at least the protection of a map. Catherine Morland, for example, warmly defends her brother James for not keeping a horse and gig of his own: 'I am sure he could not afford it' (*NA* 89). Elinor Dashwood prevents her sister Marianne from accepting a horse from Willoughby and thus overburdening the family's £500 a year income. Elinor earlier encourages her mother to sell the carriage, an inappropriate expense on that income. With such an understanding, we can appreciate, along with Austen's contemporaries, why Elinor Dashwood and Edward Ferrars 'were neither of them quite enough in love to think that three hundred and fifty pounds a-year would supply them with the comforts of life' (*SS* 369), and we can calculate in pounds sterling their later happiness when they do agree to marry on £850 to £900 a year.[15] We also understand how Henry Tilney in *Northanger Abbey* is just the right man for Catherine when the happy couple retire to their cottage at Woodston on his clergyman's income 'of independence and comfort' (*NA* 250), plus her marriage portion of £3,000, which, invested in the government funds, of course, adds a £150 a year to their income. And as for the extraordinary good luck of Elizabeth Bennet in meeting up with £10,000 a year, 'A house in town! Every thing that is charming!' (*PP* 378), it is a telling triumph of Austen's economic ideology to turn so fabulous a landed-gentry income into the earnest, cash-conscious programme of her own rank.

But money in Jane Austen's first three novels exists for the most part as a set of restrictive anxieties attached to the romance plot by the narrowest definition of domestic economy – fear of debt. In Austen's last three novels, and in the fragmentary final piece, *Sanditon*, far more complex relationships between income and romance are held in centre focus. Debt remains an anxiety of course: Tom Bertram wreaks disaster on the family income in *Mansfield Park*; Miss Bates worries about the cost of medical care for her niece in *Emma*; Sir Walter Elliot loses his estate in *Persuasion*; and Mr. Parker seems headed for financial trouble in *Sanditon*. But the omnipresent fear of loss no longer holds sway over the narrative. Instead, Austen sets women into an active, working relationship with the economy in a world where economic choice tests the strengths and the limitations of female power.

Income takes over as the leading economic trope of *Mansfield Park*. Tom Bertram's debts, of course, are a prominent irritant, but Austen seems little interested in them or in Tom. The novel begins, instead, with the income portfolio of the 'handsome' Ward sisters: Miss Maria has done well, 'at least three thousand pounds short of any equitable claim', by marrying the wealthy Sir Thomas Bertram, Baronet, of Mansfield Park; Miss Ward, less well, being 'obliged to be attached to the Rev. Mr. Norris' and his income of 'very little less than a thousand a year'; and Miss Frances has done very badly indeed, 'fixing on a Lieutenant of Marines, without education, fortune, or connections' (*MP* 3). Marriage, says Mary Crawford, whose assessment of the state never wavers from this focus, 'is a manoeuvring business. I know so many who have married in the full expectation and confidence of some one particular advantage ... who have found themselves entirely deceived, and been obliged to put up with exactly the reverse! What is this', she asks, 'but a take in?' (46). Mary's opinion of Maria Bertram's marriage to the rich, but stupid, Mr. Rushworth simply varies the trope: '[S]he will open one of the best houses in Wimpole Street ... and certainly she will then feel – to use a vulgar phrase – that she has got her penny-worth for her penny' (394).

But, in truth, there is nothing wrong with improving one's income in this novel. Dr. Grant and Edmund Bertram engage in an earnest conversation – 'The most interesting in the world', Henry Crawford tells his sister, Mary: 'how to make money – how to turn a good income into a better' (226). Sir Thomas conscientiously travels to the West Indies to improve the income of his estates in Antigua. But Henry and Mary Crawford's notion of a better income – solely as a higher income, the common understanding of the matter – is challenged by Austen. Mary must decide whether she is willing to marry the man she loves, Edmund Bertram, on their potential married income of £1,700 a year (his moderate-to-good clergyman's income of £700 a year, plus an additional £1,000 a year from the 5 per cent interest on her £20,000 fortune), or to try for better stakes in the London market. In any pseudo-gentry accounting, £1,700 a year is a strikingly good income for a clergyman, *handsome*, but it is not good enough for Mary, who wants a house in town and the income to go with it. In the end, she wants this more than she wants Edmund.

The Crawfords, both Henry and Mary, possess an unyielding and near pathological blindness to any but the most simplistic notion of incomes. In fact, Fanny Price is the only person in the entire novel canny enough to recognize that there is an option of choice and that this complicates the common, unexamined notions of acquisition held by the rest of the characters. Austen, however, gives Fanny no power to make her opinion known. After reading Edmund's letter pledging his undying devotion to Mary Crawford, Fanny cries out in exasperation, to herself alone, of course: 'He is blinded, and nothing will open his eyes, nothing can, after having had truths before him so long in vain. – He will marry her, and be poor and miserable' (424). But even for Fanny, the dialectic stands in a kind of immiscible suspension in the phrase, 'poor *and* miserable'. She cannot escape the logic herself. Her only revenge is to 'hint' to Edmund, gently of course, of 'what share his brother's state of health' – potentially fatal illness of the heir – 'might be supposed to have in her [Mary's] wish for a complete reconciliation' with Edmund, the younger brother (459). That gets his attention. But the information is gratuitous, and it only returns choice, marriage, love, to the same corrupt relationship with money that it has been in throughout the novel, of being a 'take in'.

If this is not the opinion shared by Austen, what can we make of Fanny Price's triumph in her marriage to Edmund? Mrs. Norris' sanguine promise to Sir Thomas, 'Give a girl an education, and introduce her properly into the world, and ten to one but she has the means of settling well, without farther expense to anybody', turns out to be absolutely on the money, though not exactly as she predicts (6). Fanny's career in the Bertram family is little more, in these terms, than a low-cost/high-yield investment saga, softened happily in the anaesthesia of Sir Thomas' self-serving sentiments, but ledger-like nonetheless: 'Fanny was indeed the daughter that he wanted. His charitable kindness had been rearing a prime comfort for himself. His liberality had a rich repayment' (472), though in truth, he had tried, unsuccessfully, to unload the girl when the pressure of Tom's debts made it 'not undesirable to himself to be relieved from the expense of her support, and the obligation of her future provision' (24). The novel concludes with a rousing paean to the industrious Price children, those ideal representatives of their rank, 'all assisting to advance each other' (473). Henry Crawford with his inherited income is sent packing, and Fanny marries Edmund, happily, on his income from the Thornton Lacey living. But there is no compelling logic to make the happy couple's £700 a year clergyman's income necessarily more virtuous than the £4,000 a year inherited income of Henry Crawford (118). Henry, if Jane Austen had excused him from the obligatory sexual excess with Maria Rushworth, could have had equal, or better, title to Fanny than Edmund, as Austen admits: 'Would he have persevered, and uprightly, Fanny must have been his reward – and a reward very voluntarily bestowed' (467). Income, the economic paradigm with which Austen seeks to measure the social and moral dilemmas of *Mansfield Park*, fails to clarify.

In her next novel, Austen chooses consumer signs, those social markers so important to her own class, to explore society. The action in *Emma* rides forward on a great tide of new consumer display. Mr. Weston buys a small estate; the former Miss Taylor, now Mrs. Weston, gets a new house, a new husband, and a new carriage; Jane Fairfax receives, mysteriously, a Broadwood piano; the Coles have a new dining room and a new pianoforte that none of them can play; Emma has a new round dining table; Frank Churchill buys gloves at Ford's, and Harriet Smith buys ribbons; Mr. Elton goes to Bath for a new wife and a new carriage; Mrs. Elton boasts lace and pearls and more servants than she can remember; Mrs. Perry yearns for a new carriage; and the Martins have 'a very handsome summer-house, large enough to hold a dozen people' (*E* 27). There are also more homely items on offer: plenty of good wine at Mr. Weston's; sweetbreads and asparagus at Mr. Woodhouse's; a hind quarter of pork for Miss Bates from Hartfield; apples for Miss Bates from Donwell Abbey; arrowroot for Jane Fairfax from Hartfield; and walnuts for Harriet Smith from Mr. Martin, who walks 'three miles around' to get them, though he forgets to enquire for the novels she had mentioned. What can it all mean?

Mr. Knightley proves himself the hero of the piece by possessing the sensibility that is the key by which these material goods are to be understood. He keeps warning Emma, over and over, that *things* are not what they seem, or, at least, they are not what *she* thinks they seem. Consumer signs, it is true, provide the system of order that keeps everyday life ticking along in *Emma*. Servants and carriages, for example, bring the Box Hill episode to a welcome close: 'The appearance of the servants looking out for them to give notice of the carriages was a joyful sight' (374). Tea saves Mr. Weston from more unwanted news of Maple Grove: 'They were interrupted. Tea was carrying around, and Mr. Weston, having said all that he wanted, soon took the opportunity of walking away' (310). 'The saddle of mutton' sets the pace of conversation at Randalls (119), and tea sets the time for departure. 'Mr. Woodhouse was soon ready for his tea; and when he had drank his tea he was quite ready to go home' (124). Finally, the length of a carriage ride provides the beginning and the end to Mr. Elton's declarations to Emma of 'violent love' (129).

But consumer goods in *Emma* also trace a society in restless motion. The Coles are on the way up with their new dining room, new pianoforte, and an increase in their servants; Mrs. and Miss Bates and Jane Fairfax are on their way down with their economies, modest quarters, and one maid. Mr. Martin is on the way up, as are the Eltons, the Coxes, the Smallridges, and the Sucklings. People are passing so rapidly through the gradations of income and the consumer markers associated with them that the old rules of birth and social order are thrown into question.

Mr. Woodhouse, who likes everything that is old and settled, marks one end of the scale; Mrs. Elton, who likes everything that is new and in motion, marks the other. Emma herself is in a state of confusion, blinded by vanity and social snobbery, but also blinded by the very consumer signs that offer themselves so temptingly to her imagination. Her conclusions about Jane Fairfax's pianoforte are her most embarrassingly public mistake, but her persistent inability to judge behaviour in her society turns, like a scorpion, on the novel itself, the consumer object whose self-proclaimed mandate to interpret social signs most consistently misleads her.

The plot of Jane Austen's *Emma* is, in fact, preempted by a tale published in the *Lady's Magazine* (November 1802), a popular monthly compendium of fiction and fashion. The tale begins with eerie familiarity:

> Mr. Knightley, a country-gentleman of not very large fortune, but such as was amply sufficient for his mode of living – as he rarely visited the capital, and had an aversion to the expensive pleasures of dissipated life – had married from the purest affection, and an esteem which grew with his knowledge of its object ... a deserted orphan [left] at a boarding-school near the residence of a relation of his whom he sometimes visited. As by this union he made no addition to his property, nor formed any advantageous connexion, he was by some blamed, and by others ridiculed. He however found himself amply compensated, both for the censure and the sneers which he encountered, by the amiable qualities and virtues of his wife; who, like himself, despised ambition, and sought only the genuine enjoyments of domestic happiness.
>
> (563)

Austen, of course, pointedly rejects the *Lady's Magazine* version of contemporary social life in the conclusion to *Emma*. Her heroine, however, swallows hook, line, and sinker the *Lady's Magazine* version of Mr. Knightley-and-the-amiable-orphan, which, of course, is exactly the admonitory point Austen intends. Cheap fiction is an untrustworthy system for interpreting social signs: Emma's fantasy of Harriet's background, for example, a classic gothic plot – 'There can be no doubt of your being a gentleman's daughter' (*E* 30); or another old chestnut, an affair of the heart between Jane Fairfax and her rescuer from the sea, Mr. Dixon; or the romance of Frank Churchill and Harriet prompted by the story of Harriet and the gypsies. Finally, when Harriet comes to Emma with her fantasy of Mr. Knightley's love, yet another rescue story, Emma falls into the trap again, exactly in the mode of the *Lady's Magazine*: 'It was horrible to Emma to think how it must sink him in the general opinion, to foresee the smiles, the sneers, the merriment it would prompt at this expense ... Could it be? – No; it was impossible. And yet it was far, very far, from impossible' (413).

It is, of course, *impossible*. If Emma had only read past the consumer signs of her society (false and misleading) to see and read the 'real' signs of social behaviour before her eyes (true and abiding), then she would not have made such a distressing hash of the situation. But here consumer fiction proves doubly false. The story from the *Lady's Magazine*, flattering fantasy as it is for tradesmen's daughters, is not necessarily wrong. Austen's society *is* experiencing major social change, fuelled in some degree by the very goods – novels among the first – that set themselves up as signs of social truths. The most unexpected people are indeed climbing the social ladder with the aid of money and the social markers it buys. Austen rejects the *Lady's* story for a more acceptable ideological resolution – Harriet Smith gets a farmer and Emma Woodhouse gets Mr. Knightley – but a conflicting set of social patterns, also explored in Austen's novel, points the other way. Mr. Knightley might just as well have married Harriet as not. After all, Austen's *Emma* is only one novel among many vying to promote its own reading of the 'real' signs of social behaviour.

Persuasion turns to *credit* as the issue that opens the economy, but with a spin that sets the topic apart from the compulsive debtors (Wickham, Willoughby) found in Austen's early works. Austen sends her two old-style debtors in this novel, Sir Walter Elliot and his daughter Elizabeth, to Bath for an early, embalmed retirement. Credit, *good* credit that is, becomes the talisman for future expectations in *Persuasion*. In fact the central romantic dilemma of the novel is, by extension, one of credit: whether Anne Elliot should have waited for Captain Wentworth, as she wanted to do. That is, should she have taken him on credit, or should she have remained with her dreadful father and sister in the conservative, but unhappy position of an unvalued dependent as Lady Russell persuaded her to do? The answer, according to Anne, is a negotiated qualification, but one turned strongly to the side of credit: 'Tell me', Captain Wentworth asks Anne, 'if, when I returned to England in the year eight, with a few thousand pounds, and was posted into the Laconia, if I had then written to you, would you have answered my letter? would you, in short, have renewed the engagement then?' Anne's answer is short, but decisive: 'Would I!' (*P* 247).

Anne marries Wentworth and thus joins the active, hard-working and prosperous pseudo-gentry rank she has learned to admire, a class of people who work for their living and know how to live within their means, as opposed to her father, the 'spendthrift baronet', or even as opposed to her gentry brother-in-law, the slack, unfocused Charles Musgrove, future heir to Uppercross, who agrees with his wife in only two things: 'the want of more money, and a strong inclination for a handsome present from his father' (44). The upbeat credit ideology of *Persuasion* rests on two assumptions: first, that the future holds prosperity for the British economy, and second, that a person who works for a living will pay his bills to uphold 'the character', as Lady Russell terms it, 'of an honest man' (12). 'And *woman*', she might have said, for in *Persuasion* Austen makes women active managers of the family income. 'While Lady Elliot lived', Austen notes, as the first in a string of good women managers in this novel, 'there had been method, moderation, and economy', which had 'just kept' Sir Walter within his income (9). When bill collectors begin to hover around Sir Walter, Lady Russell and Anne, both excellent economists, recommend 'vigorous measures' of economy that could have released him from debt in a reasonable amount of time (12–13). When Admiral and Mrs. Croft negotiate for the lease on Kellynch Hall, the lawyer, Mr. Shepherd, notes that Mrs. Croft 'asked more questions about the house, and terms, and taxes, than the admiral himself, and seemed more conversant with business' (22). Mrs. Harville in Lyme is another model economist, and on a very small income (113). Mrs. Smith, in Bath, remains cheerful and competent on an even smaller income (154).

Partnership marriages become the keynote of the new economic arrangement, demonstrated by the Harvilles and the Crofts for the edification of the future Captain and Mrs. Wentworth. Wentworth and Anne, 'a sailor's wife', *both* belong 'to that profession which is, if possible, more distinguished in its domestic virtues than in its national importance' (252). The income of the happy couple is reported as well, stamping Austen's seal of economic approval on the marriage at the highest reaches of pseudo-gentry prosperity: they will have £1,250 from the interest on Wentworth's £25,000 prize money, plus a small addition from the interest on one-third of the £10,000 of Anne's mother's fortune (when Sir Walter is able to pay it), *and* the promise of more money to come in the navy. It is as if Austen has single-handedly revised the economic priorities of her society: a higher credit line for the pseudo-gentry Wentworths, and a lower one for the baronet Elliots.

In *Sanditon* the economic future is not so cloudless. Mr. Parker, land-owning gentry, has invested heavily in a seaside bathing spa, Sanditon, where it appears likely that he is about to experience some financial rough weather. Investment as 'speculation' seems to be the economic focus of the piece. The failure of Austen's brother Henry's bank in which her uncle, Mr. Leigh-Perrot, and her brother Edward lost huge sums of money in March, 1816, may well be the inspiration for this new line of economic exploration – *Sanditon* was roughed out less than a year after the bankruptcy, between January and March, 1817, when illness forced her to put the fragment aside unfinished. It seems likely that the fragility of Mr. Parker's hold on the economy will be a central issue. Mr. Parker's partner in the enterprise is Lady Denham, a parsimonious, tyrannical old woman, and a fearful investor, who will be no support when economic storms arrive. His wife, weak, dependent, and ignorant of business, does not promise to be any assistance either, and his two sisters, professional invalids, are equally ineffectual. 'Activity run mad', thinks the heroine, Charlotte Heywood, who is a shocked witness of their fumbling interference in the Sanditon enterprise (*MW* 410).

Austen, as usual, sets out squarely the social and economic corners of her universe. There is the usual cast of economic scavengers: younger relatives of Lady Denham with a hungry eye for an inheritance, and, of course, the overspending Miss Beauforts, pretenders to elegance. There is the figure of conservative economics, Charlotte's father, Mr. Heywood – farmer, land-owner with modest investments in the funds – who seems to represent a sound, but old-fashioned and rather out-of-the-fray position. And then there is Mr. Parker, the 'enthusiast' for Sanditon, his financial speculation. The investment will probably not be allowed to go under completely: the town is attractive, the sea is beautiful, and there is the competent younger brother of Mr. Parker, Sidney, who puts in a brief appearance right before the fragment breaks off – 'well bred', 'very good looking', '7 or 8 & 20', and perhaps a future suitor for the heroine (425). Sidney suggests a Jane Austen signature hero for the future: a younger son, rich by 'collateral' inheritance (371), so not himself landowning gentry, though a pseudo-gentry member of such a family – of 'superior abilities', 'a very clever Young Man', 'always said what he chose of & to us, all' (382), and he laughs at the youngest brother, Arthur, for being 'so delicate that he can engage in no profession' (385).

From the start of her career, Austen is a shrewd observer of the economic terrain of her class, though always from the chilly and exposed position of an economically marginal female member of it – herself related to the landed gentry through the good fortune of her brother Edward (adopted by wealthy gentry relations), but really no more than a maiden-aunt visitor to his estate and his class.[16] In fact, the shadow of the single woman without money, Charlotte Lucas syndrome, continues to haunt her works to the end. In *Sanditon*, Clara Brereton fits the position, and though she is only vaguely sketched-in, her economic position is clear enough: 'more helpless & more pitiable of course than any – a dependent on Poverty – an additional Burthen on an encumbered Circle' (379).

Joseph Wiesenfarth's useful distinctions between the novel of manners and the gothic novel in *Gothic Manners and the Classic English Novel* (1988) provide a probe for examining the unresolved presence of this economic shadow.[17] The novel of manners presents a rational 'case', Wiesenfarth argues, whereas the gothic novel presents a 'riddle'. Obviously, Austen presents a 'case' for the operation of money in each of her novels – in fact, she presents several different cases. On the other hand, the single, unprovided woman carries in her very existence a gothic 'riddle' that underscores the moral entanglements cast up by her anomalous position in the economy. In the early novels, money comes to her through courtship windfalls – Mr. Collins is one of these – a resolution that Austen rejects in her last three novels to mount the 'case' for more rational relationships to the economy for women. But in each of these later novels, the 'case' regularly falls short before the immovable plight of the single woman without money. Fanny Price, Jane Fairfax, even Anne Elliot, are, in the end, left dependent upon purest chance for their entrance into the monied world of the 'case'. Moreover, the moral identity of each one of these women must first be asserted *against* the economic 'case' that eventually defines her social identity. Austen acknowledges the moral confusion when she has Emma say feelingly of Jane Fairfax, whose secret engagement to Frank Churchill would never have been condoned by his rich, capricious aunt: 'Of such, one may almost say, that "the world is not their's, nor the world's law"' (*E* 400). Anne Elliot's situation is equally ambivalent. In Anne's situation, where 'advice is good or bad only as the event decides' (*P* 246), the clarity of right and wrong, which is the rightful province of romance, edges towards Wiesenfarth's 'gothic confusion', a tribute to that deeper game of desire, the elusive force that Austen has pursued all along.

NOTES

1 David Spring, 'Interpreters of Jane Austen's Social World: Literary Critics and Historians', *Jane Austen: New Perspectives*, ed. Janet Todd (New York and London: Holmes and Meier, 1983), pp. 53–72.
2 R. S. Neale, in *Bath, 1680–1850: A Social History* (London: Routledge and Kegan Paul, 1981), writes that, 'If ... a woman through death or desertion should find herself the sole support of a family, the impoverishment of the family was virtually certain' (279–80).

3 See Edward Copeland, 'Introduction', *Women Writing about Money: Women's Fiction in England, 1790–1820* (Cambridge: Cambridge University Press, 1995), pp. 1–14.

4 The major exception for men in Austen's novels occurs in *Persuasion* where Captain Wentworth's profits from his naval career are reported in lump sum only: a fortune of £25,000.

5 See Copeland, *Women Writing about Money*, pp. 22–33. Contemporary domestic economists include Samuel and Sarah Adams, *The Complete Servant*, first published 1825 (Chichester: Southover Press, 1989); James Luckcock, *Hints for Practical Economy, in the Management of Household Affairs, with Tables, Shewing Different Scales of Expenses, from £50 to £400 Per Annum* (Birmingham: James Drake; London: Longman, *et al.*, 1834); John Trusler, *The Economist* (London: printed for the author, 1774).

6 Deirdre Le Faye, *Jane Austen: A Family Record* (London: The British Library, 1989), pp. 14, 19, 23.

7 Samuel and Sarah Adams, *The Complete Servant*, p. 16.

8 Edward's potential income of £300 a year comes from the Delaford living of £200 a year, plus his personal income of £100 a year from an inheritance of £2,000 (*SS* 276).

9 Le Faye, *Jane Austen: A Family Record*, p. 67.

10 Ibid., p. 131.

11 Ibid., p. 102.

12 W. Bence Jones, 'Landowning as a Business', *The Nineteenth Century*, vol. II (1882), p. 254. Cited by F. M. L. Thompson, *English Landed Society in the Nineteenth Century* (London: Routledge and Kegan Paul, 1963), pp. 25–6. Sir Thomas Bertram's fortune in *Mansfield Park* is a marked exception, severely shaken by the eldest son Tom's gambling debts and expenses in London and by poor returns from his West Indian estates.

13 Gary Kelly, *English Fiction of the Romantic Period, 1789–1830* (London and New York: Longman, 1989), p. 19. See also, Nancy Armstrong, *Desire and Domestic Fiction: A Political History of the Novel* (Oxford: Oxford University Press, 1987), pp. 8–10.

14 William Chester Jordan, *Women and Credit in Pre-Industrial and Developing Societies* (Philadelphia: University of Pennsylvania Press, 1993), cites studies of rich widows with disposable capital, but concludes that 'risk-taking English women investors' in the early modern period seem 'exceptional' (pp. 67–9). Susan Staves examines the limitations of women's economic independence in *Married Women's Separate Property in England, 1660–1833* (Cambridge, MA: Harvard University Press, 1990); also, Staves, 'Pin Money', *Studies in Eighteenth-Century Culture*, 14 (Madison: Wisconsin University Press, 1985), 47–77; Ida Beatrice O'Malley presents a general account in *Women in Subjection: A Study of the Lives of Englishwomen before 1832* (London: Duckworth, 1933), pp. 22–6; and Kaplan, in *Jane Austen among Women*, cites anecdotes from Jane Austen's own neighbourhood (pp. 43–61).

15 Edward and Elinor's joint income comes from the following sources: £100 a year interest from Edward's inheritance of £2,000 (*SS* 276); £50 a year from the interest on Elinor's £1,000 inheritance (4) – Mrs. Ferrars mistakenly thinks Elinor has '*three*' (373); £250 a year, 'at the utmost', from the Delaford living

(374), though valued by Colonel Brandon at only £200 a year (283); finally, £500 a year from Mrs. Ferrars' grudging marriage gift of £10,000 (374).

16 This is how her favourite niece, Fanny Knight, remembered her visits: 'Both the Aunts (Cassandra & Jane) were brought up in the most complete ignorance of the World & its ways (I mean as to fashion &c) & if it had not been for Papa's marriage which brought them into Kent, & the kindness of Mrs. Knight, who used often to have one or the other of the sisters staying with her, they would have been, tho' not less clever & agreeable in themselves, very much below par as to good Society & its ways.' Le Faye, *Jane Austen: A Family Record*, p. 253.

17 Joseph Wiesenfarth, 'Introduction', *Gothic Manners and the Classic English Novel* (Madison: The University of Wisconsin Press, 1988), pp. 3–22.

9

GARY KELLY

Religion and politics

For Jane Austen and the majority of her contemporaries, religion and politics were inextricably intertwined and of central ideological and material interest, and had long been so. Austen belonged to the Church of England, or Anglican church, established as the state church in the sixteenth century. It was Protestant, headed by the monarch, and episcopal in structure. Its theology and ecclesiastical structure were a compromise between Roman Catholicism and non-Calvinist Protestantism. Anglican theology was Arminian, rejecting the Calvinist doctrine of predestination and affirming salvation by a combination of true faith and good works, free will and divine grace. There were some groups who rejected various aspects of the established church and its theology, however, and who were accordingly known as 'Dissenters' or 'Nonconformists' and excluded from certain civil rights. These differences and inequalities resulted in social, cultural, and political tensions that reached a particular crisis in Austen's day.

The Church of England itself was not monolithic, however. Since the late seventeenth century a 'High Church' group had advocated alliance with government to suppress religious Dissent and became associated with the Tory faction in politics. A 'Low Church' or 'Latitudinarian' movement advocated an 'Erastian' policy subordinating church to state and tolerating religious differences within a national 'Broad Church'. This group became associated with the Whig political faction which favoured a constitutional monarchy ruling in collaboration with the landed class and supported by a broad coalition of public opinion that would include most Dissenters. The Whigs dominated politics from the Hanoverian succession in 1714 and brought the established church into the patronage system by which the political, social, and economic life of the country was managed. As a result, the Church of England became increasingly secularized and integrated in the civil order and culture which were dominated by the upper and upper middle classes.

These relations between religion and politics conditioned links between religion and social class.[1] Certain classes were more likely than others to benefit from the social status and patronage connections conferred by membership in the established church. These included the upper class or landed gentry and most of the upper middle classes, including the elite professions to which Austen's family belonged, and many well-to-do middle-class people in 'trade', or commerce and manufacture. Many of their lower-class dependents identified with these interests and thus remained Anglicans. Within the Church of England, however, Methodist and Evangelical movements had developed in the eighteenth century, appealing mainly to groups within the working and middle classes. The various Dissenting sects appealed mainly to those outside the dominant social order, especially the town-based commercial and professional middle class and the skilled working class, or artisans. By Austen's day, however, many Dissenters were demanding full civic rights and the social status and political influence they felt they merited.

By the time Austen reached adulthood these relations and tensions between religion and politics had again become the subject of intense public debate. In the late 1780s Dissenters renewed their campaign for parliamentary repeal of their civil disabilities. In the early 1790s the French Revolutionary government legislated religious toleration, showing Dissenters what might be done in Britain. Many Dissenters believed religious toleration could not be achieved in England without broader political reform, and many supported other reform movements such as feminism, prison reorganization, relief of the poor, and abolition of the slave trade. It soon became difficult to propose the French Revolution as a model, however, with successive episodes of Revolutionary violence, war between France and its neighbours, the Jacobin Terror of 1793–4, the rampant commercialism and moral permissiveness of the Directory period in the mid-1790s, and the long military and imperial struggle against Napoleonic France from the late 1790s to 1815. The term 'Jacobin', referring to radical French Revolutionaries, was used by counter-revolutionaries in Britain to discredit any kind of reformer, including Dissenters, Methodists, and Evangelicals.

Austen wrote the early versions of *Pride and Prejudice* and *Sense and Sensibility* just as public opinion in Britain was becoming decisively counter-revolutionary. During the mid-1790s, reform legislation was defeated in Parliament, Antijacobin organizations harassed reformers, and government repression broke up reform societies and drove many reformers into exile. By the early 1800s, when Austen finished and sold the manuscript of *Northanger Abbey*, public opinion rallied against Napoleonic France in a new 'Romantic' nationalism. Many reformers subsumed their earlier aims in broad schemes of social and economic improvement, some turned their reformist political enthusiasm into zealous religious activism, and others promoted common social, cultural, and political identities rather than particular and contested ones. Religion was used to promote post-revolutionary social mediation, harmony, and national unity, and to justify movements of ideological indoctrination, cultural reformation, and social control. Austen wrote the rest of her novels and rewrote her earlier ones towards the end of this period of prolonged crisis, a crisis in which she and her family, closely connected to the established order in church and state, had a direct interest.

As a novelist, Austen had an additional interest in this crisis, however. At that time novels of all kinds were in effect fictitious and narrative 'conduct books', or manuals for social and private life in the upper and upper middle classes that comprised the reading public. Yet most prose fiction was considered inartistic, unrealistic, intellectually shallow, overly stimulating or even addictive, and thus morally and socially corrupting. The 'modern novel', as it was often called, was distinguished from the 'romance', with the former supposedly representing 'probable' characters and incidents in contemporary life, especially 'fashionable' or courtly society, while the latter was thought to present eccentric characters in improbable circumstances and exotic or unusual locations. Accordingly, some critics defended the 'modern novel' as more 'realistic', but others condemned it for spreading false upper-class values and social expectations. Both the 'modern novel' and the 'romance' were condemned for distracting readers from 'solid and useful reading', and encouraging imagination, fantasy, and desire through fictitious narratives of social advancement through love and marriage, at the expense of the reason, self-discipline, and pragmatism supposedly required in 'real' middle-class life. Since 'modern novels' were widely thought to encourage social and cultural emulation of the decadent courtly upper classes by the middle classes, some blamed them for contributing to the supposed moral decline that had precipitated the Revolutionary crisis in Britain. Since 'romances' were widely believed to inspire a taste for the improbable and sensational, some blamed them for exposing gullible readers to the appeal of Revolutionary 'speculation' and violence. Such negative associations were reinforced by the belief that most novels of any type were written by and for women, who were widely seen as the vulnerable point in class solidarity, the social order, and national and imperial strength. In fact, men were as active as women in writing and reading novels.[2]

As Austen wrote her first full-length novels, some writers were attempting to reform the novel artistically, morally, and intellectually, thereby making it a more effective instrument in the Revolution debate, since it could reach readers who would seldom pick up a polemical pamphlet or political treatise. These writers incorporated in their novels explicit social, cultural, and political critique; new aspects of social, cultural, and linguistic reality; and elements from more prestigious learned and literary discourses. They also developed new formal devices and restructured established ones, especially narration, plot, and character. The most prominent of these novelists were 'English Jacobins' led by Robert Bage, William Godwin, Mary Hays, and Mary Wollstonecraft and including Dr. John Moore, Charlotte Smith, Mary Robinson, and perhaps Ann Radcliffe. Antijacobin or 'loyalist' critics condemned many of these novels as unrealistic 'political romances'. Antijacobin novelists such as Elizabeth Hamilton, Jane West, and Hannah More satirized their opponents' politics, private lives, and literary innovations, and claimed to present 'reality' rather than political fantasy in their own work. Austen knew the work of most if not all of these novelists.

In the 1800s and 1810s, just before Austen wrote her later novels and rewrote her earlier ones, certain writers tried adapting the novel to create a post-Revolutionary social consensus for national unity and imperial defence. Novelists such as Maria Edgeworth, Sydney Owenson (Lady Morgan), Jane Porter, and Walter Scott appropriated elements from historiography, popular literature, social studies, and political economy in order to represent various kinds of relationship between 'national' history, identity, and destiny and the individual and the local community. Both loyalist and reformist novelists used narration, characterization, and language in new ways to represent nation and empire as socially diverse and needing unifying values. Footnotes and other learned apparatus were often used to give authority to such representations. Some novelists, such as Maria Edgeworth, Amelia Opie, Elizabeth Hamilton, and Hannah More devised new techniques of formal realism and focused on supposedly 'ordinary' characters in everyday settings experiencing commonplace events, thereby suggesting that the public political sphere was remote from 'reality' as lived by most people. Austen knew the work of some, if not all of these novelists, too.

She would have known and understood both the interconnection of religion and politics and the way other writers used the novel to disseminate their religious and political views during the period when she herself was writing novels. She left little direct comment, however, in her novels or her letters, on these matters. According to her family she practised an unostentatious yet consistent and mainstream Anglican faith. Scattered remarks on religion in her letters indicate that she placed great importance on taking holy communion, regarded religiosity unfavourably, and sometime between

1809 and 1814 came to view the Evangelicals with less disapproval than before (*L* 170, 280). She also left three highly penitential manuscript prayers (*MW* 453–7). Like most Anglicans of her time, she seems to have had a 'latitudinarian' outlook, though she preferred Thomas Sherlock's High Anglican sermons 'almost to any' (*L* 278). She left even fewer comments on politics, though her letters show that she followed current events and especially naval affairs, as they involved two of her brothers. Her few references to the novels of her time do not constitute a significant body of criticism.

Paucity of direct comment does not necessarily mean indifference to issues of religion and politics and their representation in the novel, and it is likely that she saw these issues and representations as a woman of her religion and class. Her father and two of her brothers were Church of England clergymen, so she had both a familial and a personal commitment to the established Church. She also had an interest in the social hierarchy that supported and was supported by the Church. Her brother Edward was adopted as heir by a gentry family and thereby joined the historically dominant social class. It was he who provided his sisters Cassandra and Jane with the home at Chawton where Jane wrote (or rewrote) all her novels. Yet Austen could sympathize with reformers' claims for merit over inherited rank and status. Two of her brothers, Francis and Charles, went into the navy, a profession open to merit, and did well. In addition, Austen would know that writers from Mary Wollstonecraft to Hannah More called for women of merit to reform the domestic and local sphere and thus, indirectly, the public and political sphere. It seems likely, then, that a woman like Austen would support the historic hierarchical social structure and constitution of church and state, yet could recognize that they should be open to merit – including female merit in the domestic sphere – if they were to avoid the closedness and rigidity that many blamed for causing the social and political upheavals of the Revolution and its aftermath.

Since Austen's day, critical and scholarly interest in her religion and politics has focused on her novels. Interest in their religious aspect appeared soon after she died but reflected changes in religion and the Church that took place after her time. Much of this interest has centred on her representation of clergymen – the Rev. Henry Tilney and the Rev. Richard Morland in *Northanger Abbey*, Edward Ferrars in *Sense and Sensibility*, the Rev. William Collins in *Pride and Prejudice*, the Rev. Philip Elton in *Emma*, Edmund Bertram and the Rev. Dr. Grant in *Mansfield Park*, and the Rev. Charles Hayter and the Rev. Dr. Shirley in *Persuasion*. They have been seen as realistic representations of what one twentieth-century historian calls 'the church in an age of negligence' and what another sees as the culmination of a century of secularization or laicization of the Anglican church.[3] By Austen's day clergymen of all sects engaged in party politics, the patronage systems in church and state were intertwined, and the Anglican clergy increasingly came from the landed gentry and pursued that class's way of life. The clergy was viewed as one 'learned' or elite profession among others, not necessarily requiring a special spiritual calling, though there were exceptions, especially among Methodists and Evangelicals.

Only after her death did such movements effect widespread changes in religion and the established church, and these changes affected the way readers and critics interpreted Austen's treatment of religious and ecclesiastical matters in her novels. As early as 1818 her brother Henry felt it necessary to assure readers that the most important fact about her life was that she 'was thoroughly religious and devout', was 'well-instructed' on 'serious [i.e., religious] subjects', and that 'her opinions accorded strictly with those of our Established Church'. By the 1830s, when her novels began to be regarded as literary classics, the Church of England had changed considerably from what she had experienced in life and represented in fiction. In 1837, for example, John Henry Newman, leader of the Oxford and Tractarian movements for spiritual and ecclesiastical reform of the Church of England, found that her parsons were 'vile creatures' and that she herself had 'not a dream of the high Catholic [i.e., Anglican] ethos'. Such views persisted into the twentieth century: in 1931 a magazine for religious Dissenters concluded, 'we need never regret that the days of Jane Austen are gone beyond recall and that her type of clergyman no longer controls the religious life of rural England'.[4]

Others approved of Austen's apparent reticence about religion and secularized attitude to it. In 1816 a reviewer praised *Emma* 'because it does not dabble in religion; of fanatical novels and fanatical authoresses we are already sick'. In 1870, Richard Simpson praised Austen because she 'let the church stand in the churchyard, and did not attempt to transport it into her novels'. Twentieth-century academic and professional critics, predominantly secular in outlook, have questioned the relevance of Austen's religion to her fictional art. In an exchange of letters in the *Times Literary Supplement* for January and February 1944, Q. D. Leavis argued that Austen's personal beliefs could only interest the literary critic if they were manifested in the novels. In 1967 Laurence Lerner argued that, however pious Austen the person may have been, Austen the novelist did not believe in God, because 'a belief or a value only matters artistically if it is artistically present' in the writer's work.[5]

Others did find Austen's religion to be 'artistically present' in her novels.

Richard Whately was a latitudinarian and anti-Evangelical and later an anti-Tractarian and reforming Archbishop of Dublin; in 1821 he declared in the influential *Quarterly Review*, 'Miss Austen has the merit (in our judgment most essential) of being evidently a Christian writer: a merit which is much enhanced, both on the score of good taste, and of practical utility, by her religion being not at all obtrusive.' Edmund Knox, the late nineteenth-century conservative theologian and Evangelical, and later Bishop of Manchester, praised *Mansfield Park* for giving 'a convincing and reasoned estimate of the Church in country life'. In 1939 Canon Harold Anson argued that Austen's novels are religious not because they contain religious controversy or 'a strong ecclesiastical motif', as in the novels of Anthony Trollope, but because they show 'the underlying principles upon which men live their lives and by which they judge the characters of others'.[6] This has become the dominant view of those critics who find Austen to be a religious novelist.[7] Some critics have even argued that her portrayal of clergymen was intended to promote greater spirituality and social responsibility in the church.[8]

Discussion of Austen as a political novelist has developed fairly recently, and has also reflected differing political interests of times later than her own. Through the nineteenth century her novels were seen as indifferent to or above the politics of her day, for better or worse. Such views reflected the tendency of many though not all Victorian critics and writers to distinguish art from politics and to place the former above the latter. This critical tradition continued into the twentieth century and Austen's supposed neglect of the politics of her day has been seen as the necessary condition of her novels achieving 'classic' literary status.[9] Certainly politics are less obvious in Austen's novels than in those of the English Jacobins and Antijacobins, but during a period of political crisis this fact would itself make a political point. Furthermore, the novels' few direct references to politics are satirical. This fact may still make a political point, however. Some critics argue that to mock politics is to disparage the importance of the 'masculine' public and political sphere in relation to the 'feminine' domestic and local sphere. Others argue that ignoring politics casts doubt on the knowability or reality of the public and political sphere in contrast to the domestic sphere.[10]

After the mid-twentieth century, increasing numbers of critics challenged the view that Austen ignores politics. This shift was signalled in the 1950s by Rebecca West. West accepted the older view that Austen's novels 'contain no mention of the Napoleonic wars' because 'she had nothing to say about them', but also insisted that Austen 'was not apolitical, for she had much to say about those parts of the social structure which she had opportunities to observe', including 'the inequality presumed among people who were in fact equal, and who had to be dishonest to ignore their equality'. Since then historians and critics have identified particular political themes in Austen's novels, including the French Revolution, imperialism and capitalism, Regency politics, and the culture of Sensibility as an inspiration for cultural, social, and political 'innovation' and insubordination.[11]

Yet those who agree that Austen addresses politics in her novels disagree on the nature of those politics. Some see her as a political 'conservative' because she seems to defend the established social order.[12] Others see her as sympathetic to 'radical' politics that challenged the established order, especially in the form of patriarchy.[13] Conservativism meant something different in Austen's day than it does now, however, and criticism of patriarchy, or the system of hierarchical gender relations, did not necessarily involve criticism of patronage and paternalism, or the system of hierarchical class relations. Austen, like many men and women of her class, could support partial reform of this system without advocating its overthrow. Thus some critics see Austen's novels as neither conservative nor subversive, but complex, criticizing aspects of the social order but supporting stability and an open class hierarchy.[14]

What most readers could agree is that, if politics concern relations of power, then Austen's novels deal with politics in private and local life. This was the conventionally accepted subject of the novel of manners and the conventionally accepted domain of the woman writer. Yet readers in Austen's day were accustomed to seeing such politics as a metonym or metaphor for the politics of the public sphere. Though many readers may have found Austen's novels free from political or religious doctrine, they do contain both particular and general references to religious and political topics of her day.

Mansfield Park, for example, contains Austen's most extensive discussion of the clergy, and indicates her sympathy with Evangelicalism. The richly comfortable but unimposing and unused chapel at Sotherton could symbolize critically the 'church in an age of negligence'. Mary Crawford's reluctance to be a country clergyman's wife (*MP* 91–4) contrasts with Fanny Price's eagerness for the role, and Fanny disapproves when Henry Crawford says he could be a clergyman only if he could have a fashionable London congregation able to appreciate his artistry as preacher (341). Later readers' preference for Mary over Fanny exemplifies a secularization of literary culture since Austen's day that has made it difficult to understand how Anglicans such as Austen would have considered it vital in the Revolutionary aftermath to fill country vicarages with Edmunds and Fannys rather than Henrys and Marys.

Northanger Abbey, completed and sold immediately after the 1790s and revised just before Austen's death, contains several direct references to politics. Henry Tilney attempts to instruct Catherine in the theory of the picturesque and she seems responsive:

> Delighted with her progress, and fearful of wearying her with too much wisdom at once, Henry suffered the subject to decline, and by an easy transition from a piece of rocky fragment and the withered oak which he had placed near its summit, to oaks in general, to forests, the inclosure of them, waste lands, crown lands and government, he shortly found himself arrived at politics; and from politics, it was an easy step to silence. (*NA* 111)

The passage refers to the contemporary debate about enclosure of common lands by local gentry, which deprived the lower classes of a historic and customary 'right' by which they could supplement their income and diet. The passage lightly mocks the tendency of political writers, especially reformists, to link small and local issues to large national ones. It also refers to the cultural convention that women were not or ought not to be interested in politics – a convention challenged by many women writers during the Revolution debate.

Immediately after this passage the difference between what were seen as the 'masculine' discourse of politics and the 'feminine' discourse of romance is treated humorously when Tilney teases Catherine and his sister about some imminent 'very shocking' event that could be either a popular uprising or publication of a new gothic romance. Tilney imagines his sister's vision of revolution and tells Catherine:

> 'You talked of expected horrors in London – ... she immediately pictured to herself a mob of three thousand men assembling in St. George's Fields; the Bank attacked, the Tower threatened, the streets of London flowing with blood, a detachment of the 12th Light Dragoons, (the hopes of the nation,) called up from Northampton to quell the insurgents, and the gallant Capt. Frederick Tilney, in the moment of charging at the head of his troop, knocked off his horse by a brickbat from an upper window. Forgive her stupidity. The fears of the sister have added to the weakness of the woman.' (113)

This was just what many people did fear, however, and troops of dragoons were raised, ostensibly to resist a French invasion but actually to suppress a popular uprising of the kind imagined here. Tilney also refers to the widely held belief that women saw such political incidents purely from a personal and familial point of view, and many women writers did treat politics in that way.[15]

A more central passage in *Northanger Abbey* contains an oblique reference to conspiracy theories of upper-class oppression and revolutionary intrigue, but rendered, as the novel requires, in personal and domestic terms. When Henry Tilney realizes what Catherine's gothic imaginings have led her to believe about his family's history he asks:

> 'What have you been judging from? Remember the country and the age in which we live. Remember that we are English, that we are Christians. Consult your own understanding, your own sense of the probable, your own observation of what is passing around you – Does our education prepare us for such atrocities? Do our laws connive at them? Could they be perpetrated without being known, in a country like this, where social and literary intercourse is on such a footing; where every man is surrounded by a neighbourhood of voluntary spies, and where roads and newspapers lay every thing open?'
>
> (197–8)

Tilney appeals to the same idea of England as an open civil society that was advanced by Antijacobins against English Jacobins' claims to the contrary in gothic 'political romances'. Such novels are what the young and naive Catherine has 'been judging from', as Antijacobin novelists had warned.

Mansfield Park also contains political allusions that most readers would have recognized. Some, at least, of the young people at Mansfield wish to perform a translation of Kotzebue's *Lovers' Vows* so that they can court a partner under cover of theatrical performance. Furthermore, the play had a dubious reputation for treating a pre-marital sexual liaison not only without moral disapproval but as a laudable expression of 'natural' love. Many readers would have known that such literature was associated with socially and politically transgressive attitudes during the 1790s. Indeed, Hannah More's widely known counter-revolutionary polemic addressed to women had called them to lead national and imperial resistance to Revolutionary and Napoleonic France by banishing such supposedly subversive literature from their homes.[16]

Post-colonial critics have recently drawn attention to the fact that the patriarch of Mansfield Park, Sir Thomas Bertram, owns property in Antigua that would have been worked by black slaves.[17] Significantly, Sir Thomas' forced absence attending to his West Indian interests allows ambitious and 'insubordinate' elements at home to introduce the subversive text of *Lovers' Vows*, suppressed only with his sudden return, though the insidious effects may be seen in the later misconduct of his daughters. This passage could dramatize a neat political allegory, with Sir Thomas representing Britain's ruling class distracted by colonial affairs and inadvertently loosing subversive forces that might overthrow the established order 'at home'. Many readers would also know that John Moore's widely read reformist novel, *Zeluco* (1789), represented a direct connection between the slave system and decadent and despotic court government. Austen's treatment of this matter is ambiguous, however. On the one hand, her apparent failure to condemn the slave system, after several decades of vociferous public campaigning against slavery and the slave trade in a broad front of reform, could be read as tacit approval of the colonial and slave systems and of firm social control in Britain. On the other hand, her apparent exposure of the limitations of patriarchal and authoritarian rule at home, and perhaps abroad, could be read as tacit approval of at least a measure of reform and liberalization.

Persuasion contains obvious references to the domestic and international political situation at the end of the Napoleonic wars. Sir Walter Elliot criticizes navy men such as Captain Wentworth and Admiral Croft because they 'spoil' their complexions by being out in all weathers and because the war has enabled them to rise in status 'too quickly'. Yet Sir Walter's own vanity and extravagance force him to rent his manor to Admiral Croft, and his daughter marries the naval captain once considered unsuitable because of his uncertain profession, but now able to purchase the estate and status of gentleman thanks to the financial rewards of his martial success in capturing French ships. Most readers would have condemned Sir Walter's criticism of a profession largely responsible for Britain's victory in the long struggle with Revolutionary and Napoleonic France. Many readers might also associate Sir Walter with the vain and extravagant Prince Regent, symbol of decadent pre-Revolutionary court culture and of the upper-class snobbery, corruption, and incompetence that had imperilled nation and empire during the Revolutionary and Napoleonic wars.

Though Austen's letters reveal little about her religious and political principles or her view of religious and political novels, they do reveal her deep concern with the art of the novel. It could be, then, that Austen addresses religion and politics in her novels less through content and theme than through literary form. As a parodist and practitioner of the novel during the period of Revolution and aftermath, Austen would have understood how other novelists of the time represented their religious and political beliefs through form as well as through theme and content. It can be argued that Austen, too, uses the novel form to embody her response, based on her Anglican faith and culture, to the related religious and political issues of her time. Through the Revolutionary crisis and aftermath many polemicists declared that sustaining this faith and culture was of vital national importance and that no person or instrument was too humble for the task. Austen might well think this could include a country parson's daughter whose instrument was 'only a novel'.

It is also true that the meaning of any novel or literary work, at least for its original readers, depends partly on those readers recognizing its resemblances to or differences from other works of a similar kind from the same period. Many of Austen's original readers would recognize that her novels seem to eschew formal elements used by novelists ideologically different from her and to adapt formal elements used by novelists ideologically similar to her. The differences could imply rejection of the politics of the former and the adaptations could imply modification of the politics of the latter. To readers with social and religious commitments similar to her own, and who took the art of the novel as seriously as she did, the form of Austen's novels can even seem consistent with a specifically Anglican view of the intertwined religious and political issues of the time.

For example, choice of narrative mode seems to have had political implications for many of Austen's contemporary novelists. Writers of the pre-Revolutionary culture of Sensibility who use the novel for social and political criticism often employ first-person narration, including the epistolary form, to focus on individual subjectivity afflicted by a supposedly corrupt and vitiated public and political sphere. English Jacobin novelists often use forms of first-person narration in this way, but also to show that individual experience and reflection suffice for political understanding and agency, and to engage readers' sympathies with the oppressed narrator-protagonist and thus with the social and political reform supposedly necessary to end such oppression. Some writers, however, such as Austen's model, Frances Burney, and most Antijacobin novelists, seem to have felt that first-person narration could engage readers' sympathies so powerfully that it disarmed judgment. One result could be to hinder development of the disciplined subjectivity considered essential to middle-class domestic and professional life. Another result could be to weaken readers' ability to resist the ideological – and sexual – seductiveness of Revolutionary rhetoric. This result was shown in several Antijacobin novels that depicted romance-reading heroines politically converted and then sexually seduced by 'Jacobin' villains skilled in the 'jargon' of 'political romances'. Consequently, most Antijacobin novelists used authoritative third-person narration, supposedly implicating the reader in a more detached, rational attitude and also serving as a formal homology for defence of social hierarchy and political authority.[18]

Austen's narrative method could be seen as mediating between such opposing political associations of form. Apparently she experimented with first-person epistolary form in the 1790s, but finally opted for third-person narration with restricted free indirect discourse, or narrator's representation of the protagonist's inward speech and thought. The effect is to retain narrative authority but allow the reader considerable knowledge of and thus sympathy for the protagonist. Austen's use of this narrative method can be read as a formal homology for a hierarchical yet open social structure, stabilized by inherited authority based on wealth and power but open to individual merit and responsive to individual rights based on it, while avoiding extremes of authoritarianism and individualism.

Her narrative method has historical religious implications, too. The Roman Catholic church insisted on the authority of priest and church, but many Protestant Dissenting sects based religious authority on individual religious experience and based ecclesiastical authority on the will of the community of believers. The Church of England took a middle way, making salvation the responsibility of the individual, though guided by priest and church doctrine and authorized by an apostolic succession of bishops claiming direct succession from Christ's disciples. Austen's narrative structure can be read as a secularized homology for the Anglican position. In this homology the protagonist is responsible for her worldly 'salvation', or moral condition and social destiny, guided by a sympathetic yet critical narrator, who allows the reader to identify with the protagonist's struggle, and thus to experience that struggle vicariously, again guided by the narrator.

Other fictional elements in the form of Austen's novels can be seen as supporting such implications of narrative method. For example, Austen's characters are fictitious, drawn from contemporary life, relatively few in number, and mostly from the professional middle class and gentry. Such a repertory enables Austen to emphasize the protagonist's moral deliberations and ethical commitments through similarities and differences of character and action, as in the stark contrast between Elinor Dashwood, her sisters, and the Steele sisters, or the challenging contrast between Fanny Price, Mary Crawford, and the Bertram sisters. Austen omits the kinds of characters found in the gothic romances, historical fiction, and regional novels, which often promoted reforming agendas. Thus her novels could be seen to imply that true or important social meaning is found not among such people and places but among the rural upper and professional middle classes she represents, and to which her family and their friends belonged. Moreover, by keeping to a relatively narrow range of character types Austen both concentrates her social satire and emphasizes moral discernment and ethical interaction in daily life and in local rural society. Such interaction was seen as the main arena of religious practice, and such a social space was the typical stronghold of the Anglican church.

Significantly, such people and places were also the basic unit of national life according to Edmund Burke's counter-revolutionary *Reflections on the*

Revolution in France (1790), and Austen uses setting to reinforce the impression that the segment of society she represents is of central importance. She avoids the exotic settings favoured in gothic, historical, and 'national' tales, many of which had reformist themes. She places her characters in settings that are predominantly domestic or semi-public, on country estates or in places of fashionable resort, where upper and professional middle classes met to create the kind of open civil society lauded by Henry Tilney.

Her range of incident is similarly narrow and includes the protagonist's solitary reflections; intimate dialogue between close friends, family members, or couples; and socializing in local civil society during visits, dinners and dances, and excursions and amusements. Occasional trips farther afield comprise the preceding kinds of incident rather than the scenes and episodes in high society favoured by 'fashionable' novelists of manners. Austen uses incidents dealing with 'the anxieties of common life' rather than 'the alarms of romance' (*NA* 201), with the exception of Colonel Brandon's autobiographical tale in *Sense and Sensibility* (*SS* 205–10), and draws the reader's attention to the fact by occasionally burlesquing sensational incidents such as murder, rape, abduction, duels, and other forms of violence found in gothic and historical romances, and even some novels of manners.

Austen reduces range and 'intensity' of incident in order to achieve three effects. The first is to emphasize moral reflection and ethical action in domestic and local life, rather than the intense sensation and experience often celebrated in the literature of Sensibility. The second effect is implicit rejection of the sensational or extraordinary as a basis for moral education of characters or readers, let alone for political action on a local or national level. The final effect is implied criticism of extremists in both past and recent history for sensationalizing issues of religion and politics, thereby polarizing public opinion, disrupting civil society, and undermining national unity.

Austen's plots may look conventional enough, but plot, too, had political and even religious implications in many novels of her time. English Jacobin novelists followed the 'necessitarian' or determinist theories of Enlightenment materialist philosophers, and so use plot to illustrate how a particular political regime conditions social practice, thereby determining individual character and necessitating certain kinds of action, usually for the worse. Antijacobin novelists deny necessary connections of this sort and assert that individuals should follow the moral and political authority of those born or appointed to it. Accordingly, Antijacobin novelists often attribute character to innate or family traits and base plots on coincidence, often with the intervention of a *deus ex machina*, or force outside the plot – usually an authoritative male. There were also religious implications to these different plot forms. The English Jacobin philosophy of determinism was widely seen as a secularized version of Calvinist Dissenters' theology of predestination. The English Jacobin belief that human reason could achieve individual and social 'perfectibility' without divine assistance was seen as a secularized version of Calvinist Dissenters' theology of salvation by faith alone. Antijacobins insisted on the limits of 'philosophy' and the need for practical virtue, or 'good works'. Paradoxically, English Jacobin and Antijacobin novels, and fiction by Evangelical Anglicans (such as Hannah More's *Cœlebs in Search of a Wife*, 1809), often present characters who are virtually perfect, irredeemably vicious, or dramatically converted at the end, exemplifying idealist or puritan principles and heightening ideological conflict.

Austen's use of plot can be read as mediating, from an Anglican viewpoint, between these different forms and their opposing political and religious implications. The central doctrine of Anglican theology asserts that God has knowledge of predestination to salvation but that individuals still have free will to be saved or damned, that good works are useful but true faith matters more, and that neither faith nor works can guarantee salvation without the intervention of grace, or divine power, infusing the individual life and actions. Austen's plots are resolved by neither the protagonist's rational will nor the force of systemic injustice, by neither a *deus ex machina* nor coincidence, but by a convergence of will and circumstance, or something like grace. Austen links this plot form to two different kinds of protagonist, the active and the passive, deployed in alternation. *Sense and Sensibility* has both kinds, *Pride and Prejudice* and *Emma* have active protagonists, and *Northanger Abbey*, *Mansfield Park*, and *Persuasion* have passive protagonists. The active protagonists err repeatedly, but act correctly and somewhat unexpectedly, at the decisive moment. Passive protagonists have correct judgment, but seem unable to act, and destined to endure rather than to prevail, until circumstances unexpectedly present the occasion to receive their merited happiness.

For active protagonists the turning point is an act of self-abnegation or humility that could be described as Christian and that seems to occur against the run of the plot and thus to be providential, or the effect of grace. Passive protagonists practise a Christian-like humility and self-abnegation throughout, though they are often undervalued by the other characters, until the mistaken selfish action of another character brings about the protagonist's obviously merited happiness. In *Sense and Sensibility* the impulsively active Marianne prides herself on the accuracy of her judgment and correctness of her actions since both are sanctioned by her 'sensibility', represented by Austen as a form of excessive will. In fact, Marianne errs repeatedly, and dangerously, until she learns some humility and then achieves, or rather receives happiness. The self-disciplined and self-sacrificing Elinor is more prominent in the novel, and seems destined to lose her happiness to the actively scheming Lucy Steele. Lucy's scheming leads her to what is obviously a morally mistaken choice, abandoning Edward Ferrars for his selfish and decadent brother, thereby leaving Elinor to be rewarded for her self-sacrifice and endurance in love. A similar pattern is used in *Mansfield Park*, with Mary and Henry Crawford as the over-reaching schemers and Fanny Price as the steadfast and enduring winner, and in *Persuasion*, with Anne eventually if poignantly rewarded for the steadfastness in love she claims for her sex against the scepticism of Captain Harville (*P* 235).

In *Emma* the protagonist, like Marianne Dashwood and Elizabeth Bennet, prides herself on her judgment and acts accordingly, almost producing her own unhappiness. Emma goes farther than Marianne and Elizabeth, however, interfering as a matchmaker in the lives of others. Her ill-judged activity produces several embarrassments, until she realizes that she loves Mr. Knightley but seems to have unwittingly encouraged him to love Harriet Smith. When Knightley seems about to tell Emma of this, she silences him to protect her own feelings, but when she sees his 'deep mortification', she sacrifices her own feelings out of love for him, and encourages him to speak. She hears that it is she whom he loves, and soon realizes, from his surprise at her reversed decision, how providential her act of self-abnegation was.

In all of Austen's novels the ending could have been other than happy, and the protagonist's recognition of her fallibility or endurance in virtue provides a turning point in the plot that enables her to achieve happiness, or shows that she deserves it. The turning point also discloses that merit and will alone cannot guarantee happiness, however; circumstances must also be propitious. This linking of character and plot could be read as an optimistic belief in the ultimate defeat of the selfish and self-serving and the ultimate triumph of the selfless and self-sacrificing. Such a reading would conform to both conventional Christian moral teaching and the secular morality advanced in many novels, including reformist novels of Austen's day. Yet Austen's linking of merit and circumstance seems to lack the sense of inevitability or determinism found in both reformist novels and many didactically religious novels of the period.

Turning points in the plotted destiny of Austen's protagonists seem unexpected, at least at the moment the protagonist and the reader encounter them, whether they be the treachery of Lucy Steele, Elizabeth's reflection on Darcy's letter and subsequent discovery of his intervention on Lydia's behalf, Henry Crawford's elopement with Maria Bertram, Emma's recognition of her love for Knightley after near-disastrous matchmaking, or Wentworth's unexpected second proposal to Anne. Yet in retrospect, protagonist and reader can see how the interaction of character and plot made the turning points possible, and even likely. It could be argued that such decisive, unexpected yet possible moments correspond to what would be recognized as instances of grace by a Christian, and especially a Christian like Austen, whose 'opinions', by her brother's testimony, 'accorded strictly with those of our Established Church' (NA, P 8). For Anglican theology places particular emphasis on grace as the instrument of salvation. It could be argued that Austen's plots depend on instances of such grace, even if apparently secular in character.

Austen does prepare the reader for these turning points and happy endings by use of comic form and tone. She excludes and even mocks the dire incidents and foreboding tone of gothic and political romance, and she builds the reader's expectation that good rather than evil will prevail, using narrator's irony, occasional comic dialogues and incidents, evident generic markers of romantic comedy, and lightness of tone. In these ways, Austen constructs the novel as a comic universe in which an omniscient yet sympathetic narrator presides over a romance plot of error, suffering, and eventual happy ending, and in which tone prepares the reader for such an outcome.

Again, this formal structure is consistent with an Anglican reading of human history as a form of romance journey in which an omniscient yet benevolent deity presides over a historical plot of human error, fall, and redemption by both free will and grace, and which instructs the reader to hope for and aspire to redemption. Such a reading differs from those advanced by opposing religious and political ideologies of the time. Anglicans had long criticized as gloomy the Calvinist theology of predestination and reserving of salvation for members of a particular sect. Anti-jacobins criticized the political purism and factionalism of French and English Jacobins as secularized forms of such exclusivism and sectarianism. Austen's use of form and tone to create a comic universe and romance plot presided over by a judging yet sympathetic and forgiving omnipotence can be read as a secular literary expression of a 'latitudinarian' Anglican position (despite Austen's admiration for the High Anglican sermons of Thomas Sherlock) that was newly appropriate for the post-Revolutionary need to reconstruct a national religious and political consensus.

Austen's novels can be read as representing the protagonist's destiny according to an Anglican view of the human condition. It can be argued that the novels also implicate the reader in this condition by using form to tempt the reader, too, into erring by misreading. In their three-volume format, title-pages, and generic elements, Austen's novels resemble the stock novel of manners, encouraging the original reader to regard them as undemanding formula fiction (unlike many later readers taught by education, the heritage industries, and television adaptations that Austen's novels are 'classics', to be read with respect and care). Such a condescending attitude to the novel was common in Austen's day, though it is rebuked in the well-known passage, 'only a novel ...' (NA 37–8). Thus the appearance of Austen's novels could encourage careless reading or misreading. Furthermore, Austen's use of third-person narration with free indirect discourse makes it possible for the reader to ignore the narrator's ironic distance from the protagonist and identify with the protagonist and her 'readings', or rather misreadings, thereby experiencing with the protagonist her romance journey through error and suffering to a well deserved 'home', which is in fact marriage as represented in the Anglican liturgy.[19]

For example, after Elizabeth rejects Darcy's proposal and receives his letter of explanation, she reviews past events and reluctantly recognizes that she has indulged her pride and prejudice in interpreting them and so misjudged Darcy and others; it is here that her romance journey of suffering and endurance begins (PP 205–9). Inclined by acquired habits of reading to identify with the protagonist, the first-time reader of the novel probably has read or misread events and characters as Elizabeth has, and will recognize this fact when Elizabeth does. The case is somewhat different with the self-doubting protagonist such as Fanny Price or Anne Elliot, who is tempted to accept the judgment of others – as the reader is likewise. Austen's narrative method discloses this kind of protagonist's subjective merit to the reader, who vicariously experiences the protagonist's romance trial of frustration and neglect until the other characters, especially the right suitor, are unexpectedly brought to extend this recognition. Again the evidence for this outcome appears in retrospect to have been there all along.

The consequences of misreading were much debated in Austen's day, and still are. Novels in general and 'romances' in particular were often condemned for furnishing readers with false images of life and encouraging fantasy and desire at the expense of the moral and intellectual discipline considered necessary for 'real life'. Austen allows her readers to indulge these desires by reading or misreading with the protagonist, despite the warnings of narratorial irony, and then teaches her readers how to read better. Chastened, the reader can reread Austen's novels with instructed interest. Austen's novels have indeed been found eminently rereadable, a fact which has made them into 'classics', or literature. Thus it could be argued that Austen used the very seductions of the novel to teach readers to overcome them, and thereby transformed what was then considered 'only a novel' into literature, as it was then coming to be understood: written verbal art of moral value, intellectual worth, and ethical utility to its readers, or at least readers of certain classes and with certain material interests.

In Austen's day these were the interests of the classes to which she, her fictional characters, and the majority of the 'reading public' belonged. In Austen's day this reading public was critically divided by interconnected issues of religion and politics, and writing of all kinds, including the novel, was used to advance or repair those divisions. Austen, too, used the novel in this way, less to address particular issues of religion and politics directly, as part of the public sphere, and more to treat these issues within the wider and, to Austen and many others, more important context of moral judgment and ethical action in everyday and local life. Like many writers of the Revolutionary aftermath, Austen sought to repair the dangerous divisions opened by differences of religion and politics in the classes her novels address. She sought to repair those differences, however, from a particular religious–political position, that of a woman involved in and supporting an open coalition of gentry and upper middle classes based on the values and teachings of the historic English national church. In doing so she created what could be called the Anglican romance.

NOTES

1 See R. D. Gilbert, *Religion and Society in Industrial England: Church, Chapel and Social Change, 1740–1914* (London and New York: Longman, 1976), part I.

2 Cf. Cheryl Turner, *Living by the Pen: Women Writers in the Eighteenth Century* (London and New York: Routledge, 1992), ch. 3.

3 Peter Virgin, *The Church in an Age of Negligence: Ecclesiastical Structure and Problems of Church Reform 1700–1840* (Cambridge: James Clarke and Co., 1989), and Norman Sykes, *Church and State in England in the XVIIIth Century* (Cambridge: at the University Press, 1934), pp. 407–8. See also Marion Lochhead, 'Literature versus Celibacy', *Quarterly Review*, 294 (April 1956), 207–17; John Walsh and Stephen Taylor, 'Introduction: The Church and Anglicanism in the "Long" Eighteenth Century', in *The Church of England c. 1681 – c. 1833*, edited by John Walsh, Colin Haydon, and Stephen Taylor (Cambridge: Cambridge University Press, 1993), pp. 1–63; Irene Collins, *Jane Austen and the Clergy* (London and Rio Grande: Hambledon 1994); Ivor Morris, *Mr Collins Considered: Approaches to Jane Austen* (London and New York: Routledge and Kegan Paul, 1987).

4 [Henry Austen,] 'Biographical Notice of the Author', prefixed to *Northanger*

Abbey and *Persuasion*, *The Novels of Jane Austen*, ed. R. W. Chapman, vol. 5, p. 8; Newman cited in *Jane Austen: The Critical Heritage*, edited by Brian C. Southam (London: Routledge and Kegan Paul; New York: Barnes and Noble, 1968), p. 117; John A. Patten, 'Jane Austen's Clergymen', *Congregational Quarterly*, 9:3 (July 1931), 310–15 (315).

5 *British Critic*, in Southam, *Jane Austen: The Critical Heritage*, p. 71; Simpson in Southam, p. 264; Laurence Lerner, *The Truthtellers: Jane Austen; George Eliot; D. H. Lawrence* (London: Chatto and Windus, 1967), p. 20.

6 Whately in Southam, *Jane Austen: The Critical Heritage*, p. 95; Knox quoted in Andrew L. Drummond, *The Churches in English Fiction* (Leicester: Edgar Backus, 1950), p. 5; Harold Anson, 'The Church in Nineteenth-Century Fiction: I – Jane Austen', *The Listener*, 21, no. 536 (20 April 1939), 841–2 (841).

7 See Edward M. Chapman, *English Literature and Religion 1800–1900* (London: Constable & Co., 1910), pp. 245–8; Rowland Grey, 'The Religion of Jane Austen', *The Bookman*, 78 (Sept. 1930), 332–4; Lesley Willis, 'Religion in Jane Austen's *Mansfield Park*', *English Studies in Canada*, 13:1 (March 1987), 65–78; Gene Koppel, *The Religious Dimension in Jane Austen's Novels* (Ann Arbor and London: UMI Research Press, 1988).

8 E. G. Selwyn, 'Jane Austen's Clergymen', *Jane Austen Society Report for the Year 1959*, 11–21; Raymond A. Cook, 'As Jane Austen Saw the Clergy', *Theology Today*, 18:1 (April 1961), 41–50.

9 See, for example, Roger Gard, *Jane Austen's Novels: The Art of Clarity* (New Haven and London: Yale University Press, 1992).

10 See, for example, Mary DeForest, 'Jane Austen and the Anti-Heroic Tradition', *Persuasions*, 10 (Dec. 1988), 11–21; John A. Dussinger, 'Jane Austen's Political Silence', *The Dolphin* (Aarhus University Press), 16 (1990), 33–42.

11 Rebecca West, *The Court and the Castle: A Study of the Interactions of Political and Religious Ideas in Imaginative Literature* (London: Macmillan, 1958), p. 93. See also Warren Roberts, *Jane Austen and the French Revolution* (1979; reprinted London and Atlantic Highlands: Athlone, 1995); Jennifer Fitzgerald, 'Jane Austen's *Persuasion* and the French Revolution', *Persuasions*, 10 (Dec. 1988), 39–43; Maaja A. Stewart, *Domestic Realities and Imperial Fictions: Jane Austen's Novels in Eighteenth-Century Contexts* (Athens, Georgia, and London: University of Georgia Press, 1993); Roger Sales, *Jane Austen and Representations of Regency England* (London and New York: Routledge, 1994); Marilyn Butler, *Jane Austen and the War of Ideas* (Oxford: Clarendon Press, 1975).

12 See, for example, Alistair M. Duckworth, *The Improvement of the Estate* (1971; reprinted Baltimore and London: The Johns Hopkins University Press, 1994).

13 See, for example, Nina Auerbach, *Communities of Women: An Idea in Fiction* (Cambridge, MA: Harvard University Press, 1978); Sandra M. Gilbert and Susan Gubar, *The Madwoman in the Attic: The Woman Writer and the Nineteenth-Century Literary Imagination* (New Haven and London: Yale University Press, 1979); Claudia L. Johnson, *Jane Austen: Women, Politics, and the Novel* (Chicago and London: University of Chicago Press, 1988).

14 See, for example, Edward Neill, 'The Politics of "Jane Austen"', *English*, 40 (Autumn 1991), 205–13, and Sales, *Austen and Regency England*.

15 See Gary Kelly, *Women, Writing, and Revolution 1790–1827* (Oxford: Clarendon Press, 1993).

16 Hannah More, *Strictures on the Modern System of Female Education* (1799), ch. 1.
17 See, for example, Edward W. Said, 'Jane Austen and Empire', in *Raymond Williams: Critical Perspectives*, edited by Terry Eagleton (Boston: Northeastern University Press, 1989), pp. 150–64.
18 See Gary Kelly, *English Fiction of the Romantic Period 1789–1830* (London and New York: Longman, 1989), ch. 2.
19 Cf. recent critics who recruit Austen to post-modern writing by arguing that she uses narrative method to question the nature of narrative authority: see Barbara M. Benedict, 'Jane Austen's *Sense and Sensibility*: The Politics of Point of View', *Philological Quarterly*, 69 (Fall 1990), 453–70; and Tara Ghoshal Wallace, *Jane Austen and Narrative Authority* (New York: St. Martin's Press; Basingstoke and London: Macmillan Press, 1995).

10

JOHN F. BURROWS

Style

Miss Crawford's countenance, as Julia spoke, might have amused a disinterested observer. She looked almost aghast under the new idea she was receiving. Fanny pitied her. 'How distressed she will be at what she said just now,' passed across her mind. *(MP* 89)

Although Julia Bertram's allusion to Edmund's forthcoming ordination is aimed at her sister and Henry Crawford, its most visible effect is on a bystander. The potency of the 'new idea' Mary Crawford is receiving is marked by the use of 'aghast', a strong word for Jane Austen, and soon afterwards by the reference to her 'rallying her spirits, and recovering her complexion'. It is also marked by the word 'idea', whose flat, modern sense of 'concept' was still enriched, in Jane Austen's use, by more pictorial connotations: Miss Crawford, the word suggests, gives one of life's long moments to a mental rehearsal of her comments on the clergy and Edmund's firm rejoinders. She then puts the question to him and, on hearing his plans, makes as graceful a gesture as her situation allows: 'If I had known this before, I would have spoken of the cloth with more respect' (89).

But the matter is too important to be dropped and she reverts to it as soon as courtesy permits: 'So you are to be a clergyman, Mr. Bertram. This is rather a surprise to me' (91). 'Surprise' is honest if low key, and the 'rather' plays it down. The anaphoric use of 'so' (where the word takes its weight from what has gone before and carries it on into the sequel) is more revealing. On this occasion it has an almost exclamatory force far removed from its ordinary task of tacking up loose syntax like that of Harriet Smith.

While its strength is evident, the precise nature of Mary Crawford's response is not easy to determine. The amusement open to a 'disinterested observer' doubtless lies in watching Millamant, in full sail, brought hard about by a sudden gust from nowhere. Fanny's sense of pity, by contrast, is addressed to what her companion must be feeling. But, even if 'distress' is the right word for it, that emotion would not take a form that Fanny could share or understand. Not for Mary a deep sense of mortification, an overpowering conviction of her own worthlessness, a lasting desire to sink out of sight. Consternation, no doubt, for her *gaucherie* in pressing her opinions upon uncertain company and not giving enough thought to the likely future of a younger son. Annoyance with Edmund for not thinking better of himself? A touch of scorn, even, for these solemn provincials, who show so little knowledge of the way of the world? But not a moment's consideration of the possibility that her opinion of clergymen may be at fault? The main point is that we are left with inferences. Although Jane Austen differs from most of her predecessors in taking us within the minds of her heroines, she follows Fielding in her treatment of some other major figures, including Mary Crawford and Jane Fairfax. With them, as with our fellows in real life, we are obliged to interpret outward signs as best we can.

The rendering of Fanny's unspoken thought in the form of direct speech ('How distressed she will be ...') lies at one end of a stylistic spectrum. The opposite pole is visible whenever the free indirect style used to render Anne Elliot's impressions and the reflective parts of the main narrative of *Persuasion* converge. If we were left, in the present case, to take Fanny's assessment of Mary's feelings at face value, the effect would be sentimental and misleading. The overt contrast between her 'unspoken speech' and the cool tone of the disinterested observer prevents us from doing so. This is an area in which Jane Austen shows increasing stylistic subtlety as her career proceeds. Whereas the unspoken thoughts of Catherine Morland are rendered in strong colours and those of Elinor Dashwood are usually couched in a stilted sort of indirect speech, the wide narrative range in the later novels from 'unspoken speech' to free indirect style admits many unobtrusive but powerful effects.

The little mismatch between Fanny and the disinterested observer also epitomizes Jane Austen's characteristic use of disjunction as a source of comic energy. It appears openly in absurd turns of phrase like '*mediocre* to the last degree' (*E* 276); 'Oh! cruel Charles to wound the hearts & legs of all the fair' ('Jack and Alice', *MW* 22); and 'Prudence obliged him to prefer the quietest sort of ruin & disgrace for the object of his Affections, to the more renowned' (*S* 406). It appears in straightforward displays of self-deception like '*We* have all the Grandeur of the Storm, with less real danger, because the Wind meeting with nothing to oppose or confine it around our House, simply rages & passes on' (*S* 381). And it appears also in large discrepancies between the apparent and the real, as in Elizabeth's original assessment of Darcy, his assessment of Elizabeth and Jane, or Admiral Croft's well-meaning attempt to enlist an ally in a good cause: 'I think we must get him to Bath. Sophy must write, and beg him to come to Bath. Here are pretty girls enough, I am sure. It would be of no use to go to Uppercross again, for that other Miss Musgrove, I find, is bespoke by her cousin, the young parson. Do not you think, Miss Elliot, we had better try to get him to Bath?' (P 173).

So far, then, our passage from *Mansfield Park* has yielded examples of such topics as generally arise in discussions of an author's literary style. The word 'aghast', so I have claimed, is unusually strong in tone for Jane Austen. She usually employs the anaphoric 'so' for a certain syntactic purpose but departs from it on this occasion. Her emphasis on sharp disjunction is essential to her comic style. The manner in which she renders Fanny's thoughts is part of a major development over the length of her literary career. Her management of narrative in such a way as to enter the minds of some major characters but not others marks a particular moment in the history of the novel as a literary form. Her use of the word 'idea' marks a moment in the history of the language. The general validity of such claims will be tested as we continue. We should first glance at what we are dealing with when we speak of style in prose fiction.

The cruel Charles of 'Jack and Alice', he who contrives to 'wound the hearts & legs of all the fair', is something more than a faithless lover and a landlord who plants his estate with mantraps. He is made the focal point of the rhetorical figure of syllepsis, in which a verb takes two different objects. This figure opposes a weary metaphor from romance ('wound the hearts') with the demotic literality of prose chronicle ('wound the legs').

That the novel is of mixed style is a simple truth which has made a persistent obstacle for scholarly analysis. As my last example suggests, the novel can draw on diverse literary and non-literary forms of language. Graham Hough identifies another difficulty: whereas the different voices of a play are all on the same epistemological plane, the chief stylistic components of a novel (from the narrative voice at its most detached to the voices of the several characters) lie on different planes.[1] Some scholars respond by confining themselves to such stylistic features as run throughout the whole. Others undertake the long and fruitless task of enumerating all feasible categories and sub-categories, setting neat lines in shifting sand. Others again, in the tradition of Henry James, bring valuable light to bear on large matters of 'composition' but are unable to connect them with the particularities of 'style'. The Russian literary theorist, Mikhail Bakhtin, carries the whole subject forward by defining the novel as essentially an orchestration of stylistic conflicts, a 'dialogic relationship' between different sorts of language.[2]

Such relationships, obviously, are most direct when the characters speak with each other. As a writer of dialogue, Jane Austen lies at a moment of transition in the history of the novel, and her own contribution is significant. Drawing upon the conventions of prose romance, her predecessors present sharp distinctions between 'high style' and 'low' in much the same fashion as their Elizabethan forebears. In 'low style,' the archaic redolence of Ann Radcliffe's Italian peasants and servants is well known. Her 'high style', even when she is representing a gentleman of the 1760s, is also remote from the quotidian: ' "This is astonishing!" said the Englishman; "of what avail are your laws, if the most atrocious criminal may thus find shelter from them? But how does he contrive to exist here!" '[3]

But other novelists of the day carried the *genre* forward. In 'low style', where they made most change, they turned from the literary to the demotic in a prose version of the 'selection of language really used' that Wordsworth advocated in the Preface to *Lyrical Ballads*. The most sustained achievement is that of Walter Scott and Maria Edgeworth in representing Scottish and Irish vernacular speech. But, in her vivid rendering of a vulgar London idiom in *Evelina* (1778), Frances Burney forestalled them both. And, though her attempts are crude, Charlotte Smith goes on from the semantic level to the phonetic: 'Oh! Lord a marcy on me! – to be shore I be got here at last! But indeed if I had a known whereabout I was a coming to, 'tis not a double the wagers as should a hired me. Lord! why what a ramshakel ould place it is!' So, again, in another of her novels: 'I ashore you, Miss, if it ad not bin that hive a somethink of an unaccountable sort of a attachment for your parson ['person'?], it is not your fortin as would ave induced me.'[4]

The speech of Thomas, the footman from *Sense and Sensibility*, shows none of this straining for effect: 'so I took off my hat, and she knew me and called to me, and inquired after you, ma'am, and the young ladies, especially Miss Marianne, and bid me I should give her compliments and Mr. Ferrars's, their best compliments and service' (*SS* 354). This easier manner allows Jane Austen an increase in versatility. Whereas Fanny Burney's poorly educated speakers, like the Branghtons of *Evelina*, can hardly be told apart, their distant cousins in Jane Austen's novels all have their separate idiolects.[5]

At the other end of the spectrum, in the management of 'high style', Jane Austen's contemporaries do not greatly differ from their forebears. Scott's heroes are as colourless as any. As he himself put it, in an anonymous review of his own early novels, they are 'all brethren of a family; very amiable and very insipid sort of young men'.[6] His emphasis is on their habitual passivity, but their habits of speech are not dissimilar. The chief characters of Maria Edgeworth's English novels often slide into affectation and extravagance. And the platitudes of the fine gentleman come as easily to

Fanny Burney's Lord Orville as to Sir Charles Grandison or any of his romance ancestors:

> 'Far be it from me,' said Lord Orville, 'to dispute the *magnetic* power of beauty, which irresistibly draws and attracts whatever has soul and sympathy: and I am happy to acknowledge, that though we have now no *gods* to occupy a mansion professedly built for them, yet we have secured their *better halves*, for we have *goddesses* to whom we all most willingly bow down.'[7]

The dignified but unpretentious English of Darcy and Mr. Knightley is so far from this kind of thing that Jane Austen's fops and coxcombs can be set in firm contrast to them while still lying well within the bounds of credibility: ' "Let me entreat you," cried Mr. Elton; "it would indeed be a delight! Let me entreat you, Miss Woodhouse, to exercise so charming a talent in favour of your friend. I know what your drawings are" ' (*E* 43).

By withdrawing, in this way, from both the higher and lower extremities of eighteenth-century fictional dialogue, Jane Austen displays a characteristic preference for 'shallow modelling'.[8] Since this allows the reader's attention to be concentrated on subtler differences of attitude among her characters, it has the paradoxical effect of intensifying their conflicts. The onward-moving energy of their disputes is another stylistic innovation. Where some of her predecessors, like Sarah Fielding and Hannah More, engage their characters in slow debates on large topics of the day like gambling, prostitution, and duelling, and some of her successors, true novelists of ideas like Peacock and George Eliot, give their large topics a fair hearing but often reduce their characters to mouthpieces, Jane Austen takes another path. Ordinary words like 'amiable' and 'family', everyday objects like a novel or a poem lately read, a pair of ornamental screens, or a portrait of a friend make focal points for unostentatiously presented but freely moving and far-reaching exchanges.

Captain Benwick, for example, goes swiftly on from discussing 'how ranked the *Giaour* and *The Bride of Abydos*; and moreover, how the *Giaour* was to be pronounced' to repeating 'the various lines which imaged a broken heart' and looking 'entirely as if he meant to be understood' (*P* 100). At this point, Anne 'ventured to recommend a larger allowance of prose in his daily study' (101). The tone of this exchange remains half-comic, but its bearing on Anne's situation is apparent. Both its lively energy and its concealed depths represent major features of Jane Austen's style.

When Mr. Knightley quarrels with Emma's use of 'amiable' and 'sensation', it is because he has been forced, step by unwilling step, into their most bitter disagreement. And when Edmund Bertram supports Fanny's idea of family prayer, he rashly begins in the belief that he is resolving a semantic misunderstanding: ' "*That* is hardly Fanny's idea of a family assembling", said Edmund. "If the master and mistress do not attend themselves, there must be more harm than good in the custom" ' (*MP* 87). But Miss Crawford's objections to public worship are more deeply seated than she has shown so far. Her only acknowledgement of what Fanny might have meant or why Edmund might speak as he does is a token-phrase, 'At any rate ...' Then she is off again, in a flurry of worldly wisdom and he must hurry to catch up. His next, more seriously considered response, including a stiff *ad feminam* rebuke ('Your lively mind can hardly be serious even on serious subjects' [87]), evokes a trenchant epigram. His final attempt is interrupted by his sister but, only a moment after this, Miss Crawford is brought low.

Eighteenth-century fiction offers few models for the sheer mobility of such exchanges. Some comedies of the period – *She Stoops to Conquer* and *The School for Scandal* are more relevant than their glittering Restoration predecessors – come nearer to the mark. But Bakhtin's claim that the novel has an omnivorous linguistic appetite suggests that Jane Austen's models may not all be literary.[9] This doctrine sets him apart from those structuralist theorists who hold that works of literature feed chiefly or exclusively off each other and are therefore to be studied as members of a more or less hermetic tradition. Jane Austen does not lend herself so easily as Burns, Scott, and Maria Edgeworth to the simplest way of supporting the idea that the language of every day affects the language of literature. Since they had no significant literary precursors in representing the Scottish and Irish verna-cular, the form taken by much of the dialogue in their writings must be explained either as an attempt to represent the speech-habits of their people or else as an elaborate construct of the authorial imagination. From such constructs, the second explanation would go, the Scots and the Irish have since derived what are now regarded as salient features of their national habits of speech. The second explanation, once set out, is patently absurd.

Because she does have literary precursors, Jane Austen's debt to the 'natural language' of her time must be approached in a different way. When Henry Tilney holds forth about 'amazingly' and 'nice', Eleanor warns Catherine that they are in danger of being 'overpowered with Johnson and Blair' (*NA* 108). Her comment glances at the fact that the late eighteenth century saw the publication, in unprecedented profusion, of English gram-mars and studies of English rhetoric.[10] Although these works are sometimes at odds with each other, they can help us to form a picture of the language as it was when George Austen was a young man and, afterwards, when Jane Austen was a girl.

Jane Austen's letters make it clear that she and her family were keenly interested in niceties of usage and amused by solecisms of every kind. In her novels, the dialogue shows many traces of this attitude. John Thorpe omits his pronouns in just the way that Buchanan deplores as a 'Style too much used by Tradesmen' (108). The Steele sisters are his rivals here but they surpass him in the habit of confusing past tense with past participle as in 'I drunk' and 'I have drank'. Lowth calls this 'a very great Corruption' (85) and Buchanan calls it 'a ridiculous Solecism' that began among 'Females and mean Authors' (178). Such affectations as Mrs. Elton's 'caro sposo' and 'Hymen's saffron robe' (E 308) draw unfavourable comment from Campbell and Blair.

In modern use, to turn to something more pervasive, the contracted forms of auxiliary verbs are used so freely in conversation and personal letters that the full forms can sound pedantic. But, while granting that some contractions make for a 'clashing together consonants of most obdurate sound', Campbell would relax the general prohibition then prevailing. Following 'the animadversion of some of our ablest pens, Addison, Swift, Pope, and others', he says,

> contractions of every kind have ever since been in disgrace, even those of easy pronunciation, *and which had been in use long before* [italics added] ... And though I am sensible that *wasn't, didn't, shouldn't,* and *couldn't* are intolerably bad, there are others of more pleasant sound, to which our critics, without any injury to the language, might have given a pass ... Some indulgence, I think, may still be given to the more familiar style of dialogues, letters, essays, and even of popular addresses. (Campbell III.iv.404–5)

Throughout her writings, from *Volume the First* to *Sanditon*, Jane Austen almost never uses any of those contractions that Campbell regards as 'intolerably bad'. A few contractions of less 'obdurate sound' like 'that's', 'don't', and ''tis' occur in the speech of her well-spoken characters. But she treats most of the contractions that we take for granted nowadays as the province of the vulgar. As this would suggest, they occur most freely in *Sense and Sensibility* and *The Watsons*. They rarely occur in *Northanger Abbey* and *Persuasion* (where the manuscripts may well have been purified after Jane Austen's death). In the later novels, they are most freely used by Lieutenant Price and Harriet Smith and, now and then, by consciously 'smart' characters like Mary Crawford and Tom Bertram.

It emerges, then, that in a linguistic area where Fanny Burney is profuse but undiscriminating and where a modern reader may not even notice what is going on, Jane Austen makes consistent and exact distinctions among her characters in a manner consonant with the prescripts of her day. Within the novels themselves, these distinctions serve various expressive purposes. They also add weight to the idea that Jane Austen's models are not entirely literary. And, ultimately, they raise important questions about the processes by which, and the purposes for which, society creates its national and even tribal codes,[11] processes in which Jane Austen's novels certainly participate. In the course of the eighteenth century, 'correct usage' became an important shibboleth for the English gentry and was to serve its purposes long and well. If this seems to put undue weight upon small points of usage and if Campbell's rationalizations about more and less obdurate sounds seem comical, a modern instance may be worth a moment's thought. Those of us who now say 'Anyone who wants their hat' are forsaking logic for a gender-driven shibboleth. Those others of us who were brought up to say 'Anyone who wants his hat' and who will rephrase, however awkwardly, rather than give way have logic on our side – but at the price of living in the past. We all have our stylistic niceties and our own reasons for observing them.

But most of us would now agree that those who habitually contract their auxiliary verbs, those who often turn to slang, and even those who slip into tautologies like 'a faithful promise' (NA 196) and 'the sort of self-evident proposition which many a clearer head does not always avoid' (MP 89) need not be denied all good society. We may nevertheless find it possible to agree that there is a truly admirable lucidity and not merely a reinforcement of tribal solidarity in the sort of prose which was the staple of educated English in Jane Austen's day. Of the many personal letters and periodical essays that survive to represent it, I take two tiny specimens, both written in Jane Austen's lifetime. My purpose is to suggest that we need not seek particular models for Jane Austen's more articulate characters and need not feel that our inability to recover the spoken English of her day leaves us entirely ignorant of what, at its best, it must have been. This gives rise to the objection that a style permeable to the world around must lack individuality: as I hope to show a little later, that is not the case.

My first specimen is from Hester Thrale's letters to Samuel Johnson, published in 1788, which were well known to the Austen sisters. Mrs. Thrale's customary effusiveness is parodied in one of Jane Austen's letters and genially derided in another (L 44, 156). But when Johnson rebuked her for allying herself with Gabriel Piozzi after her husband's death, she answered him, point by point, with an unaffected dignity:

> Sir – I have this Morning received from You so rough a Letter, in reply to one which was both tenderly & respectfully written, that I am forced to desire the conclusion of a Correspondence which I can bear to continue no longer. The Birth of my second Husband is not meaner than that of my first, his sentiments are not meaner, his Profession is not meaner, – and his Superiority in what he professes – acknowledged by all Mankind.[12]

My other specimen is taken from a letter of thanks from Edward Gibbon to his old friend Lord Sheffield (1789).

> I could not easily forgive myself for shutting you up in a dark room with parchments and attorneys, did I not reflect that this probably is the last material trouble you will ever have on my account; and that after the labours and delays of twenty years, I shall at last attain what I have always sighed for, a clear and competent income, above my wants, and equal to my wishes.[13]

While they cannot be mistaken for each other, these two writers obviously have much in common, and stand at a remove from such breathless adherents of the epistolary exclamation mark as Maria Edgeworth. They share a moral vocabulary, a carefully marshalled syntax, and an exactitude of focus. In such passages, we are not far from Darcy and Mr. Knightley. With only a slight relaxation in their formality, we are within easy reach of Frank Churchill, Mary Crawford, and Anne Elliot. And, with a necessary adjustment of perspective, Jane Austen's narrative style is also in clear view.

The most notable feature of Jane Austen's narrative is that there is so little of it. It comprises only about three-fifths of the words used in her six novels and, in *Emma*, only a trifle over half. (Something like a quarter of the narrative component, moreover, is couched in 'free indirect style', some of which verges on dialogue.) While there are novels, including those of Ivy Compton-Burnett and *The Awkward Age*, where the proportion of narrative runs lower still, they are decidedly the exception. What is it, then, that makes for the deficiency? Jane Austen's narrative, in the first place, avoids the sort of commentary that conceals deficiencies in the dialogue, telling even the inattentive reader what the characters have just been saying. In her novels and those of other canonical writers, interpretative commentary is usually associated with disjunctions, often ironical in cast, between dialogue and narrative. The passage cited at the beginning of this essay is a fair specimen.

Most canonical novelists, however, give more attention than Jane Austen to descriptions of person and place. One reason why she can afford to leave much unsaid is that, when they were written, her novels were so immediate in time and place. If, by contrast, the re-creation of a lost national culture lies at the heart of Walter Scott's whole literary enterprise, he must needs stand, as he does, at the opposite end of the descriptive spectrum from Jane Austen. The immediacy of her emphasis can now best be recovered from the letters and diaries of her time.

The youthful letters of Emily Eden, for example, shed a clear and often amusing light on life in circles not unlike those frequented by Henry and Mary Crawford. The Eden family, it is true, were Whig grandees rather than country gentry. But as one reads what Emily, who was born in 1797 and whose earliest surviving letter comes from 1814, tells her older sister and her own friends of what she sees and hears, the life of Jane Austen's characters generally and of the Crawfords in particular comes constantly to mind. A sister has just heard from Miss Milbanke that she is engaged to marry Lord Byron. Their Mama does not think he is likely to make any woman very happy, but they hear that he 'is going to be a good boy, and will never be naughty no more'.[14] She receives a letter about the 'worldliness' of a man who has 'a notion that it don't signify what people do, so they keep it quiet, and make no open *scandale*' (*Miss Eden's Letters* 72). Her brother reports that an early attempt by Lady Melbourne to do something about the failure of her son's marriage ended abruptly when she found 'the happy couple at breakfast, and Lady Caroline drawling out – "William, some more muffin?" – and everything made up' (3). On a visit to Newby Hall, she is given a bedroom 'peculiarly liable to murder and that sort of accident', swarming with ghosts and banditti, 'only I was much too sleepy to lay awake and look at them' (24). A visit to Derbyshire brings Radcliffean memories of the Pyrenees: 'some people might think it verging on the extreme of picturesque and call it wild, but I love a mountainous country' (88). Her style is light-hearted and inventive, and it is punctuated by the polite slang of the day. The woman who will accompany her brother when he goes as Governor-General to India lies in the future – but the England of Jane Austen is always close at hand. Although her 'gothic' account of the bedroom was written in 1818, some months after the publication of *Northanger Abbey*, it need not be an echo of that novel. By 1826, she will allude to 'the immortal Collins ... "Pride and Prejudice" Collins' (104). For the rest, however, I think it likely that we are seeing independent versions of the same kind of thing and being reminded that Jane Austen had no need to set it all out in lavish detail.

In those passages where Jane Austen's narrative does take on a truly descriptive cast, a strong dramatic function is rarely far to seek. The early passages about the Devon countryside give rise to suggestive disagreements among the Dashwoods and their visitors. The account of Darcy's estate gives substance to Elizabeth's joking claim that she must date her love for him 'from my first seeing his beautiful grounds at Pemberley' (*PP* 373). Similar purposes are served, in their several ways, by the portrayal of the park at Sotherton, the summer day at Donwell Abbey, and the little sojourn at Lyme Regis.

These full-bodied passages differ only in degree, of course, from the common fabric of Jane Austen's narrative prose, that which Graham Hough characterizes as 'objective narrative' and which he distinguishes, on one side, from 'the authorial voice' and, on the other, from the sort of 'coloured narrative' that flows easily into free indirect style.[15] Objective narrative, he rightly claims, makes up those many passages where 'the facts are presented to us as facts … uncontaminated either by the subjectivity of the author or that of any of the characters' (Hough, 'Narrative and Dialogue in Jane Austen' 204). It is couched in 'the common form of decent educated discourse' (207), much like that of the best-spoken characters, and it derives an underlying strength from an accepted scheme of values, 'Christian morals in a temperate English version' (209). With a single reservation, one can readily accede. Like many other commentators, Hough takes Samuel Johnson as Jane Austen's model for this way of writing. As I have tried to show, many other admirable models were available. And, in any event, her style is generally so much lighter and more spirited than Johnson's that a brief Johnsonian parody is enough to set the curmudgeonly side of John Knightley in high relief:

> 'A man,' said he, 'must have a very good opinion of himself when he asks people to leave their own fireside, and encounter such a day as this, for the sake of coming to see him … Here are we setting forward to spend five dull hours in another man's house, with nothing to say or hear that was not said and heard yesterday, and may not be said and heard again to-morrow.'
>
> (E 113)

Jane Austen's 'coloured narrative' reveals her increasingly subtle parodic skills. The treatment of the gothic style in the narrative of *Northanger Abbey* and of the picturesque in *Sense and Sensibility* is clear and powerful. But in the Chawton novels, an 'over-literary' touch or two can be enough to mark some significant distortion in a character's perspective. In such phrases as 'the fair mistress of the mansion' (E 22), Emma Woodhouse is established as a new female quixote, rescuer of romantic orphans like Harriet Smith, lodestone for wandering princes like Frank Churchill, social arbiter of all Highbury, and patroness of worthy people like the Coles, with whom she 'left a name behind her that would not soon die away' (231). 'Delighted to connect any thing with history already known, or warm her imagination with scenes of the past' (MP 85), Fanny Price looks vainly for traces of medieval antiquity in the chapel at Sotherton. Mary Crawford sets off the episode which has served us as a focal point by evoking a counter-image of a past in which 'the former belles of the house of Rushworth did many a time repair to this chapel' (MP 87). Bakhtin's idea of a dialogic relationship between different sorts of language goes to the heart of Jane Austen's shifts of narrative voice and of the stylistic modulations that convey them.

And nowhere more than in the juxtaposition of her 'authorial voice' with all the rest. For this voice breaches the Jamesian illusion, the 'precious illusion' that, for the time being, the world within the story is the reader's only world. On some occasions, where it scarcely breaks the surface of the narrative, Jane Austen's authorial voice encourages observant readers to keep their wits about them: Jane Fairfax's 'account to her aunt contained nothing but truth, though there might be some truths not told' (*E* 166). On others, where a certain asperity can be felt, it is often highlighted by an epigrammatic polish. The visitors to Sotherton are shown 'many more rooms than could be supposed to be of any other use than to contribute to the window tax, and find employment for housemaids' (*MP* 85). Dinner at the Coles' offers 'the usual rate of conversation; ... nothing worse than every day remarks, dull repetitions, old news, and heavy jokes' (*E* 219). Miss Bates 'had no intellectual superiority to make atonement to herself, or frighten those who might hate her, into outward respect' (21). Mary Crawford is not alone in thinking marriage 'a manouevring business' (*MP* 46), for, after all, 'It is a truth universally acknowledged, that a single man in possession of a good fortune, must be in want of a wife' (*PP* 3). And unmixed pity for Mrs. Musgrove is not easily achieved. Even if her lamentations for her worthless son were not slightly factitious, an aesthetic difficulty would remain: 'A large bulky figure has as good a right to be in deep affliction, as the most graceful set of limbs in the world. But, fair or not fair, there are unbecoming conjunctions, which reason will patronize in vain, – which taste cannot tolerate, – which ridicule will seize' (*P* 68).

In this aspect, Jane Austen's authorial voice is aptly said to betray a 'regulated hatred'.[16] In another, of no less importance, it speaks for a regulated but unconventional sense of literary purpose. Catherine's return to Fullerton, 'a heroine in a hack post-chaise' (*NA* 232), makes for a little pretence of authorial self-mockery. Emma's response to Mr. Knightley's proposal of marriage need not be made explicit ('What did Emma say? Just what she ought, of course. A lady always does' [*E* 431]). The period that must elapse before 'the cure of unconquerable passions, and the transfer of unchanging attachments' (*MP* 470) can be effected is best left for readers to determine. The sort of guilt and misery that darkens the ending of *Mansfield Park* for many of its characters is best left to 'other pens' (461).

By placing a number of the more satirical and the more compositional remarks that are offered in Jane Austen's authorial voice side by side, one gains an increased awareness of her willingness to disrupt the smooth surface of her fiction. Almost every passage cited in my last two paragraphs has caught the attention of her critics. How they – how we – should respond to these outspoken comments is, with one proviso, a matter for each one of us. Our entitlement ends, I maintain, when we begin to infringe upon her 'intellectual property' by giving free rein to our subjectivity: for (to use a topical phrase for an unfashionable doctrine) her moral right to be met on her own terms is tacitly asserted in the style of every page she writes.

My own assertions need firmer support than the conventions of literary argument can ordinarily yield. A conventional account of an author's style might consist, like my argument so far, in a series of propositions about its several facets, each supported by examples from that author's work and by comparisons with the work of other authors. Such evidential strength as it might claim would consist in nothing more secure than the acceptability of the propositions and the aptness of the associated examples and comparisons. Especially at a time when style itself is widely regarded as a subject for impressionistic flights and when 'the author' and even 'the authorial function' are commonly treated as empty vessels, such 'evidence' may seem deficient and the strong claims that ended my preceding section may seem imprudent.

Statistical analysis, likewise, can never yield absolute support for any proposition. The possible occurrence of an exceptional case cannot be excluded and the link between data and inference is always likely to be imperfect. As a complement to the methods of literary argument, however, it has virtues that are gaining increasing attention as its applications become more sophisticated. It offers quite another perspective on a problem and, instead of relying upon a few select examples, it can embrace all members of a chosen class of phenomena – all instances, even, of word-types like *and* and *the*.

For a glimpse of these possibilities, I have analysed selections of several thousand words apiece from the personal letters of a dozen writers ranging from the seventeenth century to the early twentieth, and compared them with some extracts from Jane Austen's writings – a set of her own letters; the fictional letters of Darcy, Frank Churchill, and Mary Crawford; and the 'histories' recounted by Colonel Brandon, Willoughby, and Mrs. Smith. The question at issue is whether the Austen extracts, though differing in literary kind, have enough in common to distinguish them from the other, formally more homogeneous set of texts. If so, the claim that it is possible to identify Jane Austen's style is strengthened.

Apart from Jane Austen, the letters are by: Edmund Burke (1729–97); George Gordon, Lord Byron (1788–1824); Emily Eden (1797–1869); Maria Edgeworth (1767–1849); Henry James (1843–1916); William King, Archbishop of Dublin (1650–1729); Katherine Mansfield (1888–1923); Mary Wortley Montagu (1689–1762); Dorothy Osborne (1627–95);

Walter Scott (1771–1832); Jonathan Swift (1667–1745); and Virginia Woolf (1882–1941).

The data used for the present demonstration consist of frequency-counts for the sixty most common word-types. These amount, all told, to about half the word-tokens used in each text. Over the last ten years, data of this kind have been yielding worthwhile results in the field of computational stylistics. They can do so because the very common words have closely constrained functions: as a result, their relative frequencies across a range of texts mark subtle but remarkably consistent differences of reference, of syntax, and of emphasis. Through the use of appropriate statistical methods, like principal component analysis, these frequency-counts enable us, therefore, to identify significant resemblances and differences among the members of a set of texts.[17]

Figure 1 shows how the common words of the present set of texts respond to principal component analysis. Those words which behave most like each other lie towards the four extremities and are opposed by the words that behave least like them. (To behave alike, in this context, is to exhibit concomitant frequencies by occurring more – or less – frequently in the same texts as each other.) Some predictable sets of partners lie at the northerly edge of the figure, where *she/her* reflect a common referential tendency, while *by/from/of/to* and *which/who* reflect two sorts of connective tendency. These last are opposed, in the extreme south, by the relative pronoun *that* in territory where *I/you* make natural partners. The western extremity has *my/me* not far from *I/you*; *he/him/his*; and a set of past tense and subjunctive forms of the major auxiliary verbs. These last are accompanied by the infinitive form of *to*. The definite and indefinite articles lie at the eastern extremity, with *an* not far inland from *a*.

Readers who are not interested in statistical technicalities may prefer to envisage Figure 1 as an abstract space in which the words are allowed to array themselves according to their frequency-patterns in the present group of texts. Let us consider the stylistic implications of one small set of entries. In Figure 1, *which* and *who* lie at almost the opposite extremity from the relative pronoun *that*. This means that when the first two occur more often than usual, the third is very likely to occur less often (and vice versa). Such sharp contrasts of frequency mark the difference between texts in which relative clauses are mostly embedded and those in which they are appended. Since we are not comparing the work of British and American writers (*that* being the preference of most Americans), the opposition we are seeing is between writers whose syntax tends, at least in one significant respect, to be formally constructed and those whose sentences show an affinity for the spoken word. The location of *I* and *you* in the neighbourhood of *that*

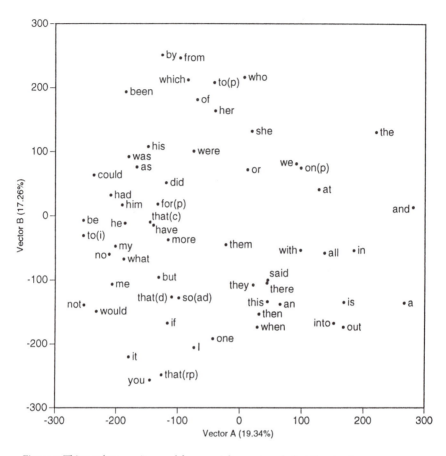

Figure 1 Thirteen letter-writers and four special cases (word plot) (for the sixty most common words of the main corpus)

supports this interpretation. The presence just there of *it* is also a mark of the vernacular: when that pronoun abounds it tends to be in frequent use as a 'place-holder' ('It is about time', 'it is a good thing', and so on). The crucial point is that the interconnection of word-counts, represented in Figure 1, carries us beyond the study of separate verbal entities and reveals an aspect of their interrelationships, the very substance of the language in action.

Figure 2, constructed by a technique that aligns the word-frequencies for each text against the pattern of Figure 1, gives a clear stylistic significance to the results. The entries for the twelve sets of personal letters form a loose cluster, with Jane Austen's personal letters standing out as a thirteenth, most northerly member. The fictional letters of Jane Austen's characters lie

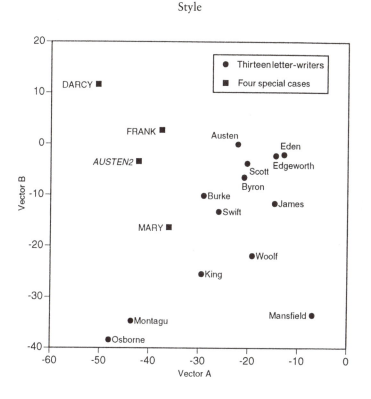

Figure 2 Thirteen letter-writers and four special cases (based on the sixty most common words of the main corpus)

further to the north and west, along with *AUSTEN2*, the entry for her fictional 'histories'. The result of the analysis, therefore, is unequivocal: despite their differences in literary form, the five Austen entries can be distinguished from the rest.

This is no place for additional analyses. But I shall offer a few more comments on the shape of these two figures. Darcy's letter to Elizabeth is in many ways the most formal of all these texts, its syntax marked by a more than usual proportion of embedded relative clauses and prepositional phrases. Its referential structure is marked not only by *she/her/he/him/his* but also by its retrospective verb-forms. Such features explain why it lies so far from the more colloquial and more descriptive letters that yield the most easterly entries and from the highly personal *I/you* letters that lie furthest to the south. Taken in this light, the location of the entry for Mary Crawford's oppressively intimate letters to Fanny is easily understood. Most of the sets of personal letters lie in rough chronological order from south-west to north-east with the most demotic of them lying, a little out of order, at the latter extreme. But the three most recent of these sets are all displaced towards the eastern extremity, the territory of strong descriptive markers like *a/an/the*. The feverishly impressionistic letters in which Katherine Mansfield tells Middleton Murry of her own grave illness and describes the things that take her mind off it set her among the furthest to the south and furthest of all to the east. The unique compound of high frequencies for *I/you/a/an/the/and/is* moves her letters away from all the rest. But the present analysis was not designed to examine such large, Bakhtinian matters as evidence of chronological change across a range of texts. Its purpose, which it satisfies, was to show whether these specimens of Jane Austen's literary and non-literary writing can be distinguished from the rest.

This outcome is much like those yielded by similar analyses of many other texts by many other writers. But the identification of authorial 'signatures', the stuff of literary forensics, is not the only use of computational stylistics. In my own *Computation into Criticism* (to stay with Jane Austen), this sort of analysis showed potent contrasts between narrative and dialogue, with 'free indirect style' emerging as an intermediate form. It showed remarkable similarities and differences among her characters. And, especially among her later heroines, it showed subtle but revealing forms of change. In literary studies generally, computational methods of analysis offer us new instruments. They are least useful in treating powerful but infrequent stylistic effects, where traditional methods are at their best. But they give an unprecedented access to many small touches that good readers recognize but can seldom quite define.

'Style', it seems, is not a belletristic fancy but a real presence, recognized as long ago as Aristotle and now responsive to straightforward computational procedures. That makes it a good ground on which to contest the doctrine, widespread in recent years, that literary studies should admit the unfettered expression of our precious subjectivities. 'Myself creating what I saw' (*E* 344), the evidence suggests, is neither necessity nor desideratum but an intellectual blind alley.

How, then, should we think of style? Now that so many national and regional varieties of English are accepted, style cannot reasonably be regarded as either a conformity to or an apotheosis of a preferred variety. It is now more fruitful, I suggest, to regard it as whatever marks the distinct identity of an author or a school, a set of loosely consistent features ranging from the surface to the depths, from phenomena that can readily be listed, classified, or counted to those larger 'compositional' phenomena whose existence they register.

In Jane Austen's case, as in any other, every reader will have a different perspective – just as the watchers at the windows of James' house of fiction look from different angles over the same ground. But while their interpretations of the novels differ greatly, her published critics (those readers whose opinions are on record) show a broad consensus on such important stylistic features, many of them now measurable, as her economy of description, her customary formality of tone, her subtle mingling of styles, and her creation of so smooth a surface that every ripple repays our attention.

NOTES

1 Graham Hough, 'Narrative and Dialogue in Jane Austen', *Critical Quarterly*, 12 (1970), 201.
2 For a characteristic discussion of the subject, see his 'Discourse in the Novel', in Michael Holquist, ed., *The Dialogic Imagination: Four Essays by M. M. Bakhtin* (Austin: University of Texas Press, 1981), pp. 259–422. Bakhtin's ideas are not all congenial to our present enterprise. In his concern for the evolution of the novel as a genre, he holds that it is trivial to focus on the style of any single novelist and brushes aside the fact that large movements consist of small moments. In emphasizing the stylistic differences among the various facets of a novel, he makes too little of those characteristics that do pervade them all.
3 Ann Radcliffe, *The Italian* (1797) (London: Oxford University Press, 1968), p. 2.
4 Charlotte Smith, *Emmeline* (1788) (London: Oxford University Press, 1971), p. 10; and *The Young Philosopher* (1798) (New York: Garland, 1974), IV:221.
5 Such individual differences are examined in my *Computation into Criticism: A Study of Jane Austen's Novels and an Experiment in Method* (Oxford: Clarendon, 1987).
6 [Walter Scott,] review of *The Black Dwarf* and *Old Mortality*, *Quarterly Review*, 16 (1817), 430–80: reprinted in John O. Hayden, ed., *Scott: The Critical Heritage* (London: Routledge, 1970), p. 115.
7 Frances Burney, *Evelina* (1778) (London: Oxford University Press, 1968), p. 107.
8 Mary Lascelles, *Jane Austen and her Art* (Oxford: Clarendon, 1939), p. 95.
9 Mikhail Bakhtin, 'Discourse in the Novel', *passim*.
10 These works include: James Harris, *Hermes* (1751); Samuel Johnson, *Preface to A Dictionary of the English Language* (1755); Robert Lowth, *A Short Introduction to English Grammar* (1762); James Buchanan, *The British Grammar* (1762); George Campbell, *The Philosophy of Rhetoric* (1776); and Hugh Blair, *Lectures on Rhetoric and Belles Lettres* (1783).
11 See E. D. Hirsch Jr., *Cultural Literacy: What Every American Needs to Know* (Boston: Houghton Mifflin, 1987), ch. 3.
12 R. W. Chapman, ed., *The Letters of Samuel Johnson, with Mrs. Thrale's Genuine Letters to Him* (Oxford: Clarendon Press, 1952), III:175.
13 J. B. Bury, ed., *Autobiography of Edward Gibbon* (London: Oxford University Press, 1959), p. 231.
14 Violet Dickinson, ed., *Miss Eden's Letters* (London: Macmillan, 1919), p. 3.
15 Graham Hough, 'Narrative and Dialogue in Jane Austen', 203–4.

16 D. W. Harding, 'Regulated Hatred: An Aspect of the Work of Jane Austen', *Scrutiny*, 8 (1940), 346–62.
17 For a detailed account of these procedures and a large-scale comparison between tragedies of two literary periods, see J. F. Burrows and D. H. Craig, 'Lyrical Drama and the "Turbid Mountebanks": Styles of Dialogue in Romantic and Renaissance Tragedy', *Computers and the Humanities*, 28 (1994), 63–86.

11

ISOBEL GRUNDY

Jane Austen and literary traditions

Jane Austen inherited no obvious, no precisely defined tradition: not the classical canon which her brothers studied at school, not (like so many of her literary granddaughters) the canon as studied for a B.A. in English literature; not the full sweep of her predecessors in English fiction, many of whom remained unknown to her; not the intellectual framework offered by any regular course of study. 'Her reading was very extensive in history and belles lettres' (*NA*, *P* 7). But it was desultory. She was never in a position, even had she wished it, to work through the kind of subject-bibliography which Emma is always drawing up; instead, she was dependent on titles which happened to come her way.

What came her way was by no means negligible. She was luckier than some of her heroines: Marianne Dashwood, who thinks her family library 'too well known to me' to provide 'anything beyond mere amusement' (*SS* 343), or Catherine Morland, who says, 'new books do not fall in our way' (*NA* 41). Austen's first library, her father's, ran to more than 500 books.[1] Though her school experience was brief and insignificant, most of the usual school books were accessible at home. Most importantly, the whole family were avid book-borrowers and book-exchangers. Chawton, scene of her most sustained and productive period of writing, had a better reading group than she had found at Steventon and Manydown, as she was at pains to point out.[2] Her letters teem with every possible kind of reference to books: simple reports of what she or the family is reading; opinions; quotations applied sometimes straightforwardly but more often with multiple layers of irony; loving, joking mention of details from novels in which she treats them just like real life. Only a highly literary sister would write to a brother about to visit Sweden: 'Gustavus-Vasa, & Charles 12th, & Christiana, & Linneus – do their Ghosts rise up before You?' (*L* 214). This remark alone would place Austen squarely in the centre of the Enlightenment tradition of European learning of the long eighteenth century.

We have, therefore, a paradox of real knowledge and expertise combined with real intellectual deprivation (of which she probably became more conscious as her literary career gathered momentum). She picked her reading matter for herself from a wide range of rich and multiple traditions; but she knew no tradition systematically or comprehensively. One result of this situation is that she never assumes the role of disciple or student, let alone that of pedagogue. She recognizes no canonical status, acknowledges no literary authority. She assumes the sufficiency of her own taste as guide to literary value, admiring authors because she likes them and not because of their currency value as great or respected names; when she admires a Great Name she expresses that admiration in terms of personal friendship, not literary appreciation.[3]

She seems not to have thought in terms of a Great Tradition. She does not, like many of her contemporaries, seek to raise the status of the novel and confer authority on her own fictions by heading chapters with literary quotations. Nor does she seek to endow fictional characters with status and value by making them familiar with great writers. Henry Fielding uses the latter technique for Parson Adams and Will Booth;[4] but both are popular among contemporaries of Austen whose literary quality is questionable. Eleanor Sleath, for instance, in *The Orphan of the Rhine* (one of Isabella Thorpe's choices) is unreliable as to grammar but uses Shakespeare, Milton, Pope, Burns, and other canonical authors to head her chapters; her heroine at thirteen is keen on Ariosto and Petrarch. Sleath's next novel, *The Nocturnal Minstrel*, quotes Ariosto in Italian and Horace in Latin.[5]

Austen's way of using the tradition is not Sleath's. Books are of service to her novels because of the daily uses that people make of their reading, in conversation, argument, and the shaping of imaginative experience. She presents them through the minds of her characters, coloured and differentiated by the imagined reader.[6] They are a vital part of the flow of life surrounding her; knowledge of books is, for her, continuous with other forms of knowledge.

I hope to establish here the broad outlines of Jane Austen's reading, and some slight sketch of the uses to which she puts it in her fiction. From an early age she read like a potential author. She looked for what she could use – not by quietly absorbing and reflecting it, but by actively engaging, rewriting, often mocking it. Evidence of her reading comes largely from her letters; it is, therefore, always fragmentary. At most times the Austen family group would be reading some book together; Jane would be reading another book on her own. Her letters mention only a very small proportion of all these books; and what they mention is not designed to convey meaning to a twentieth-century reader, but only to the letter's original recipient, who shared all kinds of private knowledge with which to make sense of what the letter says.

Almost every item of evidence, therefore, requires analysis and explanation, and this must necessarily be speculative. Austen's references to authors do not flatly deliver approval or disapproval: she has less direct, but perhaps more interesting, impressions to convey. This is not to say that her approval or disapproval is unimportant. As with characters, so with books: judgment, both moral and intellectual, is an important part of the response she solicits. But judgment is invited (against Mrs. Norris and Mr. Elton, for Miss Bates and Mrs. Smith) under the cloak of amusement and pleasure in the quirks of individuality. In the same way Austen does not, like a reviewer, attach quality rankings to books. She leaves it to her readers (the beloved recipients of letters, the anonymous public of novels) to discover her judgments for themselves. She does not praise or analyse George Crabbe: instead she launches a long-running joke about her hopes of seeing him in London and her efforts to detect his marital status from his writings, culminating in a resolve, elaborated with curlicues of fantasy, to marry him now he is a widower. She disguises her admiration for Thomas Clarkson, historian of the slave trade, and for Charles Pasley, writer on British governance in India, under the same metaphor of a woman assessing a man as husband material.[7]

A disciple who mocks discipleship under the guise of husband-hunting, a critic who mocks assessment of poetry under the guise of vulgar personal curiosity, is not one to signpost her favourites or her influences, if any. In fact in her own work she is chary of influence, taking pains always to avoid anybody else's manner of doing anything. She is little given to direct imitation, let alone allusion, let alone the canonical epigraph as chapter-heading.

In the teeth of her reticence and non-cooperation, I shall endeavour to reconstruct an outline of her extremely catholic reading, with some comments on its contribution to her work, although traces of influence have often been carefully erased. I shall comment on her relationship with books as it appears in her letters (where the issues of revelation and concealment are different from what they are in her published work) and on the reading of her fictional characters (not only what they read, but how they in turn use their reading).

We no longer find it easy to believe Austen's claim to be 'the most unlearned, & uninformed Female who ever dared to be an Authoress' (L 306). She was, after all, crafting a graceful but absolute refusal of James Stanier Clarke's invitation to build a novel around a clergyman 'entirely engaged in Literature', who, as she herself noted, would discourse 'on subjects of Science & Philosophy' and 'be occasionally abundant in quotation & allusions' (*L* 296–7, 306). The meaning of 'occasionally' here is not 'from time to time' but 'to match the occasion'. Clarke means the kind of clergyman whose response to the daily events of life draws *habitually* on the tags and phrases provided by his reading. Such a man is moulded by his 'Classical Education', his 'very extensive acquaintance with English Literature, Ancient & Modern'. We may suppose that Austen, as she made, 'with all possible Vanity', her boast of ignorance, felt profoundly grateful to be disqualified from writing about him; occasional abundance in quotation is not something that appeals to her.

Most of her own quotations and allusions are deliberately mismatched to their occasion. She takes a rhapsodic description of natural beauty and yokes it by violence with news of an unsatisfactory social occasion: ' "T'is Night & the Landscape is lovely no more", but to make amends for that, our visit to the Tyldens is over' (*L* 226). She echoes Falstaff's (disingenuous) appeal to time measured by Shrewsbury clock, on no better excuse than the fact that someone involved in her story 'once lived at Shrewsbury, or at least at Tewksbury' (*L* 64). The target of her mockery here is the seizing of occasions for quotation, and the vapidity of the tags quoted.

Austen's letters consistently debunk literary tradition, but of course such debunking is a tradition in itself. The Augustan writers loved to make fun of reference to canonical authors: mocking not the authors themselves, but pedantic dependence on them. Pope's 'I cough like Horace', Henry Fielding's mock-epic descriptions of vulgar brawls, innumerable half-submerged references in Johnson's letters, indulge themselves in this kind of fun. Austen herself, in mocking avid Shakespearians, is nonetheless also indicating familiarity with *Henry IV*, Part I.

Today acceptance of Austen's 'ignorance' at face value has given place to steady growth in critical attention to her reading and her influences. A century ago, just as the university syllabus for English literature was beginning to emerge, the American literary journalist William Branford Shubrick Clymer began the 'placing' of Austen in literary history. Together with her contemporary Sir Walter Scott, he said, she marked the half-way point between Richardson's day and Clymer's own.

> Richardson, Fielding, and Smollett, the first novelists in England (for Defoe's stories of adventure are not precisely novels as the term is now understood), had been followed by a romantic and by a sentimental school, the former growing from Horace Walpole, through Clara Reeve and Mrs Radcliffe, to Scott; and the latter including men so dissimilar as Sterne, Mackenzie, and Goldsmith. The sentimentalists were virtually a thing of the past, and the romanticists were in full career when Jane Austen, cutting loose from both

influences, set again on a firm basis the realistic study of manners taught her by Richardson and Fielding ... She belongs to a small group of women who excelled in what has been well called 'fictitious biography'; of that group – comprising Miss Edgeworth, Miss Ferrier, and herself ... she is incontestably the finest artist.

Her work, he says, is the slender thread which carried the strain of realism safely through the Romantic age from the hands of Fielding and Richardson to those of Thackeray and Trollope.[8]

This account is now itself historical. It is an early act of canon-construction, open-minded and non-rigid in its judgments. Four female contemporaries of Austen's appear (though not Frances Burney), along with several men – Horace Walpole, Henry Mackenzie, Goldsmith as novelist – who did not retain their place in a central canon.

Canon-construction also involves pigeonholing. Austen is a novelist; fiction must be her tradition. In fact she cares nothing for generic boundaries, but a great deal for the way the tradition of fiction flowed outwards to mix with those of history, and essays, and drama, and poetry. The English novel was seen in her day as a legitimate heir of Shakespeare, working as it did with dialogue and character and passion and interaction. Defoe did not yet enjoy the paternal status which historians of the novel later accorded him, and the works of Defoe's female predecessors and contemporaries (Behn, Davys, Barker, Aubin, Haywood) had already been forgotten. For Austen as for Clymer the great age of the novel had dawned with Samuel Richardson and Henry Fielding. Fiction moved between the poles represented by these two, and Austen, alert to their unlikenesses, learns from and disputes with each.

More recent critics have charted the broad range of influences on Austen's art. Detailed and sensitive attention has been paid to the ties that link her with the Augustan tradition of Addison and Johnson, to the landscape writing of Gilpin, and to a broad range of fiction including that by women, by Richardson,[9] and by her immediate contemporaries. She has been discussed as a novelist of ideas, with views on political, philosophical and legal issues of her day.

This new willingness to take her seriously as a thinker does not involve forgetting her own statements about disliking to be taken *too* seriously. Now we know she never turned her back or closed her ears to the intellectual debates raging around her, we should also remember her necessarily tenuous and deliberately oblique relation to such debates. She says that 'a Woman ... like me' *cannot* abound in quotation and allusion; none of her writings suggests for an instant that she wanted to. Quoting many writers, she almost without exception quotes them 'slant'. Whether to read this as female outsidership or as traditional Augustan irony is a matter of taste. While maintaining the superiority of the Chawton to the Steventon reading club, she inveighs against 'enormous great stupid thick Quarto Volumes'. For herself, she 'detest[s] a Quarto', does not want to learn 'everything in the World', and prefers 'a Man who condenses his Thoughts into an Octavo' (L 206). Such anti-pedantry is not anti-intellectualism; but it keeps a deliberate toehold in irresponsibility.

Both in letters and fiction, Austen mock-curtseys to or answers back at books which have caught her interest, disregarding their canonical or non-canonical status. Her reprocessing often makes strange bedfellows. For instance, Oliver Goldsmith's *History of England*, a text regularly fed to passive pupil consumers, is pressed into service in her *History of England*, 1791; but so is the essence of innumerable novels treating the opposition between Queen Elizabeth and Mary Queen of Scots – which, for devotees of the novel, was a more compelling pair of alternatives than Roundhead and Cavalier.[10] Goldsmith on the one hand, historical novelists on the other: the sixteen-year-old Austen takes the classic ruling that literature should combine instruction and pleasure, and divides it between two parties, neither of which, therefore, conforms fully to the rule.

It is safe to assume that even at this age Austen would know this classical rule, would know it was propounded by the Roman poet Horace, and would know the much-quoted tags (*utile dulci*, useful and sweet, and the slightly less hackneyed *jucunda et idonea*, merry and proper) in which it was embodied. Above all, however, she would know, more deeply and feelingly with advancing years, every shade of pedantry, or superiority, or self-importance, with which such tags were trotted out in mixed conversation. Her enquiring mind and retentive memory could not fail to pick up a good smattering of classical learning: what she did not pick up was any faith that these fragments carried the stamp of exceptional value. Like George Eliot later, she connected the idea of classical authors with the idea of little boys studying them.[11] For her the ancients remained subject to the same kind of critical scepticism (whether feminist or Augustan scepticism) as other sources. She calls a woman in childbed a 'sister in Lucina'; but she detects 'pedantry & affectation' in the title of Hannah More's *Cœlebs* [that is, celibate or bachelor] *in Search of a Wife*, 1808: 'Is it written only to Classical Scholars?'[12]

These are not the uses to which the classics are put by a devotee of a Great Tradition. Austen did not turn to the Latin language for authority or authorization. Yet, though she dislikes pedantry, I would not accept that she dislikes scholarship.[13] She went to some trouble to ensure factual accuracy in works by herself and her nieces. She likes to let foolish characters expose their foolishness by garbling texts. John Thorpe categorically misstates what is and is not contained in Burney's *Camilla, A Picture of Youth*, 1796: he has got only as far as chapter 4 of a voluminous novel, as readers of it will recognize. In the first chapter of *Sanditon* Mr. Parker garbles the context of a quotation from Cowper: what Cowper praises as a virtue in an old woman is confusingly converted into a deficiency in a seaside resort. The reader feels licensed to despise these inadequate readers – but no more than we feel free to despise Mrs. Elton for garbling a traditional saying or cliché by making Surrey, instead of Kent, 'the garden of England'. Mrs. Elton is an inadequate listener in just the way that Thorpe and Mr. Parker are inadequate readers.

While she came to the classics filtered through the minds of others, Austen had direct, almost continuous contact with another body of texts whose roots lie far back in antiquity. The texts of the Christian religion, and of the Anglican branch of it, were variously written by nomadic desert chiefs and priests, by poorly educated rural folk in a province of the Roman Empire, by a Roman ex-civil-servant (St. Paul), and by English Renaissance churchmen. They were either written or translated nearly two hundred years before Austen as a child first became familiar with them; their language was obsolete as well as their morality (in the Old Testament) often alien or unacceptable.

The Bible (Authorised Version or King James Bible) and the Book of Common Prayer, as Austen used them, dated from 1611 and 1662 respectively; but they were closely based on work done by Tyndale and Cranmer during the sixteenth century. Linguistically, therefore, they were a door opening backwards into 'English Literature, Ancient'; and they were familiar to her in a way that only a few texts become familiar to anyone: familiar from daily or weekly or yearly repetition, aloud, marked with the different speech habits of the different voices that pronounced them.[14] Even if she had never read the Bible herself (as she did) she would have heard the passages appointed to be read at the services of the church (no doubt with varying degrees of expertise). The passages appointed for Sundays and for the great festivals would be heard every year. The book of Psalms would be worked through during the church's year; in addition, certain psalms, as well as canticles and prayers, occurred every week as part of the service.[15] The prayers which Austen wrote herself reflect her familiarity with prayer-book rhythms: her words compose themselves into an order which is perfectly in tune with Elizabethan liturgical discourse, foreign to her usual practice but none the less securely hers.[16]

Austen's fictional style or styles may seem remote indeed from anything in the Bible or prayer-book: not only from ancient annals or martial poetry, but from St. Paul's letter-sermons and St. John's apocalyptic visions. Careful scrutiny, however, reveals the traces left by some of these familiar cadences. The almost prehistorical authors of the Old Testament have bequeathed her their rapidity and spareness of narrative, the New Testament writers their remarkable ability to enter the common mind and to conjure an illusion of verisimilitude by means of a single detail – the qualities that Auerbach notices when he writes about St. Mark's gospel in *Mimesis*.[17] The Bible, Austen's daily bread, must have helped her to plot the moral consequences (momentous for them) of Elizabeth's feeding her vanity with Wickham, or Emma's feeding hers with Harriet, while most novelists needed at least the *idea* of some momentous causes for what deeply affected their heroines. The Bible also helped to keep her rhythms free from the verbosity which afflicts so many of her contemporaries. In narrative passages (a comparatively small part, but an important one, of her novels) her taste for brief declarative sentences is something she shares with the gospels. 'Henry and Catherine were married, the bells rang, and every body smiled' (*NA* 252). That is in its way a very New Testament sentence.

These original Anglican texts had their later descendants. As well as listening regularly to sermons, Austen read them in printed form, subscribed to one collection, and transcribed her father's sermons (*L* 388 n. 12; xvii–xviii). Jacobean churchmen and later preachers contributed their copia and orotundity, their preference for using two words where one would do, if not directly to Austen then certainly to Mr. Collins.[18]

After the Bible, Shakespeare is 'part of an Englishman's constitution' (*MP* 338). The implications of Henry Crawford's remark reach beyond his intention, particularly in view of the exclusion of women from public life, and of Austen's generally mocking attitude to the institutional or property-owning approach to texts. It is, perhaps, an English birthright to know Shakespeare, as Edmund Bertram says, 'in bits and scraps', to refer parrot-fashion to Shrewsbury clock without recalling anything about Falstaff's deplorable conduct on the battlefield and without being able to tell Shrewsbury from Tewkesbury. (I believe that the frequent, minute inaccuracies which are sometimes stigmatized as misquotation are better seen as what the eighteenth century accepted as 'ease': a sign that quotations come from knowing an author 'pretty thoroughly', not from thumbing through texts; that the relation of reader to author is relaxed and unpedantic. Changing Shrewsbury into Tewkesbury is a different class of inaccuracy.)

Austen takes familiarity with Shakespeare for granted; but she makes a good deal hang on Fanny Price's delight in Crawford's reading; and at least once I believe she makes a good deal hang on a quotation from Shakespeare.

Ronald Blythe, who believes that Highbury society is essentially Philistine, omits from his sparse enumeration of its literary references a Shakespearian quotation from Emma. 'The world is not theirs, nor the world's law', she says of governesses, echoing (approximately) what Romeo says of the starving apothecary who sells him poison.[19] This is an interesting case. Some might argue that it proves Emma, like Catherine Morland, to have been reading selectively, on the lookout for pathos to grace the speech of a heroine. But, quite apart from the fact that Emma leans less towards the role of heroine than that of producer or director, quite apart from the fact that her reading of *Romeo and Juliet* got all the way to the last act, her picking her example of pathos from this speech about need and oppression, contempt and beggary, rather from the emotional pathos of the lovers, indicates a strong mind reading against the grain, ignoring hackneyed phrases but taking sustenance from a canonical text for her own independent thinking. Her Shakespeare allusion is one of several straws in the wind to suggest that marriage to the tirelessly, practically benevolent Mr. Knightley will suit her down to the ground.

Those critics are surely right who see Austen's natural place in the course of English literature as being among the Augustans. She knows the established canon: Addison, Pope, Gay, the Swift of *Gulliver's Travels*,[20] Thomson, Gray, Goldsmith, and Charlotte Lennox, whose *Female Quixote; or, The Adventures of Arabella*, 1752, renews her admiration on rereading (*L* 116). Marianne Dashwood's requiring Willoughby to admire Pope 'no more than is proper' (*SS* 47) may imply that only *Eloisa to Abelard* and *Elegy to the Memory of an Unfortunate Lady* are acceptable to her; or it may be a sly hint that Marianne's acquaintance with Pope has not extended so far as these rather early, highly emotional poems.[21] In a letter Austen writes, ' "Whatever is, is best." – There has been one infallible Pope in the World' (*L* 245), which besides repeating a well-worn anti-Catholic joke is surely a signal that she relished Pope the poet's insight as well as his *ex cathedra* manner.

Austen's best-loved authors are those with Augustan affinities: apart from Crabbe, they are Richardson, Johnson, Cowper, and Burney. To all these she pays the compliment of frequent and familiar reference. Not only does she quote them from memory, as she quotes Shakespeare or Pope; she also takes liberties with them, using them freely as part of the background of her life. She 'could not do without a Syringa' for the garden because of the way Cowper described it; she writes that 'like my dear Dr Johnson ... I have dealt more in Notions than Facts' (*L* 119, 121). This is what Johnson says he does in his *Journey to the Western Islands of Scotland*, with which Austen thus demurely ranks her own letter.[22] At one point she owned a set of the standard poetry anthology, Dodsley's *Collection of Poems*, originally published in 1748. Her Augustan texts are not limited to books. She is able to project on Cassandra's mind's eye the whole trajectory of Hogarth's 'Harlot's Progress', by observing that if she travelled to London with nowhere to stay, 'I should inevitably fall a Sacrifice to the arts of some fat Woman who would make me drunk with Small Beer' (*L* 88, 12).

Cowper threads through Austen's novels, loved passionately by Marianne and soberly by Fanny Price, and quoted by Mr. Knightley. Edward Ferrars, having been judged deficient in spirit and animation by Marianne on the basis of his reading of Cowper aloud, demonstrates both qualities in imagining how Marianne, if she had money, would buy up every extant copy of Cowper and other favourites, 'to prevent their falling into unworthy hands'. His combination of shyness, secret anguish, and whimsical humour in private might even suggest a hint of Cowper in character.[23]

Richardson's *Sir Charles Grandison*, 1753–4, and Burney's *Camilla* probably share the palm for frequency of mention in Austen's surviving letters, though *Evelina, or, A Young Lady's Entrance into the World*, 1778, runs them close. (*Camilla*, so far as we know, is the only novel which she honoured by continuing its story beyond the ending, as she sometimes did for her own books). She indulges in comic self-identification with their heroines: 'I shall be just like Camilla in Mr Dubster's summer-house'; 'Like Harriet Byron I ask, what am I to do with my Gratitude?' (In each case the joke lies in the discrepancy between the heroine's situation and Austen's less extreme one.)[24] But minor characters, minor situations in these novels are reckoned to be equally memorable. She writes of the thirst for travelling 'which in poor James Selby was so much reprobated' or of 'Our own particular little brother', confident that her correspondent will pick up her allusions.[25] John Thorpe cannot get through *Grandison*, but thinks *Tom Jones* the best novel written until Matthew Lewis' charnel gothic *The Monk*, 1796. Thorpe's admiration is damning indeed, and from it we might surmise that Austen prefers Richardson to Fielding. Yet what could be more Fieldingesque than the technique she uses to undermine Fielding here, the technique of praising with loud damns from a bad judge? Thorpe praising Fielding, dispraising Richardson, owes something to the famous scene in *Tom Jones* where Partridge praises the loud voice and stiff action of the actor playing Claudius, and dispraises Garrick as too natural to be good acting. To attribute favourites to Austen is not to suppose she failed to appreciate the rest of the Augustan tradition.[26]

Johnson is a special case in Austen's letters and novels. Opinions shared with him pervade her fiction at a deep level vital to meaning and structure. She knew his correspondence with Hester Thrale, which the latter published in 1788, as well as letters printed in Boswell's *Life*, 1791. Her letters resemble his in their minute detail and in their guessing games of half-submerged, shorthand reference. She might have modelled all her letters to Cassandra on his injunction about the need for 'petty talk upon slight occurrences', for letters to prevent the 'great inconvenience of absence, that of returning home a stranger and an enquirer'. The letter in which she quotes his 'more in Notions than Facts' is explicitly presented as an exercise in the art of writing a letter with nothing to say: what he called the 'great epistolick art'.[27]

Besides his minute particulars, Austen relished Johnson's habits of playful intertextuality and hidden meanings. Thus he implies an equation of himself with Lovelace's rakish friends when he writes, 'So I *comforted and advised him*.' When she writes 'Now this, says my Master will be mighty dull', she is assuming the language and therefore the mantle of the Johnson–Thrale correspondence, in which Henry Thrale is regularly 'my Master'. In the passage mentioning ordination, which has been so widely misread, the real joke lies in Austen's claim that she is making 'a complete change of subject' – which turns out to be a change from *Pride and Prejudice* and its reception to *Mansfield Park* and its planning. She presents herself as someone too egotistical to write of anything except her own works, though 'I will *try* to write of something else; – it *shall be* a complete change of subject.'[28]

Austen makes Cowper stand generically for rural, domestic life and Johnson for urban, social life when she writes (of a manservant who prefers the country) 'He has more of Cowper than of Johnson in him, fonder of Tame Hares & Blank verse than of the full tide of human Existence at Charing Cross' (*L* 250). In calling this preference 'a venial fault', she implies that she herself might side with Johnson, in spite of Cowper's remarkable power to unite in his support Marianne Dashwood, Edward Ferrars, Fanny Price, and George Knightley. Another kind of opposition between Johnson and Cowper implicitly underlies *Sense and Sensibility*: between Elinor's Johnsonian attempts to combat grief and depression through mental activity, and Marianne's Cowperesque savouring of melancholy. Fanny Price unites Johnson and Cowper, sense and sensibility.

While so many of her characters thus admire Cowper, their narrator is consistently Johnsonian. The spoof aphorism which opens *Pride and Prejudice* is not mockery of Johnson, but Johnsonian mockery: he too loves to burlesque the aphoristic manner with unreliable matter, as he does with the 'great truth', 'In a Man's Letters you know, Madam, his soul lies naked.' Marianne in her penitence and self-knowledge acquires Johnsonian sentiments and Johnsonian cadences: 'His remembrance can be overcome by no change of circumstances or opinions. But it shall be regulated, it shall be checked by religion, by reason, by constant employment.' When Elinor smiles to see her sister 'introducing excess' into her scheme for rationality and self-control, she might have practised exactly the same smiles in response to a reading of *Rasselas* (*SS* 347, 343). While Henry Tilney uses Johnson's dictionary to overpower ladies in debate (as if he is copying Johnson in 'talking for victory' as well as in his linguistic views), the novelist draws on Johnson's ideas about history to allocate to both Eleanor Tilney and Catherine: the latter's perception of history as a dark record of wars and pestilences, the former's philosophical speculations as to the reliability of sources (*NA* 107–9).

Critics have noted that Fanny Price and Anne Elliot are both reliant on Johnson for their moral thinking. (It is with Johnson that Anne seeks to counter the influence of Scott and Byron on Captain Benwick.) His effect on Emma is perhaps more surprising, but equally important. In her Box Hill experience of causing pain through over-eagerness to display her wit, she follows in the footsteps of a number of *Rambler* examples (e.g. nos. 16, 101, 141, 174) of the potential of intellectual excellence to lead its possessor astray. In her struggles for self-knowledge, when presented with detachment and irony, she recalls young female characters who take up their pens in the *Rambler* (e.g. nos. 51, 55, 62, 84, 191); but in her thoughts in the final chapters, in her steady aspiration after self-knowledge, rationality, and candour, she recalls the persona of Mr. Rambler himself.

Austen's tradition did not close with Johnson's death or with Boswell's *Life* – which, along with his *Journal of a Tour to the Hebrides*, the Austen family sought out to buy (*L* 22). Throwaway reference to the plays of Hannah Cowley suggests they had an established status in her mind.[29] She also read pedagogical works, books of travel, history, political and medical pamphlets. At dates close to their publication, the Austens read Francis Lathom's *The Midnight Bell*, 1798, Samuel Egerton Brydges' *Arthur Fitz-Albini*, 1798 (which receives perhaps Austen's worst review ever), Genlis' *Alphonsine* (which displeased by being indelicate),[30] Southey's *Letters from England*, 1807, Anne Grant's *Memoirs of an American Lady*, 1808, and Henrietta Sykes' *Margiana, or Widdrington Tower, A Tale of the Fifteenth Century*, 1808.[31]

Austen's judgments of those publishing contemporaneously with herself are complicated by a new element of irony and indirection: that of feigned or exaggerated envy and rivalry. In another reminiscence of Johnson, she repeatedly asserts her refusal to admire any work that might compete with her own. Hannah More, Jane West, Sir Walter Scott, all fall under this ban. She first implies prejudice against Scott (feeling not 'very much pleased' with *Marmion*, though perhaps she ought to be); then promotes him to the honour of affectionately inappropriate citing and quoting; then, when he switches from poetry to fiction, reverts to rivalry, and does not 'mean to like Waverley if I can help it – but fear I must'.[32]

In this context, her judgments on contemporaries are particularly slippery to assess. The accolade to Edgeworth (the only novelist, with herself and her niece, she is willing to like) is considerable. Her delight in Barrett's satirical *The Heroine*, her disappointment at Sarah Harriet Burney's debut in *Clarentine*, 1796, are directly expressed and can be trusted. So can her recommendation of Germaine de Staël's *Corinne*, 1807.[33] A relative, Cassandra Cooke, author of *Battleridge*, 1799, is apparently exempt from professional envy. But when Austen salutes Elizabeth Hamilton as 'such a respectable Writer', the compliment *may* be as back-handed as 'good Mrs West' or the expectation that *Ida of Athens* by Sydney Morgan (later Owenson) must be 'very clever' because written in only three months.[34]

There has been debate over the question whether Austen's literary judgments reflect any partiality towards her own sex (who, by this date, dominated the field of fiction). Such partisanship, like concern for her own fame, she would express only by indirection, with playful hyperbole or understatement. One can hardly mistake her treatment of the 'very Young Man, just entered of Oxford, wears Spectacles', who 'has heard that Evelina was written by Dr Johnson'. His so easily believing (and so authoritatively communicating?) what he has heard invites the reader to convict him of having a prejudice against women writers and no ear for style (*L* 43). When Austen disliked Sir Jenison Gordon for uttering 'once or twice a sort of sneer at Mrs Anne Finch', it seems probable that the sneers were directed at Anne Finch, Lady Winchilsea, an important poet of a century earlier. She was well known by the name she bore before her husband inherited the title; she lived at, and loved, and wrote about, the Finch family seat at Eastwell (where, during a visit, the sneers were uttered), and lay buried in the church there.[35] This sentence is *probably* Austen's strongest expression of solidarity with another women writer; but as so often her meaning remains obscure.

Austen's own sex is exempt neither from her serious literary judgment nor from her outrageous teasing. Mary Brunton's *Self-Control*, 1811, is 'excellently-meant, elegantly-written', but its failures in nature and probability invite, and receive, severe ribbing. *Rosanne; or, A Father's Labour Lost*, 1814, by Laetitia Matilda Hawkins, is 'very good and clever, but tedious'. Delightful on religion and other serious subjects (the heroine has a father influenced by Voltaire and a governess believing in human perfectability), it becomes, 'on lighter topics', improbable and absurd. The flamboyant *Wild Irish Girl*, by Sydney Owenson, later Morgan, would be worth reading in cold weather if only 'the warmth of her Language could affect the Body'. Hester Piozzi's colloquialisms are taken off in a sentence which is repeatedly, ramblingly prolonged by further second or third thoughts tacked on the end.[36] Mme de Genlis' *Olimpe et Theophile* is energetically repudiated for tormenting its characters; even at Austen's 'sedate time of Life', she tells her niece Caroline, she could not reread it 'without being in a rage. It really is too bad! ... Don't talk of it, pray' (L 310). Here Piozzi and Genlis, though they are targets of mockery, are also offered a slightly dubious compliment: Austen has clearly enjoyed the former's self-indulgence in the slapdash and slipshod, and been moved, albeit against her better judgment, by the latter's sentiment.

For failure of original thought, for re-hashing of stereotypes (by writers of either sex), she has no mercy. In fiction she reprobates 'thorough novel slang', 'the common Novel style': diction like 'vortex of Dissipation', characters like the handsome, amiable young man who loves desperately and in vain (L 277). The cant of critics fares no better. Early in her career, in *Northanger Abbey*, and at its end, in *Sanditon*, she holds up in disgust the well-worn phrases: 'threadbare strains of the trash with which the press now groans'; the 'mere Trash of the common Circulating Library' (NA 37; MW 403). The pedagogical tradition (which dealt largely in stereotypes) gets short shrift. Catherine Morland is right to hate the lamentable 'Beggar's Petition' by the Rev. Thomas Moss.[37] Lydia Bennet is never more sympathetic than when she meets James Fordyce's *Sermons to Young Women*, 1766, with yawning and interruption, in contrast to her sister Mary's eternal copying of extracts.[38]

Austen treats the exaggerated conventions of the novel of terror rather differently from other stereotypes. Her father borrowed from the library at least one novel admired by Isabella Thorpe: Francis Lathom's *The Midnight Bell*.[39] Austen's delight in Henrietta Sykes' fifteenth-century *Margiana* equals Henry Tilney's in Radcliffe's *Udolpho*; as usual she signifies pleasure by pretending the action is real, and pretending she can participate. The family, she says, 'like it very well indeed. We are just going to set off for Northumberland to be shut up in Widdrington Tower, where there must be two or three sets of Victims already immured under a very fine Villain' (L 164).

She responded rather similarly to Mrs. Rachel Hunter of Norwich, using her twice (in collaboration with two of her nieces) for the favourite game of taking fiction to be true stories about actual people. Twelve-year-old Fanny Austen (later Knight) used the opening story from Hunter's *Letters from Mrs. Palmerstone* to convey a private message about her own behaviour;[40] Anna Austen (later Lefroy) received a letter ostensibly addressed in the third person to Mrs. Hunter herself, chatting about the most pathetic characters in her *Lady Maclairn, the Victim of Villainy*, 1806. Since Austen also alluded to another episode in *Lady Maclairn* in the elopement of Lydia Bennet,[41] she surely felt some affection for Hunter.[42]

It would take too much space to set about tracing the ways in which Austen learned from the writers who made up her tradition: how she developed her mastery of balance from Pope, wisdom and playfulness from Johnson, gendered power-struggle and immediacy of representation from Richardson, relation of books to life from Lennox, pathos and domesticity from Cowper, grotesquerie from Burney, etc. She tends to stand a little outside the beaten paths of discipleship. While she reflects some of Johnson's opinions, she never calls on his authority or copies his style. She avoids both the unmixed models of virtue and vice and the heavy-handed poetic justice which often characterize the followers of Richardson.

Each of Austen's works occupies a particular position in relation to the community of literary texts. She commonly defines her characters in part through their reading habits; and the text itself inevitably engages in dialogue with texts by others. The juvenile volumes First, Second, and Third make explicit reference to sixteen works or writers.[43] Their parodic spirit gives way to the self-sufficient imaginative world of *Lady Susan*, where books are never mentioned, but where the epistolary novel's traditional inclusion of some callously self-seeking, cynical character is transformed by the simple device of switching this person's gender. Emma Watson turns thankfully to a book in time of trouble, for 'the employment of mind, the dissipation of unpleasant ideas which only reading could produce' (*MW* 361). If her reading is fiction, it depicts a level of society closer to the one she has just lost than to the one she has just found, for *The Watsons'* low level of social and financial status is its chief claim to originality. It was conventional for a heroine's financial affairs to have a certain substance. (Eliza Parsons was creating fictional problems involving £4,000 at a time when she was in danger of debtors' prison for the sum of £12.[44]) *The Watsons* presents, in Elizabeth, a woman who is vulgar and obsessively concerned with getting married, yet who has none of the complementary negative qualities of an Anne Steele or a Mrs. Bennet, but only a warm heart and strong sense of duty. Even in this fragment Austen has found space to challenge several conventions of the contemporary novel.

Sense and Sensibility and *Northanger Abbey* each makes fun of a particular literary ideology; yet the Dashwoods are probably Austen's most studious family, and Catherine is far better educated than many readers notice. Elinor's pity for Lucy Steele's lack of education, her 'illiterate' state, is genuinely felt. Marianne's 'knack of finding her way in every house to the library, however it might be avoided by the family in general' is not an aspect of her behaviour that needs modification (*SS* 127, 304). Mrs. Dashwood can allude to a little-known novel by Richard Graves (*Columella, the Distressed Anchoret*, 1776) and expect to be understood by her daughters and Edward Ferrars.[45] Plans of study (Marianne's after her heart is broken, and their mother's for young Margaret) are subjected to some teasing from the narrator. Still, the atmosphere overall is far more favourable to reading and study than is usual in either of *Sense and Sensibility*'s two prototype genres: the novel of misguided reading, like Lennox's *Female Quixote*, or the novel of good and bad sisters, as written by Elizabeth Helme, Jane West, and others. If books and ideas have led Marianne astray, encouraging her to seek intensity of emotion as the greatest good, then books and ideas, and especially meditation and self-examining, are to play some part in her redemption. This makes another highly original resolution of a familiar fictional dilemma.

Catherine Morland is educated squarely within the Augustan tradition. She resists the 'trembling limbs' and emotional blackmail of Moss's aged beggar; but she has no trouble learning a poem from fifty years earlier, 'The Hare and Many Friends' by the under-rated John Gay (a little gem of irony and black humour). The hunted hare evidently wrings her heart as the beggar does not. At fourteen her dislike for 'books of information' is matched by delight in those which are 'all story and no reflection'. At seventeen she has read Shakespeare, Pope, Thomson, and Gray, even if only in order to comb them for aphorisms and sentiment.[46]

Austen's supposed dislike of scholarship is hard to square with Henry Tilney. He has scholarly tastes; he delights in the cut-and-thrust of argument; on linguistic niceties he overpowers ladies with Johnson's dictionary and Hugh Blair's *Lectures on Rhetoric*. His sister (herself a reader of the historians David Hume and William Robertson) thinks the scholar in him liable to prevail over the gentleman. Where Edgar Mandlebert as Camilla's mentor acts repressively, issuing no instructions but finding fault later, Henry behaves like a skilled tutor, eliciting Catherine's ideas, consistently questioning received opinion, playing down his pleasure in conscious intellectual superiority (*NA* 106–14).

Northanger Abbey famously defends novels by setting them, too, squarely at the centre of the literary tradition. Novels exhibit 'genius, wit, and taste'. They display, in 'the best chosen language', 'the greatest powers of the mind ... the most thorough knowledge of human nature ... the liveliest effusions of wit and humour'. This praise would be as apt for Pope or Johnson as for Burney and Edgeworth. But while novelists shine so brightly, says Austen, modern men of letters (reviewers, editors, anthologizers) do not; the revered

Spectator is really guilty of the 'improbable circumstances, unnatural characters' of which the novel stands accused.[47]

While she defends her own 'literary corporation', Austen engages it in debate. Having introduced Henry challenging received opinion (the cliché that women write better letters than men) she quickly issues her own challenge to Samuel Richardson's opinion 'that no young lady can be justified in falling in love before the gentleman's love is declared' (*NA* 29–30). This was also, famously, the view of Camilla's father;[48] so *Camilla*, explicitly lauded by the narrator, is also criticized, implicitly but radically, in the action.

Catherine must learn to throw off her gothic illusion and cease to expect in life the trappings of villainy: concealment of suspected horrors, as in Ann Radcliffe's *Mysteries of Udolpho*, 1794, or ancient texts testifying to female suffering, as in Parsons' *Castle of Wolfenbach*, 1793 (one of Isabella's favourites), Eliza Kirkham Matthews' *What Has Been*, 1801, and many, many more. But first and more importantly she must learn to throw off the social timidity which makes her vulnerable to the Thorpes' social tyranny, as Evelina was vulnerable to that of the Branghtons. Catherine trapped in John Thorpe's carriage, breaking her word to the Tilneys against her will, strongly recalls Evelina trapped in Lord Orville's carriage which has been borrowed in her name against her will. If Radcliffe is reproved, Burney is endorsed; so is Johnson, who made one woman advise another to consider herself 'a being born to know, to reason, and to act'.[49]

Literary reference is less central to *Pride and Prejudice*. Burney contributes the novel's title;[50] but *Cecilia*'s pride and prejudice belong to the older generation, while Elizabeth's and Darcy's are their own. Elizabeth may be less of a reader than Elinor, Marianne, or Catherine, but her impromptu comment on picturesque grouping shows she knows her Gilpin (*PP* 53). Free spirit that she is, she is hedged around with ineffectually repressive texts: her father's library, Mary's improving books,[51] the gender-obsessed Fordyce, with whom Mr. Collins replaces more solid Christian thinkers.

Mansfield Park is another battleground of texts. It has been shown that Austen was familiar with contemporary pro- and anti-slave-trade debates. (Johnson's letters on the Mansfield case would have brought the matter to her attention, even if she had not read and fallen 'in love with' Thomas Clarkson.)[52] Issues of governance at Mansfield therefore (like Mrs. Norris's Popean meanness to servants) are related to issues of governance in the West Indies, whence Sir Thomas returns as more of an oppressor than he was before. But behind the heavyweight 'books of information', used for this novel only, stand the familiar books of imagination which feed all of Austen's work. Sir Charles Grandison and his loving extended family provide a silent commentary on that of the Bertrams. The caged starling in Sterne's *Sentimental Journey* (which is agonized over but never let out) provides a sudden, shocking parallel to Maria's prospects in marriage. Kotzebue's *Lovers' Vows* (a play of passion, translated by the radical Elizabeth Inchbald, 1798) offers the delusory escape of fiction. Fanny keeps both her heart and mind alive with books. Cowper (well known as an opponent of the slave trade) is her *alter ego*, Lord Macartney on China her serious reading, Crabbe and (especially) Johnson her relaxations (*MP* 156, 392). Against her heartfelt reading of, for instance, Scott (86, 281) is set the uncommitted facility with which the Crawfords can summon Milton or poems of seduction, or imitate an imitator of Pope (43, 161, 292).

The literary situation in *Emma* resembles that in *Pride and Prejudice*. Emma is a woman of action who knows the world of ideas through bibliographies, but never actually reads the books; still, her use of Shakespeare is significant. Mr. Knightley is an outdoors man, a glutton for practical work; yet he is familiar with Cowper. Books are not forgotten. Robert Martin's knowledge of Goldsmith's *Vicar of Wakefield*, 1762, and the *Elegant Extracts* edited by Vicesimus Knox in 1789, his ignorance of Radcliffe or Regina Maria Roche, mark him squarely as an unmodish, middlebrow reader; only Harriet finds this dismaying. Mrs. Elton, raised like Catherine Morland on Gay's 'Hare and Many Friends', shows it by shatteringly inappropriate quotation.[53]

Austen's last completed novel brings two of her traditions, the writers of feeling and the writers of thinking, into direct confrontation for the soul of the bereaved Captain Benwick. As Anne urges him to read moralists, letter-writers, and 'memoirs of characters of worth and suffering', Johnson makes another masked appearance in the text at two levels. Along with sermon-writers like Austen's favourite Thomas Sherlock (*L* 278), he is the most obvious moralist for Benwick to read; he is also an important source of Anne's own creed of activity and benevolence and self-control. Anne shows that knowledge of fiction can be illuminating, not misleading: she compares herself both with an exaggeratedly self-abnegating romantic heroine of Matthew Prior and with the awful Miss Larolles in Burney's *Cecilia*, 1782.[54]

Austen's final novel, the fragment *Sanditon*, would have been her most literary. Charlotte Heywood's reading habits recall Anne's: she is 'a very sober-minded young Lady, sufficiently well-read in Novels to supply her Imagination with amusement, but not at all unreasonably influenced by them' (*MW* 391–2). Comparing herself with Camilla leads her to deliver a mental *coup de grace* to that tale of outrageous female suffering which had haunted Austen's imagination for years: 'She had not *Camilla*'s Youth, & had no intention of having her Distress' (390). The misreaders here are male: Mr. Parker and Sir Edward Denham. Sir Edward can quote without conveying meaning of any kind (by repeating, for instance, 'Oh! Woman in our Hours of Ease – ' without a verb, without a statement). He races from Scott to Burns to Montgomery[55] to Wordsworth to Thomas Campbell and back; but none of these writers is to blame for his incoherence. As always in Austen, what matters is what you make of your reading. Sir Edward's intellectual digestion malfunctions: he draws 'only false Principles from Lessons of Morality, & incentives to Vice from the History of it's Overthrow ... only hard words & involved sentences from the style of our most approved Writers' (404–5).

Austen returns at last to Lennox's *Female Quixote*, to reverse the gender of its protagonist and to present, so far as I know unprecedentedly, a man misreading the world in the light of his misreading fiction. In a typically daring reversal, the female protagonist is a reader in calm control of her texts.

Her literary traditions give depth to Austen's fiction. It depicts a society whose overall level of interest in ideas and books is very high, in which novels rank with poetry, drama, and 'Essays, Letters, Tours & Criticisms' (404). For her and for her central characters books and life are not divided; books are a vital part of life. In this as in other matters, her manner of proceeding sets her squarely in the steps of Richardson and Burney, Johnson and Cowper, and closely in touch with neglected fields and forgotten chambers, with John Gay and Richard Graves, Rachel Hunter and Henrietta Sykes.

NOTES

1 D. J. Gilson, 'Jane Austen's Books', *The Book Collector*, 23 (1974), 27.
2 *Letters*, 3rd ed., collected and edited by Deirdre Le Faye (Oxford and New York: Oxford University Press, 1995), pp. 198–9. Twelve years after visiting Dawlish she remembered its 'particularly pitiful & wretched' library (L 267).
3 Sometimes her stance is jokingly appropriative: Dr. Edward Percival wrote 'Moral Tales for Edward to give to me' (L 145).
4 *Joseph Andrews*, 1742, I, ch. 17; *Amelia*, 1751, VIII, ch. 5.
5 *The Orphan of the Rhine*, ed. Devendra P. Varma (London: Folio Press, 1968), p. 31; *The Nocturnal Minstrel*, ed. Varma (New York: Arno Press, 1972), pp. 1, 64, 209. Austen owned Ariosto's *Orlando furioso* in John Hoole's translation, 1783, copy later bought by Virginia Woolf (Gilson, 'Jane Austen's Books', 30–1).
6 Lascelles says this of her presentation of the natural world (*Jane Austen and her Art*, 1939 (London: Athlone Press, 1995), p. 1).
7 L 218, 220–1, 243, 198.
8 'A Note on Jane Austen', *Scribner's Magazine*, Feb. 1891, repr. in B. C.

Southam, ed., *Jane Austen: The Critical Heritage: Volume II 1870–1940* (London and New York: Routledge and Kegan Paul, 1987), pp. 199–200.

9 See, among several valuable studies, Jocelyn Harris, *Jane Austen's Art of Memory* (Cambridge: Cambridge University Press, 1989).

10 Its popularity was fostered though not begun by Sophia Lee, *The Recess*, 1783–5.

11 She wrote for Frank some verses which 'seemed to me purely classical – just like Homer & Virgil, Ovid & Propria que Maribus' (*L 170*).

12 *L 224, 172. She had another reason to dislike More, whose Strictures on the Modern System of Female Education, 1799,* called novels a principal source of moral corruption: 'The glutted imagination soon overflows with the redundance of cheap sentiment and plentiful incident' (422–3).

13 In his edition of *Emma*, Ronald Blythe says she disliked it 'very much' (Harmondsworth: Penguin, 1966), p. 467.

14 Perhaps the nearest parallel for Austen would be the motley collection of plays her family performed at home, from Susanna Centlivre and (probably) Fielding to Richard Brinsley Sheridan. Deirdre Le Faye, *Jane Austen: A Family Record* (London: British Library, 1989), pp. xvi–xvii.

15 Said rather than sung. See Irene Collins, *Jane Austen and the Clergy* (London: Hambledon, 1994), p. 181.

16 See Bruce Stovel, ' "The Sentient Target of Death": Jane Austen's Prayers', Juliet McMaster and Bruce Stovel, eds., *Jane Austen's Business* (London: Macmillan, 1995), pp. 192–205.

17 Erich Auerbach, *Mimesis: The Representation of Reality in Western Literature*, 1946, trans. Willard R. Trask (Princeton: Princeton University Press, 1953), pp. 40–9. Auerbach does not, regrettably, mention Austen.

18 *PP* 105–6. Note his repetitions and self-elucidations, his *firstly, secondly, thirdly*.

19 *E* 400. 'The world is not thy friend, nor the world's law' (*Romeo and Juliet*, V. i; *E*, ed. Blythe [Harmondsworth: Penguin, 1966], pp. 467–8).

20 *L* 47.

21 Catherine Morland finds a line to remember in the *Elegy* (*NA* 15).

22 Samuel Johnson, *Journey to the Western Islands of Scotland*, ed. Mary Lascelles (New Haven: Yale, 1971); to Boswell, July 7, 1774. Lascelles borrowed the phrase *Notions and Facts* from Johnson *and* Austen, as the title of a book, 1973.

23 *SS* 18, 47, 92; *MP* 56, 431; *E* 344.

24 *L* 357, 6, 234; also 9, 220.

25 *L 93, 38. It is unfortunate that this new edition does not index authors or titles of books, so that these allusions remain untraceable in the volume. Evelina* is referred to on pp. 120, 302.

26 *Tom Jones*, XVI, ch. 5. This novel enters her letters in connection with the dashing Tom Lefroy's white coat, *Tristram Shandy* in connection with a praiseworthy servant, *Robinson Crusoe* only as a servant's reading (*L, 93, 95*).

27 To Hester Thrale, *The Letters of Samuel Johnson*, ed. Bruce Redford (Princeton: Princeton University Press, 1992–4), III:50, 89.

28 *L* 202. Italics added. See also Johnson, *Letters*, II:328

29 As well as being acted by request of Eliza de Feuillide at Tunbridge Wells in 1786 (*L* 74; *MW* 65; Le Faye, *Jane Austen: Her Life and Letters. A Family Record*, 57).

30 *L* 15, 22, 115.

31 *L* 141, 164. Attribution from Virginia Blain, Patricia Clements and Isobel Grundy, *The Feminist Companion to Literature in English: Women Writers from the Middle Ages to the Present* (New Haven: Yale University Press, 1990).

32 *L* 131 (1808), 194 and 202 (1811, 1813), 277 (1814).

33 *L* 278, 255, 120, 161.

34 *L* 252, 321, 166.

35 Austen, who was particular about modes of address, normally uses 'Miss Finch' for the present-day Anne Finch, and 'Mrs Finches' for her and her sister (*L*, 106; e.g. 8, 38, 107, 108).

36 'He is more comfortable here than I thought he would be, & so is Eliz: tho' they will both I believe be very glad to get away, the latter especially – Which one can't wonder at *somehow*' (*L* 44). Footnoted as referring to Piozzi's edition of Johnson's letters, this is far more likely aimed at her *Observations in the Course of a Journey through Italy* ..., 1789, whose style was widely reprobated as too like gossipy speech.

37 *NA* 14. Written when its author was an undergraduate and frequently anthologized or reprinted in periodicals, it voices a flatly pathetic appeal to 'Pity the sorrows of a poor old man!' Moss, *Poems on Several Occasions* (1827), pp. 18–21.

38 *PP* 68. Against her expectations, however, Austen enjoyed Thomas Gisborne's *Enquiry into the Duties of the Female Sex* (*L* 112).

39 *L* 15; *NA* 40.

40 *L* 107; *Letters from Mrs. Palmerstone to her Daughter, Inculcating Morality by Entertaining Narratives* (1803), first story.

41 Hunter's eloping Lydia resembles Austen's in character; her family resembles Austen's in reaction. *Lady Maclairn*, III: 223; IV: 144–8.

42 *L* 195, 407 n. 3, 408 n. 6, 269. Cf. Deirdre Le Faye, 'Jane Austen and Mrs Hunter's Novel', *N&Q*, 230 (1985), 335–6; Isobel Grundy, 'Rachel Hunter and the Victims of Slavery', *Women's Writing: The Early Modern Period*, ed. Janet Todd and Marie Mulvey Roberts, 1 (1994), 25–34.

43 Fergus, *Jane Austen: A Literary Life*, p. 39.

44 Blain *et al.*, *Feminist Companion*, p. 835.

45 There is something highly instructive in way she uses, casually and unexplained, the name of its protagonist, and the way that Austen scholars (versed in the classical tradition but not in that of eighteenth-century fiction) at first supposed she meant an obscure Latin writer who shares that name (*SS* 103 and Chapman's note at 384).

46 *NA* 14–16. Her mother later selects for her improvement a periodical, *The Mirror*, which, although written by Henry Mackenzie, belongs not in the sentimental but the social-Addisonian category. Mrs. Morland is mistaken in thinking that pedagogy can help in this crisis; but her choice of pedagogue is traditional and sound. (Alyson Bardsley and Jeff Ewing pointed this out on the Eighteenth-Century List.)

47 *NA* 37–8. Some surprise has been expressed at Austen's finding the *Spectator*'s language coarse; but a word-count of a few terms like 'whore' and 'cuckold' would explain her reasons.

48 'A Sermon', *Camilla*, v, ch. 5.

49 *NA* 87–8; *Evelina*, II, letter 23; *Rambler* 133.

50 Burney, *Cecilia*, final chapter. The words 'pride and prejudice' also occur in Robert Bage's *Hermsprong; or, Man as he is not*, 1796, which Austen owned (Gilson, 'Jane Austen's Books', 31).

51 Mary even parodies Evelina's Mr. Villars in the aftermath of Lydia's loss, with parrotted comment on female reputation: 'no less brittle than it is beautiful' (*PP* 289; *Evelina*, II, letter 8).

52 *L* 198. R. W. Chapman once supposed this referred to Clarkson's *Memoirs of William Penn*, 1813; but his *History of the Abolition of the African Slave Trade*, 1808, is immeasurably more likely.

53 She embarrasses Jane Fairfax and no doubt amuses Emma with 'For when a lady's in the case, / You know all other things give place' (lines 41–2) – originally said by a bull intent on sex (*E* 454).

54 *P* 150, 116, 189. Lady Mary Wortley Montagu thought the 'monstrous folly' of Prior's heroine in 'Henry and Emma' (1709) likely to lead young readers astray. *Complete Letters*, ed. Robert Halsband (Oxford: Clarendon Press, 1965–7), III: 68.

55 Presumably James Montgomery (1771–1854), another poet who wrote against the slave trade.

12

CLAUDIA L. JOHNSON

Austen cults and cultures

Ever since Henry James, early in this century, observed that a 'body of publishers, editors, illustrators, [and] producers of the pleasant twaddle of magazines' found 'their "dear", our dear, everybody's dear, Jane so infinitely to their material purpose', two things have been abundantly clear: first, that Austen has been not a mere novelist about whom one might talk dispassionately, but a commercial phenomenon and a cultural figure, at once formidable and non-threatening; second, that many of Austen's most acute admirers have been unhappy with this extravagant popularity. An Austenian descendant himself, James aims his criticism not so much at Austen but at her faddish commodification by publishers and marketers. He had a point. Since 1832, Austen's six novels were available separately in the *Standard Novels* series published by Richard Bentley. But even though Bentley reprinted the novels at various times in the coming decades, joined by other printers once his copyrights expired, Austen's novels were hardly best sellers. Indeed, she remained an artist admired intensely by a few, such as George Lewes and Thomas Macaulay. 'Janeitism' – the self-consciously idolatrous enthusiasm for 'Jane' and every detail relative to her which James is alluding to – did not burgeon until the last two decades of the nineteenth century. It was spurred on by J. E. Austen-Leigh's *A Memoir of Jane Austen* in 1870, which provided biographical information about the quaint and saintly obscure spinster aunt who lived in a quieter time, and by Bentley's deluxe *Steventon Edition of Jane Austen's Work* in 1882 (the first collected edition of Austen's novels), which included *Lady Susan*, the *Memoir*, a frontispiece portrait of Austen, and woodcuts of Chawton Church and Steventon Parsonage, and which thus put most of Austen's famous little 'world' into a tidy bundle.[1] Janeitism boomed with the wider publication of Austen's novels singly and in sets, ranging from Routledge's cheap issues of 1883, and the Sixpenny Novel series starting in 1886; to Macmillan's 1890 issues, lavishly if inanely illustrated by Hugh Thomson; to the quasi-scholarly ten-volume set of R. Brimley Johnson for Dent in 1892, reissued five times in as many years.[2]

Aggravated by such commercial promotion, James denounces the 'special bookselling spirit' which, with all its 'eager, active interfering force' (rather like a nautical Mrs. Norris), whips up a 'stiff breeze', driving the waters of reputation above their natural levels, and flooding the literary marketplace to promote the sales of its own titles. Though inclined to disparage Austen as an unconscious artist, James acknowledges that she would not be so 'saleable if we had not more or less ... lost our hearts to her' in the first place.[3] But the truth is that James cannot stand the fact that Austen is loved in the wrong ways by the wrong sorts of people, people evidently incapable of assessing her just value, or discriminating her real merits.

If James, revolted by middlebrow culture and its purveyors, lambastes the ubiquity of Austeniana in 'pretty reproduction in every variety of what is called tasteful ... form', how would he recoil today, when Austen comes to us in dazzling movies from Hollywood and the British film industry featuring our favourite stars, in more ponderous BBC adaptations, in published sequels, imitations and homages, on radio broadcasts and editorial pages, on bumperstickers announcing 'I'd rather be reading Jane Austen', on book bags and T-shirts sporting Cassandra's portrait of her sister, on coffee mugs averring, via Kipling, that there is no one to beat Jane when you're in a tight place? Clearly, once her reputation thrived beyond a small circle of enthusiasts, Austen's appeal has been wide enough to be a worry, for it reaches beyond the authority of those who consider themselves entitled to adjudicate not only who but how it is proper to enjoy 'great' literature.

Other essays in this volume treat Austen and her novels as an object of study. This essay addresses not Austen's works *per se*, but our reception of them, the ideas about culture Austen has been thought to represent, and the uses to which we have put her and her achievement. Needless to say, the extent to which any writer can be pondered independently from her or his reception remains a vexed question. But Austen is a cultural fetish; loving – or hating – her has typically implied meanings well beyond any encoded in her works. Because she has proved essential to the self-definition of so many contending interests – people who see themselves as delicate escapists or as hard-nosed realists, as staunch defenders of morality or as exponents of ludically amoral theatricality, as elitists or democrats, as iconoclasts or conventionalists, as connoisseurs or as common readers – it is conspicuously difficult to disentangle the 'real' Austen from the acknowledged or unacknowledged agendas of those discussing her.

One vociferous segment of Austen's reading public missing from the above assortment are professional academics, and I omitted us solely for the purpose of more exclusive emphasis here. The claim to unbiased enquiry is foundational to our enterprise as teachers and students, but we too have been an interested and decidedly high-handed party contending for access to the real Jane Austen, and thus stand to learn a great deal from recognizing how some of our most basic assumptions about how to read her novels were calculated to consolidate the authority of a new professorate, with its distinctive programme and concomitant visions of class, gender, and national identity, and at a time when the novel was still entering the curriculum at Oxbridge (having been included decades earlier in the curricula of US colleges and universities, where classical models held less sway). What follows is not an exhaustive analysis of Austenian criticism among diverse readerships for the past two centuries, but a more modest attempt to historicize our notions about her, in the hopes of demonstrating the numerous ways in which she has been a cultural presence.

Modern Austenian criticism begins not with a literary critic or a novel scholar, but with psychologist D. W. Harding. The fundamental principle of his pathbreaking 1940 essay is that Austen's 'books are ... read and enjoyed by precisely the sort of people whom she disliked'. To be sure, this was not the first time anyone had argued that Austen's relation to her subject matter was satirical rather than reverential – one thinks, for example, of Mrs. Oliphant's remarks on the 'feminine cynicism' and '[quiet] jeering' in Austen's works.[4] Nor, as James' remarks above indicate, was this the first time anyone asserted the superiority of his own powers of discrimination by trashing others' love of Austen as mindless, excessive, or otherwise undisciplined. But it was, I think, the first time anyone claimed that Austen herself was above her admirers, and attempted to place criticism on a proper footing by rescuing her from them.

But who were these admirers, and what is it precisely that Harding is trying to get away from? Not the hoi polloi, the philistine Janeites James had castigated, for whom an admiration of Austen stood as an example of high culture in its least challenging form, and for whom an admiration of her works served as a badge of gentility. The social and political horizon had radically changed, and when Harding thinks of Janeites, men of the upper classes come to his mind, the 'exponents of urbanity', the 'sensitive', and 'cultured', the 'Gentlemen of an older generation than mine' who disseminate Austeniana 'through histories of literature, university courses, literary journalism, and polite allusions'. Because we now live in a cultural environment when it can be assumed that literature written by women is literature written for women, it may at first seem counter-intuitive that, in its most influential forms, the Janeitism of the early twentieth century was, with the prominent exception of Shakespearian scholar Caroline Spurgeon, principally a male enthusiasm shared among publishers, professors, and literati such as Montague Summers, A. C. Bradley, Lord David Cecil,

Walter Raleigh, R. W. Chapman, and E. M. Forster. At the Royal Society of Literature in particular Austen's genius was celebrated with an enthusiasm that would be regarded as dotty in the conferences or classrooms of today. Far from regarding their interest in Austen as level-headed 'work' necessitated by the complexity of her novels, Janeites flaunt it as ecstatic revelation: she was not merely their *dear* Jane, but their *divine* Jane, their *matchless* Jane, and they were her *cult*, her *sect*, her *little company (fit though few)*, her *tribe* of ardent adorers who celebrate the *miracle* of her work in flamboyantly hyperbolic terms, archly suggesting – to my ear at least – the incommensurateness of their fervour to the primness of its object. Although their zeal is genuine, the self-parody implicit in these pronouncements tells us that we are in an insider's society of scholar gentlemen at play.[5]

Janeites constituted a reading community whose practices transgress the dogmas later instituted by professional academics presiding over the emergent field of novel studies – dogmas holding, for example, that it is inappropriate to talk about characters as if they were real people or in any way to speculate upon their lives before, after, or outside the text itself; that biographical information about an author is irrelevant at best and heretical (i.e., a 'fallacy') at worst; that the business of studying is serious indeed, requiring analytic skills and specialist knowledges available through courses of study at colleges and universities; that Austen's novels are essentially about marriage, and that the courtship plot – rather than, say, the category *character* – is the major event in her fiction. To exemplify and to account for ways in which Janeite reading practices resist these truths *not* universally acknowledged, I will turn briefly to Rudyard Kipling's 'The Janeites', a story often alluded to in Austen criticism, but quite obviously not very often or very carefully read.

A story within a frame story, 'The Janeites' is set in a London Masonic Lodge during 1920, where shell-shocked veteran Humberstall talks about a secret society into which he was inducted while serving under the supervision of Sergeant Macklin as an officers' mess-waiter with his World War I artillery battery in France.[6] One day as the officers discuss whether or not 'Jane' died without leaving 'direct an' lawful prog'ny', Macklin (who is very drunk) loudly interrupts the officers' conversation with the claim 'She *did* leave lawful issue in the shape o' one son; an' 'is name was 'Enery James' (124). Puzzled that the superior officers, far from punishing such insubordinate intrusiveness, actually order him to be taken off to bed and cared for, Humberstall finds out more about the secret club whose membership brings such extraordinary privileges. After selling him the password ('*Tilniz an' trap-doors*', a phrase from *Northanger Abbey*), Macklin imparts to him the mysteries of Jane, which make the horrors of the front companionable: 'It *was* a 'appy little Group' (132), Humberstall later murmurs nostalgically. When half the battery is killed in a German artillery attack, Humberstall is the only Janeite to survive. As he struggles to board a hospital train, only to be put off by a chattering nurse insisting the train is too crowded, Humberstall implores the head nurse to 'make Miss Bates, there, stop talkin' or I'll die', and the head-nurse – evidently an initiate herself – recognizes a fellow's password and eagerly obliges, even filching a spare blanket for his comfort (136).

As a story both about readings and readers of Austen's novels 'The Janeites' is highly suggestive. Unlike virtually all academic readers of Austen since the 1950s, Janeites in foxholes do not think Austen's novels are about courtship and marriage. The love story plot is less-than-inevitable for them. In their civilian lives, they are chilly towards women (Jane 'was the only woman I ever 'eard 'em say a good word for' [123] Humberstall remembers), and chary of domesticity (the senior Janeites are a Divorce Court Lawyer and a Private Detective specializing in adultery cases). Even Humberstall himself, having been discharged from an earlier stint of service, can so little tolerate the company of his mother, sister, and aunts that he actually re-enlists. Of course, the Janeites recognize that novels are 'all about young girls o' seventeen ... not certain 'oom they'd like to marry', but for them (unlike non-Janeites in the story) this narrative fact is levelled with other narrative facts that also constitute part of what the novels are 'all about' – including 'their dances 'an card parties 'an picnics, and their young blokes goin' off to London on 'orseback for 'aircuts an' shaves', a detail which, like the wearing of wigs, is especially engaging to a hairdresser like Humberstall. As far as Austenian plots are concerned, 'there was nothin' *to* 'em nor *in* 'em. Nothin' at all' (128).

Defended by mere school lads, equipped with superannuated cannons, and mobilized by a dilapidated train rather than modern transport caterpillars, the Janeites' battery is pitifully doomed. As readers they cathect onto Austen's novels precisely because they appear to have no plots. Again, unlike current students and scholars of narrative, for whom plot bears virtually all significance in narrative, Janeite readers resist plot with all its forward-moving momentums, its inevitabilities, and its closure, and they dwell instead on atemporal aspects of narration, such as descriptive details, catchy phrases, and especially characterization. As in the bulk of belletristic Janeite commentary from the mid-nineteenth century on, Janeites in the foxholes rhapsodize over the verisimilitude of Austenian characters. By identifying characters and things in their own experience and renaming them according to Austenian prototypes the soon-to-be-slaughtered Janeites piece out their brutally shattered world.

Because Janeites outside Kipling's story would be decried as escapists taking solace in the supposedly rehabilitative placidity of Austen's world, it is worth stressing that Kipling's Janeites do not quite fit this model, and indeed are drawn to Austen precisely because she is like the world of the foxholes. Their Jane Austen – as distinct from the Austen celebrated in the prefatory poem as 'England's Jane' (120) – is never described by them as a repository of ethical wisdom, nor is she linked with a feminine elegiac ideal of England whose very vulnerability is what knightly menfolk are fighting to protect. At the end of the story, Humberstall avidly reads Austen's novels not because they enable him to recapture the safe world which war has not shaken, but because they remind him of the trenches: 'it brings it all back – down to the smell of the glue-paint on the screens. You take it from me, Brethren, there's no one to touch Jane when you're in a tight place' (137).

Since many within the academy and outside of it as well often assume that Austen and her admirers are hyper-conventional, it is also worth emphasizing that Janeite confederacies had rather little truck with bourgeois domestic morality. Kipling's story mentions two exclusive societies – the Masons and the Janeites – but several details suggest that Austen's fiction promoted a secret brotherhood of specifically homoerotic fellowship too. When Humberstall chalks the names of Austenian characters onto the casements of the guns, he rouses the ire of the Battery Sergeant Major, who reads Humberstall's cockney spelling of 'De Bugg' for De Bourgh as a reference to sodomy. Determined to punish him and Macklin for 'writin' obese words on His Majesty's property', the BSM takes the case to the officers on the grounds that "e couldn't hope to preserve discipline unless examples was made' (131). What he does not foresee is that the officers will not discipline one of their own: they dismiss the charges after perfunctory admonitions, send the BSM away, and proceed to entertain themselves by quizzing Humberstall on Jane. The narrator, not a Janeite, closes the story by observing that Austen was 'a match-maker' and her novels 'full of match-making' (138), and by hinting at a secondary character's marriage to Humberstall's sister. And as if this were not going far enough, Kipling attaches a sequel-poem entitled 'Jane's Marriage', in which Jane enters the gates of Heaven and is rewarded by matrimony to Captain Wentworth. But these efforts to instate the marriage plot are not only risible (after all, Wentworth is both fictional and already married!) but are also at odds with the spirit of Janeiteism narrated within the story, and thus the frame itself appears to be a sop thrown to 'a pious post-war world' which requires what the narrator has already called 'revision[s]' and deletions (129). Janeites are committed to club rather than domestic society. The reproduction in which they are interested pertains not to spouses and children – in fact, they are as barren of 'direct an' lawful prog'ny' as Austen herself, leaving no issue we know of, the surviving Humberstall being a stranger to women. The reproduction they engage in is the dissemination of Janeite culture itself. Just as Austen brought forth Henry James, Janeites bring forth other Janeites by recruitment, peopling the world with Austenian characters, thus continually enlarging her world beyond the confines non-initiates are wont to dismiss as narrow. Macklin is highly satisfied when Humberstall renames the guns after Austenian characters – 'He reached up an' patted me on the shoulder. "You done nobly", he says. "You're bringin' forth abundant fruit, like a good Janeite"' (130).

As Kipling's story suggests, early twentieth-century Janeitism is a construction that emerges from specific historical needs. Before World War I, Frederic Harrison described Austen as a 'heartless little cynic ... penning satirettes against her neighbours whilst the Dynasts were tearing the world to pieces, and consigning millions to their graves'.[7] Harrison of course deplored Austen's supposed isolation from the real world, but once the Dynasts of our own century went at it, many Janeites loved precisely this ahistoricity, indulging in a fantasy about the elegiac Austen which Kipling's story both conjures and also, in my view, undermines. To Janeites outside Kipling's story, her novels evoke a world *before* history blew up, *before* rules and codes lost their efficacy, particularly in defining masculinity in relation to other men. Christopher Kent has shown that Austen's novels were actually recommended to British veterans suffering post-traumatic shock syndrome in the years following the war.[8] For soldiers whose minds were shattered by Dynastic history, the (in)famously limited dimensions of Austen's fictional world could feel rehabilitative; her placid interiors could feel manageable; her scepticism about the turbulence of sexual passion could feel a relief; her triviality could feel redemptive. Assumptions about *feminine* propriety embedded within this fantasy about Austen – about transparency, restraint, and poise – helped to shore up masculine lucidity and self-definition when these, along with English national identity itself, were under threat. The notion, then, that Austen could be therapy for people whom history has made sick has an origin in global crisis and in a profound yearning for a world still sufficient to its own forms and rituals.[9]

Harding and the tradition of academic criticism he inaugurated ridiculed the idyllic figure of 'England's Jane' whose work 'provide[s] a refuge for the sensitive when the contemporary world grew too much for them', and he refers with contempt to those who place her beyond the ugly world of politics, crisis, and machine guns.[10] But the Janeitism of this period was more productive than he admits. For one thing, it gave us Chapman's *The Novels of Jane Austen*, published by the Clarendon Press in 1923, and ever since acknowledged to be the authoritative edition of her works. Because novel studies have since moved to the centre of university curricula, while Greek and Latin departments are struggling to survive, it is easy to forget that Chapman's was the first scholarly edition of any English novelist – male or female – ever to appear. His title page touted that 'The [Texts are] based on a Collation of the Early Editions', and, as reviewers were quick to note, he treated Austen's novels with a scrupulousness customarily reserved for classical authors. What prompted such anomalous magisteriality at such a moment? The answer can be found in the collection of short essays Chapman wrote during his own wartime duty in Macedonia, where he recurs to his birthright as a classically educated English gentleman as if to bolster his morale in an alien world: he recites Horace's odes from memory on long marches or on quiet nights at observation posts; he animadverts on the decline of English syntax, on proposals for British spelling reform which would 'involve us in dangers and inconveniences of unsuspected magnitude'; he muses on his passion for collecting silver spoons, closing on a note of imperial melancholy: 'There are no spoons in Macedonia.'

Given Chapman's sense of his stewardship to English culture, felt acutely during his isolation from it, it is no wonder that he declared 'To restore, and maintain in its integrity, the text of our great writers is a pious duty.' Having fondly remembered not only Horace's odes, as it turns out, but also 'a series of summer evenings in Perthshire, when a lady read *Persuasion* to admiration', Chapman places Austen alongside Samuel Johnson as a monument to the redemptive glory of England's bygone days.[11] To be sure, Victorian publishers preserved Austen too, and with hype loud enough to offend James' ears. But while their volumes, replete with Victorian-styled illustrations and typography, perforce made Austen one of their own, the edition Chapman prepared to preserve this treasure in its 'integrity' includes chronologies of plot events based on early nineteenth-century almanacs, reproductions of Regency fashion plates and dancing manuals, and not least of all facsimiles of the original title pages, thus placing Austen safely within the national past the better to secure her there as a refuge from the present. Most of Chapman's reviewers recognized and gratefully approved of this enterprise: the reviewer for *The New Statesman* specifically praises the illustrations and historical apparatus for helping to make Austen's novels 'a *refuge* from present realities'; while *The Edinburgh Review*, likewise bemoaning its modernity, maintains that 'It is something to have escaped, if only for a moment, from this "world" that is "too much with us" to that other world, the leisured, "country-featured" and homely world of Jane Austen'.[12] Pressing Austen into the service of this national nostalgia, Chapman not only piously preserves the past, of course, but decides exactly *which* past to preserve, tracking down allusions to Shakespeare, Johnson, and Cowper with indefatigable energy, but passing over references to slavery in Antigua or riots in London as if they and the unrest to which they allude did not exist. *That* past – which so compels our generation, with its very different premiums on ideological rupture and political conflict – was not to the purpose of Chapman and his fellows.

Although some of the methods, if not the motives, of Janeiteism would surface in later academic criticism under the banner of historicism, it was foundational to the practice of Austenian criticism in the academy to discredit the Janeites such as existed in Kipling's story, in the Royal Society of Literature, and of course in later Jane Austen Societies in England and North America. Deploying an invidious distinction between the 'attentive' and 'urbane', Harding accomplished this by asserting that Austen's admirers are her worst readers: '[S]he is a literary classic of the society which attitudes like hers, held widely enough, would undermine.' Harding's own qualifications as a good reader, it is implied, derive from his own rigorously tough-minded alienation from upper-class mores, an alienation Austen herself is said to have shared. Claiming Austen would never 'have helped to make her society what it was, or ours what it is', Harding trumps the Janeite 'posterity of urbane gentlemen' by disaffiliating Austen from them and the doddering, weak-minded complacency they are said to represent.[13]

Harding's depiction of Austen as a subversive opponent of dominant values proved helpful to the next generation of academics, especially feminists, who also considered Austen at odds with dominant values, and to all readers who took candidly non-moralistic and non-moralizing pleasure in her sarcasm. But Harding's intentions were anything but open-minded, and his immediate heirs were not slow to elaborate the nasty class- and gender-inflected attacks implicit in his essay. Defining Janeite escapists as effete gentlemen, Harding hinted that Austen was in some ways more of a real man, astringent and unblinking, than they were. F. R. Leavis is more direct in *The Great Tradition* (1948), which is among other things a running diatribe against Janeite extraordinaire, Lord David Cecil. Leavis dignifies Austen as well as the great tradition of English fiction she originated by insisting on her moral seriousness, and accordingly, the leisured amateurism of Janeites – with their fondness for entertainment, performance, and comedy – is noxious to him. His class-based attack upon Lord David, which includes charges of decadence, aestheticism, over-sophistication, and evil, contains a homophobically charged gender component as well, for when Leavis casts aspersions on Lytton Strachey and the culture of Bloomsbury, he is aiming to taint Lord David by association.[14]

Citing the 'feral' animosity of writers like Twain, Lionel Trilling opined that Austen aroused 'man's panic fear at a fictional world in which the masculine principle, although represented as admirable and necessary, is prescribed and controlled by a female mind', but Trilling's explanation misrepresents the problem as a conflict between the two sexes rather than as a conflict about sexuality *per se*, regardless of the sex of the offender in question.[15] The history of Austenian criticism has often been darkened by the umbrage Austen-haters have taken against her representations of men as idle creatures absorbed in village tittle-tattle, and male Janeites have had much to endure at the hands of a world that frowns upon their passion. H. W. Garrod's 'Depreciation', a virulent attack upon Austen and her admirers both, was written 'for a pleasant occasion, and in lightness of heart' as a lecture to fellow members of the RSL. But its misogyny is still toxic, and it spatters onto men as well. Garrod opens by questioning the virility of Janeites in his audience: 'There is a time to be born and a time to die, and a time to be middle-aged and read Miss Austen. Some men are born middle-aged, some achieve middle age of their preference, others have it thrust upon them.' A man content to read novels by 'a mere slip of a girl', Garrod suggests, must somehow be womanish as well. Having feminized themselves not simply by idolizing a woman writer – which is bad enough – but even worse by then idolizing a sharp-tongued woman who fails to honour the virility of men, Janeites by Garrod's account are doubly queer.[16]

What makes Harding's and Leavis' attacks on the unmanfulness of Janeites different from Garrod's and others' is that they like Austen, and seek to clear themselves from the charge of gender deviance by wresting Austen from gentlemen scholars and literati and making Austen safe for real men engaged in real study. C. S. Lewis' 1954 essay 'A Note on Jane Austen' continues this process: '[Austen] is described by someone in Kipling's worst story as the mother of Henry James', he taunts, referring to 'The Janeites', '[but] I feel much more sure that she is the daughter of Dr. Johnson'. Engaging in a frontal assault on the playful, ironized Austen – which might make her fiction in his eyes a sort of Regency *The Importance of Being Earnest* – Lewis insists that Austen's comedy is inspired by 'hard core morality' and a vein 'of religion'.

Post-World War II Austenian reception participates in that demand to consolidate and reinvigorate masculinity elsewhere visible in the larger context of British and American culture. Academic literary criticism of the 1940s and early 1950s saves Austen from her admirers and for a middle-class professorate by celebrating her acerbity and seriousness, championing her fiction as a legitimate object of study in the as yet young field of novel studies over and against the ostensibly frivolous appreciation of Janeites. But while this criticism – to which in varying degrees that of Lascelles, Watt, and Edmund Wilson could be added – conduced to the rise of Austen as an academic field, it did not as yet foster any particular method of reading narrative, nor did it privilege the marriage plot as the most important structural and thematic principle.[17] Indeed, Austen's very scepticism about romantic love is in part what qualifies her as a tough-minded fellow traveller. True, Marvin Mudrick's profoundly influential *Jane Austen: Irony as Defense and Discovery* (1952) moved in this direction, but this was by omission. For Mudrick, Austen's artistic brilliance – i.e., her formidable irony and control – results from her pathology as a woman – i.e., her formidable irony and control. Mudrick looks to Austen's novels for tender marriage plots, and is scandalized by their absence. He takes as his epigraph Harding's allusion to Austen being loved by people she hates; but while Harding likes Austen's steely lucidity, Mudrick deplores it as deviance – cast, as in Emma Woodhouse's case, sometimes as frigidity and sometimes as lesbianism.[18]

It was not until the 1960s that the marriage plot gained the prestige it still enjoys inside the academy, and this happened in a direct attempt to recuperate Austen's normality. Wayne Booth's widely reprinted 'Control of Distance in Jane Austen's *Emma*' (1961) passionately defends Emma Woodhouse's heterosexuality, which Wilson and Mudrick had doubted. Chafing at the contention that Emma has infatuations with women even at the conclusion, he links the proper reading of Austen's novels with a proper respect for the self-evidence of marital felicity in novels and outside them:

> Marriage to an intelligent, amiable, good, and attractive man is the best thing that can happen to this heroine, and the readers who do not experience it as such are, I am convinced, far from knowing what Jane Austen is about – whatever they may say about the 'bitter spinster's' attitude toward marriage.

When novels themselves lacked the cultural prestige of poetry and drama, people who studied them could be considered lightweight as well, for so long as novels were believed to be about characters, novel studies could seem to be a species of gossip of precisely the sort in which Janeites delight. But according to Booth's influential brand of Chicago-school formalism, marriage in Austen's novels is not a matter of who marries whom, as it is, say, in G. B. Stern's and Sheila Kaye-Smith's book *Speaking of Jane Austen* (1944), a Janeite repository of chit-chat, which Booth ridicules for treating characters like real people. Instead, the marriage plot becomes the novel's fundamental meaning, the telos towards which the narrative has moved since the first page. Booth endorses Mudrick's judgment that Emma's 'chief fault' is her 'lack of ... tenderness', but to him plot itself brings about 'the reform in [Emma's] character' – a reform defined solely in terms of the destiny of heterosexual love: only when she 'learns' this is she 'ready for marriage with the man she loves, the man who throughout the book has stood ... for what she lacks'; only then is the novel ready to end. Evidence is not necessary to sustain this view. Countless readers have claimed that the absence of 'love scenes' in Austen's novels must mean *something*. But for Booth, norms about gender and sexuality are encoded onto the plot, thus making the representation of the kisses or palpitations famously lacking in Austen's *oeuvre* superfluous to begin with.[19] Compare this view of the courtship plot to that of self-confessed Janeite, E. M. Forster, whose *Aspects of the Novel* (1927) was still taught in fiction courses as late as the 1970s, alongside Booth's *Rhetoric of Fiction*: 'a man and woman ... want to be united and perhaps succeed'. The compulsory nature of the love story is acknowledged here, and that compulsion has obvious ideological import. But the marriage plot as Forster sceptically presents it falls not under the headings *Plot* or *Story*, but under the heading *People*. Considering the love plot as conventional rather than structural, Forster sees it as one among many 'facts of human life' – with people, birth, food, sleep, and death – that interest people and novelists who write about them.[20]

Rescuing Austen from Mudrick, who held that she 'convert[ed] her own personal limitations into the very form of her novel', Booth succeeded in celebrating Austen's mastery over point of view and plot as a positive thing, and contributed immeasurably to the development of novel study as an analytic discipline. But discipline obviously has repressive as well as productive elements. Booth's reading is as bullying as Harding's, equating the perversity of women who indulge same-sex 'infatuations' with the perversity of novel-critics who refuse to accept a happy ending when they see one. Eve Sedgwick has remarked that Austenian criticism belongs to the knuckle-rapping (or more pruriently spanking) 'Girl Being Taught a Lesson' model of narrative analysis, where that lesson is invariably accomplished through the 'discipline' of the marriage plot.[21] As a description of academic criticism since the late 1950s, she is right. Critics as diverse as Mark Schorer, Lionel Trilling, Ian Watt, Arnold Kettle, Marilyn Butler, Tony Tanner, Patricia P. Brown, and Mary Poovey, among many others, tend to follow Booth in judging character development, formal control, and resistance or compliance with norms as mediated through marriage, as an institution and plot device.

Indeed, so entrenched is this respect and so short our institutional memory about the history of novel criticism itself that we have forgotten that there are other ways to read, and the very different reading traditions of the Janeites can accordingly now enrich our own. Many of the Janeite reading practices discussed earlier with respect to Kipling's story flourish today under less trying circumstances in the largely amateur Jane Austen Societies throughout English-speaking countries. When Mudrick wrote that Austen 'was interested in a person, an object, an event, only as she might observe and recreate them free of consequences, as performance, as tableau', he was complaining about Austen's detachment, but he might just as well have been describing the ludic enthusiasm of these amateur reading clubs, whose 'performances' include teas, costume balls, games, readings, and dramatic representations, staged with a campy anglophilia in North America, and a brisker antiquarian meticulousness in England, and whose interests range from Austenian dramatizations, to fabrics, to genealogies, and to weekend study trips, in no particular order and without any agenda-driven priority. Even though lectures by academic Austenian scholars are featured at Jane Austen Society and Jane Austen Society of North America conferences, and even though JAS's *Collected Reports* and JASNA's *Persuasions* often publish a tremendous amount in the way of sheer information, most academics I know take a rather dim view of these galas, where enjoyment rather than hermeneutic mastery is assumed to be the reward of reading, where reading is sociable rather than solitary, and where the stuff of erudition itself seems so different. On quizzes – a staple of JASNA meetings – academics fare quite poorly: having been taught to regard only certain relationships, scenes and (typically, closural) structures as significant, we rarely recollect the colour of this character's dress or that servant's name. We sometimes suffer the additional mortification of discovering our own papers becoming yet another relatively undifferentiated, unhierarchicalized item in the great repository of Austeniana assiduously collected by Janeites and compiled in newsletters and reports, printed somewhere between recipes for white soup and the latest word jumble.

Clearly more than a mood of reading is at stake here, but a method as well, one that strikes to the heart of our disciplinary self-identity. Trained to regard the text itself as a sacred boundary which must never be violated, we are confounded by the common Janeite game of imagining how a character in one novel might behave towards a character in another, or of speculating how the novels might continue *after* the wedding (a practice Austen herself authorized by gratifying the curiosity of her nephews and nieces). If for academics meaning is generally foreclosed by the comic ending of marriage, Janeites from Kipling on treat her novels instead as one capacious middle: balls, blunders, picnics, incomes, hunting-dogs, and marriages vie equally for our attention, none taking determinative priority over another, and where, moreover, all manner of 'extra-textual' material on sailors, Addison's disease, and petty-theft is welcome so long as it somehow qualifies as a Janean artefact.

The process by which academic critics deprecate Austenian admirers outside the academy is very similar to the way, as Henry Jenkins has shown, trekkies, fans, and mass media enthusiasts are derided and marginalized by dominant cultural institutions bent on legitimizing their own objects and protocols of expertise.[22] But there is an important difference: unlike *Star Trek*, Austen's novels hold a secure place in the canon of high as well as popular culture. Claiming the legitimacy of her novels as a subject for professional study has meant not assailing the *object* of amateur or belletristic study, but instead the triviality of its (non-)knowledge. But at a time when so many scholars and theorists worry that the grip of ideology upon representation is so withering that novels themselves are a form of the police, what Janeite readers supposedly do not know may help us all. By contextualizing Austenian commentary, examining the contrast between earlier reading practices and those that prevailed once novel study was professionalized, and by insisting that reading Austen is a social practice contingent upon our desires, needs, and historical circumstances, I would like to suggest that it may not be the novel that polices us, but novel criticism as a discourse that has done so. If Dr. Johnson, one of Austen's favourite writers, was correct in opining that the purpose of literature was to help us better to enjoy or endure life, then we must be glad, *pace* James, that 'Jane' is 'theirs', 'yours', and 'ours' after all.

NOTES

1 According to the *Supplement* to the *OED*, the word 'Janeite' entered the language in 1896, but the self-consciously hyperbolic zeal for her works surely pre-dates this. Although I cannot concur in his tendency to minimize the cultural importance of Janeites and anti-Janeites as an amusing controversy, I am much indebted to B. C. Southam for having uncovered so much fascinating material in his *Critical Heritage* volumes and in 'Janeite/Anti-Janeites', *A Jane Austen Handbook*, ed. J. David Grey. (London: Athlone Press, 1986), pp. 237–43. For a brief but informative sketch of the term 'Janeite', see Lorraine Hanaway, ' "Janeite" at 100', *Persuasions*, 16 (1994), 28–9.

2 For the publication history of Austen's novels, I am vastly indebted to B. C. Southam's invaluable 'Introduction' to *Jane Austen: The Critical Heritage, Volume II: 1870–1940*, (London and New York: Routledge and Kegan Paul, 1987), especially pp. 58–70; David Gilson, *A Bibliography of Jane Austen* (Oxford: Clarendon Press, 1982), pp. 211–34; Geoffrey Keynes, *Jane Austen: A Bibliography* (London: The Nonesuch Press, 1929); and Jan Fergus' invaluable *Jane Austen: A Literary Life* (Houndmills and London: Macmillan, 1991).

3 James, 'The Lesson of Balzac' (1905), in *Jane Austen: The Critical Heritage*, vol. II, p. 230.

4 From 'Miss Austen and Miss Mitford', *Blackwood's Edinburgh Magazine*

(March 1870), reprinted in B. C. Southam, *Jane Austen: The Critical Heritage*, vol. I (London: Routledge and Kegan Paul, 1968), p. 217.

5 Quoted from Montague Summers, 'Jane Austen: An Appreciation', *Transactions of the Royal Society of Literature*, 36 (1918), 1–33. Summers' language of divine election is typical of all Janeites.

6 'The Janeites' is included in *Debits and Credits* (1926). It was begun in 1922, finished in 1923, and was first published in 1924, in a slightly different version than that published in 1926. All quotations are from *Debits and Credits*, ed. Sandra Kemp (Harmondsworth and New York: Penguin, 1987), pp. 119–140. I supply page references in the text.

7 Letter to Thomas Hardy. Quoted in F. B. Pinion, *A Jane Austen Companion* (London: Macmillan, 1973), p. 24.

8 According to Kent, H. F. Brett Smith, an Oxford tutor, served in World War I as an adviser in British hospitals, and his special responsibility was the prescription of salubrious reading for the wounded; and he recommended Austen's novels to 'severely shell-shocked' soldiers. I am much indebted to Kent's fine essay. Christopher Kent, 'Learning History with, and from, Jane Austen', in *Jane Austen's Beginnings*, ed. J. David Grey (Ann Arbor and London: UMI Research Press, 1989), p. 59.

9 D. A. Miller admits to some Janeism when he says that he once – back in the days before the AIDS crisis – believed that Austen's novels could make him well. See 'The Late Jane Austen', *Raritan*, 10 (1990), 55–79.

10 'Regulated Hatred: An Aspect of the Work of Jane Austen', in *Jane Austen: A Collection of Critical Essays*, ed. Ian Watt (Englewood Cliffs: Prentice-Hall, 1963), p. 167. Harding singles out Eric Linklater's Janeite Prime Minister in *The Impregnable Women* and Beatrice Kean Seymour's *Jane Austen*, where she wrote: 'In a society which has enthroned the machine-gun and carried it aloft even into the quiet heavens, there will always be men and women – Escapist or not, as you please – who will turn to her novels with an unending sense of relief and thankfulness.'

11 Chapman, 'Reading Aloud', in *The Portrait of a Scholar and Other Essays Written in Macedonia, 1916–1918* (London: Oxford University Press, 1920), p. 46.

12 *The New Statesman*, 22 (1923), 145; *The Edinburgh Review*, 239 (1924), 32.

13 Harding, 'Regulated Hatred', p. 170.

14 See *The Great Tradition* (Garden City, NY: Doubleday and Co., 1954), p. 19, p. 25.

15 Lionel Trilling, *The Opposing Self* (New York: Viking Press, 1955), p. 209.

16 H. W. Garrod's 'Jane Austen: A Depreciation' was originally delivered at the Royal Society for Literature in May 1928, and published in *Essays by Divers Hands: Transactions of the Royal Society of Literature*, VIII (1928): 21–40; and reprinted in numerous other places. I quote it as printed in William Heath, ed., *Discussion of Jane Austen* (Boston: Heath and Company, 1961), pp. 32–40. If Garrod launched his attack because he suspected that Janeites liked women too much, B. C. Southam would hint that Garrod himself did not like women enough: 'a clue' to Garrod's dislike of Austen lies in the fact that he was 'a distinguished classical scholar who moved to English studies in the 1920s. He spent much of his life at Oxford, unmarried, where he had rooms in Merton

College for over fifty years'; in *Jane Austen: The Critical Heritage, 1870–1940*, vol. 2, p. 154. Since many passionate Janeites, past and present, answer to this description, the 'clue' explains nothing. I examine the role Austen plays in the policing of gender as well as genre in 'The Divine Miss Jane: Jane Austen, Janeites, and the Discipline of Novel Studies', forthcoming in *boundary 2*, 23 (Fall, 1996).

17 The brilliance of Mary Lascelles' *Jane Austen and her Art* (London: Oxford University Press, 1939) I regard as exceptional to the argument I am making.

18 In *Jane Austen: Irony as Defense and Discovery* (Princeton: Princeton University Press, 1952), Mudrick holds that 'The fact is that Emma prefers the company of women' (p. 192); 'for a time at least ... Emma is in love with [Harriet]' (p. 203). On the lesbianism question specifically, Mudrick acknowledges his debt to Edmund Wilson's 'A Long Talk on Jane Austen', which first appeared in *The New Yorker*, 20 (June 24, 1944).

19 Booth's essay first appeared in *Rhetoric of Fiction* (Chicago: University of Chicago Press, 1961), pp. 243–66. I quote from pp. 260, 263, 244.

20 *Aspects of the Novel* (New York and London: Harcourt Brace Jovanovich, 1927), pp. 67–82. I quote from p. 54. In an excellent discussion of Forster's *Aspects*, Paul Morrison argues that Forster's remarks on narrative are much less emancipatory than what I suggest here. See 'End Pleasure', *GLQ*, 1 (1993), 53–78.

21 'Jane Austen and the Masturbating Heroine', in *Tendencies* (Durham: Duke University Press, 1993), p. 125.

22 *Textual Poachers: Television Fans & Participatory Culture* (London: Routledge and Kegan Paul, 1992). Jenkins draws from Michel de Certeau's *The Practice of Everyday Life* (Berkeley and Los Angeles: University of California Press, 1984) and Pierre Bourdieu's *Distinction* (Cambridge: Harvard University Press, 1979) to show how high culturalists feel tainted by the adoption of its protocols for use with respect to low culture objects, and to suggest that fans transgress against bourgeois structures of cultural valuation.

13

BRUCE STOVEL

Further reading

'It would be a delightful thing if a magazine could be started which should be devoted entirely to Miss Austen ... We are never tired of talking about her; should we ever grow weary of reading or writing about her?' So wrote Walter Stafford, 2nd Earl of Iddesleigh, in 1900, in an essay entitled 'A Chat about Jane Austen's Novels' (811). One hundred years onward, Jane Austen Societies around the world talk, read, and write about Jane Austen, and the two largest of them have for many years produced annual volumes 'devoted entirely to Miss Austen'. Furthermore, these volumes are only a small portion of the library's-worth of writing about Jane Austen, nearly all of it published since 1900. What follows is a guide to that library, discussing first biographies of Jane Austen and then criticism of the novels. As we shall see, the Earl would be delighted.

BIOGRAPHY

The dominant force in Jane Austen's life was her family, and her family has also been the dominant force in the study of her life. The major biographies of her for more than one hundred years after her death in 1817 were written by family members, and the biographies since then have relied largely on unpublished or obscurely published family manuscripts. Furthermore, the Austen family has been determined from the start to present its most famous member to the world as a figure of exemplary gentility and piety. Some five months after her death, Jane Austen was introduced to her readers as the author of her six novels, in the 'Biographical Notice' at the front of the volume containing her two posthumously published novels, *Northanger Abbey* and *Persuasion*, but this seven-page account by her favourite brother, Henry Austen, is in tone an obituary. Her life is depicted as faultless – 'She never uttered either a hasty, a silly, or a severe expression' (*NA, P* 6) – and the emphasis is upon the pious manner of her death.

Thus Jane Austen the person remained unknown to her growing readership for the first half-century after her death. Tennyson, a great admirer and rereader of the novels, could say in about 1860, 'He thanked God he knew nothing of Jane Austen, and that there were no letters preserved either of Shakespeare's or Jane Austen's, that they had not been ripped open like pigs' (cited in Gilson, *A Bibliography of Jane Austen*, 491). The public's curiosity was satisfied, and yet the author's dignity was preserved, in the first biography, *A Memoir of Jane Austen* (1870), by James Edward Austen-Leigh, Jane Austen's nephew, a clergyman and the son of her eldest brother, James. He had been sixteen when his aunt died and had known her well. His book is a tribute from someone who feels great affection for both his aunt and her novels: it is filled with reminiscences, imbued with the nostalgia of a man in his seventies for a simpler age 'before express trains, sewing machines, and photograph books' (33), and celebrates its subject's wit and high spirits as well as her domestic virtues. The book is concise (less than 150 pages), elegantly written, and cites abundantly from Austen's letters.

The main outlines of Jane Austen's life and personality are all there in the *Memoir*: the happy family life at Steventon, the precocious childhood writing as the family madcap, the attachment to Cassandra, the depression and sterility of the Bath and Southampton years, the renewed happiness and creative surge of the Chawton years, increasing admiration (from the Prince Regent among others) and her corresponding determination to maintain her privacy as the novels are published from 1811 onwards, the tragic final illness and death at forty-one. Even Austen's three brushes with love and marriage – the youthful flirtation with Tom Lefroy, the relationship with a mysterious admirer met on the Devonshire coast in 1801, the acceptance and rejection the next morning of a marriage proposal by a wealthy neighbour, Harris Bigg-Wither – are described, if in general and muffled terms. As Tennyson's remark indicates, Jane Austen was a name and nothing more to her readers before 1870; as Claudia L. Johnson shows elsewhere in this volume, the *Memoir* produces the engaging, if idealized, figure generally associated with that name.

The Austen family divulged more information in the next few decades. The first (and incomplete) edition of her letters, with a rambling 110-page introduction on Austen family life, was published by Lord Brabourne, son of Jane Austen's favourite niece, Fanny Knight, in 1884. Constance Hill's *Jane Austen: Her Homes and her Friends* (1902) cites from family manuscripts. In 1906 J. H. Hubback and his daughter Edith Hubback (the grandson and great-granddaughter of Jane Austen's brother Frank) published *Jane Austen's Sailor Brothers*, printing for the first time Jane's letters to Frank and tracing, in detail and with many anecdotes, the exciting wartime careers of Frank and Charles Austen, who both became admirals.

The 'official' biography, *Jane Austen: Her Life and Letters. A Family Record*, by William Arthur Austen-Leigh (son of James Edward) and Richard Arthur Austen-Leigh (William's nephew), appeared in 1913. It is indeed a family record, bringing together material from the different branches of the family. In the Victorian life-and-letters manner, it cites virtually every one of the surviving letters and is, in fact, largely a running commentary on the letters.

Much more readable is Elizabeth Jenkins' *Jane Austen*, which has gone through many editions since its first publication in 1938 and is, remarkably, still in print. Unencumbered by footnotes, its tale of Jane Austen's maturation as an artist and growing public success has the narrative drive of a novel – not surprisingly, since Jenkins was herself a popular novelist. She brings to life the society in which Jane Austen lived: the nuances of social rank and social occasion, the fad for the picturesque and the short-lived gothic craze, the fashions in clothes and carriages, the controversy over the Prince Regent. Like the *Memoir*, this forms an ideal place to begin reading about Jane Austen's life.

Several other popularizing biographies have appeared since then. Jane Aiken Hodge's *The Double Life of Jane Austen* (1972) takes up an idea implicit in Jenkins and makes it a thesis: that Jane Austen in private life was much more rebellious, much less conventional, than Jane Austen the dutiful family member. John Halperin's *The Life of Jane Austen* (1984) takes this view to iconoclastic extremes: his Jane Austen is consumed by smouldering resentment at her lot, incapable of love, and cynical about personal relationships, and her novels are for him correspondingly acrid. By contrast, Lord David Cecil's *A Portrait of Jane Austen* (1978) is an affectionate tribute; a picture-book in form (with 101 illustrations), elegantly written, it presents the old-fashioned Jane Austen, cultivated, genteel, sensible, principled. Cecil's book nevertheless is meant to be read, as opposed to the coffee-table books on Jane Austen, to be browsed for their pictures. Three instances of the latter are Marghanita Laski's *Jane Austen and her World* (1969), Susan Watkins' *Jane Austen's Town and Country Style* (1990), and Nigel Nicolson's *The World of Jane Austen* (1991); the last, following Hill, concentrates on the country houses in Jane Austen's life and fiction.

Meanwhile, the Austen family has gone on publishing biographical information. Mary Augusta Austen-Leigh produced *James Edward Austen-Leigh*, a memoir of her father, in 1911, and in 1920, at the age of 82, published *Personal Aspects of Jane Austen*. Both books fill in details of the Chawton years. R. A. Austen-Leigh, co-author of the *Life and Letters*, produced a series of pamphlets and articles, as well as editing *Austen Papers, 1704–1856* (1942), which contains a wealth of fascinating material:

letters by both of Jane Austen's parents, for instance, and the correspondence from Steventon of Jane Austen's witty and dazzling cousin Eliza de Feuillide. The reminiscences of Caroline Austen, the sister of James Edward Austen-Leigh and his collaborator in the 1870 *Memoir*, have been published in two slim volumes, *My Aunt Jane Austen: A Memoir* (1952) and *Reminiscences of Caroline Austen* (1986). It is Caroline who tells us an important fact: Cassandra 'burnt the greater part' of Jane's letters to her '2 or 3 years before her own death' (*My Aunt Jane Austen*, 10).

Three excellent biographies have appeared in recent years. Park Honan's *Jane Austen* (1987) is a sympathetic and thoroughly researched account: Honan, for instance, makes use throughout of unpublished family papers. Honan's main thesis is that Jane Austen was much more implicated in events of her revolutionary times than has been realized: significantly, the book's first chapter, introducing the Austen family, is preceded by an eight-page prologue following the twelve-year-old naval cadet, Frank Austen, as he rides inland to Steventon from the brutal naval academy at Portsmouth. Throughout, in fact, Honan narrates his story as if he were a novelist, providing, for instance, a ten-page account of the vacillations within Jane Austen's mind as she first accepts and then rejects Harris Bigg-Wither's proposal (189–98). Thus, despite its length (450 pages) and thoroughness, this book is highly readable.

Deirdre Le Faye's *Jane Austen: A Family Record* (1989) also makes use of family papers, but has a very different way of presenting Austen's life: her book is authoritatively factual, from the ten-page 'Chronology' of Jane Austen's life with which it begins – reprinted in this volume – to the thirteen pages of family pedigrees (including a two-page chart entitled 'Origin and Descent of Biographical Information') with which it ends. Le Faye also draws on research of her own into parish records, county archives, wills, cemeteries, and other sources of information. The resulting account is meticulously accurate – unless one takes exception to the title page, which identifies this book as a revised and enlarged version of the 1913 *Life and Letters*, when it is in fact a wholly new account which owes little more to the original than its chronological framework. The person who reads this book, even more than the reader of Honan's, experiences Jane Austen as an actual person – sharp-edged, various, untransparent – and not as the neat hypothesis (either delightfully good or secretly rebellious) of previous biographies.

Jan Fergus' *Jane Austen* is much shorter than the Honan and Le Faye biographies, and does not make use of unpublished family papers, but has some definite advantages over them, including its very brevity (190 pages) and its critical insights. (Fergus is the author of one of the best books of

Austen criticism, *Jane Austen and the Didactic Novel* [1983], and she weaves five to ten pages of shrewd observations about each novel into the narrative.) The book is one in Macmillan's series of Literary Lives, which aim at tracing writers' professional careers and their contexts. As in her essay in this volume, Fergus provides fascinating information on the literary marketplace – the going price for a first novel, the kinds of contracts offered authors, publication runs, readership – and Jane Austen's place in it. More than ever before, Austen emerges as shrewd in her business dealings and ambitious as an author. The book's focus is on Jane Austen the professional woman: Fergus offers a carefully stated, and convincing, feminist interpretation of Jane Austen's personal situation and of her novels. More forthrightly feminist is Deborah Kaplan's *Jane Austen among Women* (1994); using fresh research, Kaplan defines Austen's life by examining those of other women in her family circle and neighbourhood.

Each of the biographies by Honan, Le Faye, and Fergus offers a state-of-the-art portrait of Jane Austen. Two books by George Holbert Tucker are carefully researched and very readable: *A Goodly Heritage: A History of Jane Austen's Family* (1983), which devotes ten to fifteen pages to each of the family members in turn, and *Jane Austen the Woman* (1994), which has chapters on topics such as Jane Austen and Scandal or Jane Austen's Journeyings. And Deirdre Le Faye's new edition of Jane Austen's letters (1995) contains a wealth of information in its notes, 'Biographical Index', and 'Topographical Index'. All in all, then, Jane Austen the person is no longer a cipher.

CRITICISM TO 1970

Virginia Woolf said of Austen, 'Of all great writers she is the most difficult to catch in the act of greatness' ('Jane Austen at Sixty', 15). This obliqueness makes criticism of her novels necessary, challenging, ingenious, and various. The history of that criticism can be divided into four phases, with the help of the boundaries used in B. C. Southam's two anthologies of earlier criticism, *Jane Austen: The Critical Heritage* (1968), which covers 1811 to 1870, and *Jane Austen: The Critical Heritage, Volume II: 1870–1940*. The first phase of Austen criticism thus runs from the novels' publication to 1870, the date of the *Memoir*; a second phase continues up to 1939, the date of the first valuable full-length study, Mary Lascelles' *Jane Austen and her Art* (1939); a third phase in which academic study of the novels becomes established extends from 1940 till about 1970; from that date onwards, new conceptions of Austen's achievement and rigorous new critical methods predominate. The summary of Austen criticism below outlines the high points up to 1970 and after that point, as books became more frequent and hindsight more scarce, offers a quick survey of all the critical books published on Austen's novels.

Until the publication of the *Memoir* in 1870, Jane Austen's novels had a small, if growing and appreciative, audience. No books on Austen were published during this period, and of the few essays that appeared, three are particularly interesting. Sir Walter Scott's review-essay on *Emma* in 1816 argues that *Emma* represented a major new kind of unromantic fiction. Richard Whately, reviewing *Northanger Abbey* and *Persuasion* in 1821 but displaying a shrewd grasp of all six novels, shows that Austen is like Shakespeare in her vivid, carefully differentiated characterization, that her plots follow Aristotelian principles, and that her novels present, if indirectly, 'moral lessons': 'her's is that unpretending kind of instruction which is furnished by real life' (95). Richard Simpson's 25-page 'review' of the *Memoir* in 1870 outlines an original and searching conception of Jane Austen's novels. Drawing on the *Memoir*'s account of the juvenilia, he argues that Jane Austen began as an ironic debunker of romantic love and developed her own ideal of 'intelligent love': 'Miss Austen seems to be saturated with the Platonic idea that the giving and receiving of knowledge, the active formation of another's character, or the more passive growth under another's guidance, is the truest and strongest foundation of love' (244).

After the *Memoir*'s appearance in 1870, there was a flood of new editions of the novels, many of them illustrated, and a host of new biographical and critical studies. There is a cosy, self-congratulatory quality to almost all of this new enthusiasm: as early as 1852, an anonymous author claims, 'readers of more refined taste and critical acumen feel something like dissatisfaction with almost every other domestic novelist, after they have once appreciated Miss Austen' ('Female Novelists', 136). One suspects that it is this 'refined' adulation, rather than the novels themselves, that accounts for the violent distaste for Austen's novels expressed in this period by Charlotte Brontë, Emerson, Mark Twain, and D. H. Lawrence (as well as Henry James' condescending praise).

Surprisingly little in the seven decades between 1870 and Mary Lascelles' book in 1939 is of critical interest (as opposed to curiosity value) today. Two novelists, Virginia Woolf and E. M. Forster, offer shrewd and illuminating comments in essays that, because of their authors' stature, received wide circulation in, respectively, Woolf's *The Common Reader* (1925) and Forster's *Abinger Harvest* (1936); Woolf's essay is especially eloquent, describing how different *Persuasion* is from Austen's earlier novels: 'She is beginning to discover that the world is larger, more mysterious, and more romantic than she had supposed' (22). A. C. Bradley, Professor of Poetry at Oxford and the author of *Shakespearean Tragedy* (1904), published an essay on Austen in 1911 that gave her work an academic imprimatur. Beginning with the view, 'There are two distinct strains in Jane Austen. She is a moralist and a humorist' (7), he comments on the interrelationship of these two strains and suggests that stage comedy influenced her fictional comedies; he also explores for the first time her debt to eighteenth-century writers such as Johnson and Cowper. In 1917 Reginald Farrer published a centenary tribute that was much more original, witty, penetrating, and provocative than anything since Simpson's essay. Writing for the general reader, he argues that the Jane Austen most readers know is largely a fiction produced by sentimental biography and the book trade – and that, instead, she is a conscious artist and a dispassionate critic of her own society. Farrer's comments on each of the six novels are bracing: he makes the case that *Emma* is the most complex – and best – of them.

Mary Lascelles' *Jane Austen and her Art* forms a watershed: it was the first full-length, thorough, and searching study of the novels. Jane Austen's use of language, of narrative technique, of timing, and many other artistic issues were defined and explored with precision and sensitivity. Yet the book is stimulating at the same time for its old-fashioned judgments: Darcy's long letter to Elizabeth, for instance, is considered implausible – 'so much, and such, information would hardly be volunteered by a proud and reserved man' (162). All in all, if one had to be marooned with the six novels and one critical book, this would still be the choice of many readers. Like the Jenkins biography, it remains in print some sixty years after its first publication.

The following year, 1940, saw the publication of an influential revisionist essay, D. W. Harding's 'Regulated Hatred'. Harding took Farrer's conception of Austen several steps further, presenting her as a distinctively twentieth-century figure: isolated and misunderstood, protecting her integrity as a person and an artist by subversive ironies. As a result, Austen 'is a literary classic of the society which attitudes like hers, held widely enough, would undermine' (167). This view of Austen as an isolated ironist, critical of her society, received full-length exposition in Marvin Mudrick's *Jane Austen: Irony as Defense and Discovery* (1952). Mudrick's schematic, closely argued reading of the novels is one that few readers can accept in its entirety, but that all will find thought-provoking. If criticism of the novels could no longer be innocent after Lascelles, after Mudrick it would usually be strenuous and combative.

Since then, critical books and essays – most by academics – have proliferated. Several studies from the fifties and sixties remain virtually required reading. Lionel Trilling's essays championing *Mansfield Park* (1954) and *Emma* (1957) were frequently reprinted and still make exciting reading. B. C. Southam's *Jane Austen's Literary Manuscripts* (1964) remains the standard study on its subject – and is especially useful as a guide to the juvenilia and the three incomplete novels (*Lady Susan, The Watsons, Sanditon*). Howard Babb's *Jane Austen's Novels: The Fabric of Dialogue* (1962) argues that characters define themselves by the way they use (and misuse) general concepts in conversation. Joseph Wiesenfarth's *The Errand of Form* (1967) provides a vigorous close reading of the novels, reinstating Jane Austen the moralist. Kenneth Moler's *Jane Austen's Art of Allusion* (1968) is a pioneering detailed study of Austen's debt to Burney, Edgeworth, and other novelists of her time. Perhaps the most useful book of criticism in this period is A. Walton Litz's *Jane Austen* (1965); concise, lucid, bringing into focus a great deal of previous scholarship and criticism, this volume is, like Lascelles' book, a one-volume critical compendium. Another useful compendium is *Jane Austen: A Collection of Critical Essays*, ed. Ian Watt (1963), which contains essays on Austen by Woolf, Harding, C. S. Lewis, and Edmund Wilson and critical essays on each novel.

CRITICISM SINCE 1970

Beginning in about 1970, and running parallel to the general re-theorizing of literary study in the last two decades, Austen's novels were analysed more and more as products of a specific culture. Alistair Duckworth's *The Improvement of the Estate* (1971) and Marilyn Butler's *Jane Austen and the War of Ideas* (1975) regarded them as statements in the social and moral controversies of Austen's time, as did Warren Roberts' study of Austen's politics, *Jane Austen and the French Revolution* (1979). Julia Prewitt Brown's *Jane Austen's Novels: Social Change and Literary Form* (1979) focused on society's changing conception of marriage; Susan Morgan's *In the Meantime: Character and Perception in Jane Austen's Fiction* (1980) found in the novels Austen's response to the epistemological debates of the Romantic era; Jan Fergus in *Jane Austen and the Didactic Novel* (1983) related Austen's first three novels to educational thinking. Education was the focus in D. D. Devlin's *Jane Austen and Education* (1975), Laura Mooneyham's *Romance, Language, and Education in Jane Austen's Novels* (1988), and Barbara Horwitz's *Jane Austen and the Question of Women's Education* (1991), whereas Jocelyn Harris explored Jane Austen's creative reading of earlier authors auch as Shakespeare, Chaucer, Milton, and Richardson in *Jane Austen's Art of Memory* (1989). The historian Oliver MacDonagh, in *Jane Austen: Real and Imagined Worlds* (1991), linked the novels and social history, as did Maija Stewart's *Domestic Realities and Imperial Fictions: Jane Austen's Novels in Eighteenth-Century Contexts* (1993) and Roger Sales' *Jane Austen and Representations of Regency England* (1994). James Thompson saw the novels as dramatizing the conflict between landed and exchange values in *Between Self and World: The Novels of Jane Austen* (1988). The religious context was the subject of Gene Koppel's *The Religious Dimension in Jane Austen's Novels* (1988) and *Jane Austen and the Clergy* (1994) by the historian Irene Collins. Edward Copeland has a chapter on Austen's relation to economic realities in his *Women Writing about Money: Women's Fiction in England, 1790–1820* (1995). John Wiltshire, in *Jane Austen and the Body* (1992), analyses the novels in the light of medical thinking about illness and the body. Two books that consider social rituals in the novels are David Monaghan's *Jane Austen: Structure and Social Vision* (1980) and John Dussinger's *In the Pride of the Moment: Encounters in Jane Austen's World* (1990). K. C. Phillipps in *Jane Austen's English* (1970), Karl Kroeber in *Styles in Fictional Structure: The Art of Jane Austen, Charlotte Brontë, and George Eliot* (1971), and Norman Page in *The Language of Jane Austen* (1972) concentrate on language conventions.

These specialized studies are written for the academic, rather than the general, reader. They tend to replace traditional literary criticism with rigorous attention to cultural context – though, in fact, many, perhaps most, are gracefully written, and most (for instance, the books by Brown and Morgan) provide eloquent close readings of the novels. The older kind of criticism did not simply disappear, however, and many excellent studies of Austen appeared that owed little to the changed critical climate. Stuart Tave's *Some Words of Jane Austen* (1973) is a showcase for sensitive close reading, as is Barbara Hardy's *A Reading of Jane Austen* (1976) – which, unusually, consists of chapters on topics such as Storytelling or Properties and Possessions rather than novel-by-novel treatment. Several other notable books in this category are Jane Nardin's *Those Elegant Decorums: The Concept of Propriety in Jane Austen's Novels* (1973), Lloyd Brown's *Bits of Ivory: Narrative Techniques in Jane Austen's Fiction* (1973), Darrel Mansell's *The Novels of Jane Austen* (1973), John Hardy's *Jane Austen's Heroines* (1984), Roger Gard's significantly-titled *Jane Austen's Novels: The Art of Clarity* (1992), and Juliet McMaster's *Jane Austen the Novelist* (1995) – which reprints three of the four essays in her earlier *Jane Austen on Love* (1978). Several helpful guides for the general reader appeared: Christopher Gillie's *A Preface to Jane Austen* (1974), Douglas Bush's *Jane Austen* (1975), and John Lauber's *Jane Austen* (1993), and in this category might be placed Tony Tanner's popularizing *Jane Austen* (1986), which combines post-structural terminology and old-fashioned explication (and reprints Tanner's introductions to Penguin editions of *Sense and Sensibility*, *Pride and Prejudice*, and *Mansfield Park*).

The most invigorating new approach has been feminism. Brief discussions of Austen's novels figured in several of the books that established feminism as a distinct form of literary analysis, notably Patricia Meyer Spacks' *The Female Imagination* (1975), Ellen Moers' *Literary Women* (1976), Elaine Showalter's *A Literature of their Own* (1977), Nina Auerbach's *Communities of Women* (1978), and Rachel Brownstein's *Becoming a Heroine* (1982). Two influential books contain extended discussions of Austen as a victim of the society she depicts: Sandra Gilbert and Susan Gubar, *The Madwoman in the Attic* (1979), and Mary Poovey, *The Proper Lady and the Woman Writer* (1984). A similar view of Austen's novels as enacting a constricting ideology is presented in Nancy Armstrong's chapters on *Pride and Prejudice* and *Emma* in her *Desire and Domestic Fiction* (1987). Jane Spencer discusses Austen's novels as the culmination of a tradition of women's fiction in *The Rise of the Woman Novelist* (1986). The first book devoted to Austen as a feminist was Margaret Kirkham's *Jane Austen, Feminism, and Fiction* (1983), which argues that Austen dramatizes the concerns of Enlightenment feminists of her day like Mary Wollstonecraft. Three other books that offer feminist readings of Austen's novels are Leroy W. Smith's *Jane Austen and the Drama of Woman* (1983), Mary Evans' *Jane Austen and the State* (1987), and Alison Sulloway's *Jane Austen and the Province of Womanhood* (1989). More sophisticated and provocative than any of these was Claudia Johnson's *Jane Austen: Women, Politics, and the Novel* (1989), which postulates that, in an England threatened by revolutionary France, the domestic novel became politicized, a forum in which Edmund Burke's favourite analogy of the ordered family to the conservative state could be tested. One recent essay shows how much a feminist reading opens up to view: Margaret Anne Doody's forty-page introduction to the Oxford World's Classics *Sense and Sensibility* (1990).

Of course, many recent studies fit into none of the above categories. The most fascinating of these is no doubt J. F. Burrows' *Computation into Criticism* (1987). Using computer-based statistics, Burrows describes Austen's narration (showing that the three earlier novels differ markedly from the three later ones) and identifies the 'idiolects', or distinctive speech-patterns, of her major characters. Michael Williams' *Jane Austen* (1986) applies reader-response theory to the novels, and John Odmark applies phenomenology in *An Understanding of Jane Austen's Novels* (1981). Richard Handler and Daniel Segal bring to bear anthropological ideas about ritual and class in *Jane Austen and the Fiction of Culture* (1990). Jane

Austen had a keen love of music, and two books relate her knowledge of music to the novels: Patrick Piggott's *The Innocent Diversion: Music in the Life and Writings of Jane Austen* (1979) and R. K. Wallace's *Jane Austen and Mozart* (1983). Two books of Austen criticism published in 1995 illustrate its ongoing diversity: Tara Ghoshal Wallace's *Jane Austen and Narrative Authority* and Maggie Lane's *Jane Austen and Food*.

Many helpful collections of critical essays have appeared since Watt's volume. The most notable of these are: *Critical Essays on Jane Austen*, ed. B. C. Southam (1968); *Jane Austen Today*, ed. Joel Weinsheimer (1975); *Jane Austen: Bicentenary Essays*, ed. John Halperin (1975); *Jane Austen's Achievement*, ed. Juliet McMaster (1976); *Jane Austen in a Social Context*, ed. David Monaghan (1981); *Jane Austen: New Perspectives*, ed. Janet Todd (1983); and *Jane Austen's Business*, ed. Juliet McMaster and Bruce Stovel (1996). The three volumes from the seventies are bicentennial tributes (Jane Austen was born in 1775); special issues of two scholarly journals, *Nineteenth-Century Fiction* and *Studies in the Novel*, were devoted to essays on Austen in 1975. There are several casebooks gathering critical essays on individual novels, Norton Critical Editions of *Pride and Prejudice* and *Emma*, a dozen or so monographs devoted to a single novel, and scores of valuable introductions to paperback editions (such as those by Tanner and Doody already mentioned); R. W. Chapman's scholarly editions of the novels (1923) and the minor works (1954) contain valuable textual and background information. And then there are chapters in books on larger topics, such as Dorothy Van Ghent's much-reprinted essay on *Pride and Prejudice* in *The English Novel* (1953) or Wayne Booth's chapter on *Emma* in *The Rhetoric of Fiction* (1961) or Raymond Williams' pages on Austen in *The Country and the City* (1973) or Claudia L. Johnson's essay on manhood in *Emma* in *Equivocal Beings: Politics, Gender and Sentimentality in the 1790s* (1995). The *Annual Reports* of the Jane Austen Society in England have been published since 1949, and *Persuasions*, the annual journal of the Jane Austen Society of North America, has appeared each year since 1979. The annual MLA (Modern Language Association) Bibliography lists the dozens of essays on Austen that appear in scholarly journals each year. Two earlier handbooks offer orientation. F. B. Pinion's *A Jane Austen Companion* (1973) provides a running commentary on the novels and their background, as well as items such as a glossary of Austen's usage and an index of characters and places in the novels. A more ambitious and miscellaneous reader's guide, filled with up-to-date information and critical commentary, is *The Jane Austen Companion* (1986), ed. J. David Grey, with sixty-five essays by forty contributors on a vast range of topics. David Gilson's *A Bibliography of Jane Austen* (1978) contains a list of all biography and criticism published up to 1978; since then the MLA bibliography, available now in up-to-date computer format as well as in annual volumes, has full entries on Jane Austen books and essays. Two books that contain detailed summaries of books and articles are *An Annotated Bibliography of Jane Austen Studies, 1952–1972*, by Barry Roth and Joel Weinsheimer, and *An Annotated Bibliography of Jane Austen Studies, 1973–1982*, by Barry Roth. A valuable critical tool is the three-volume *Concordance to the Works of Jane Austen*, by Peter De Rose and S. W. McGuire (1983).

Today, readers who have enjoyed Austen's novels and begin reading criticism are almost too lucky: they may be blinded by too much light. Facing shelves full of critical writing on the novels, they can hardly feel the Earl of Iddesleigh's euphoria. However, as with our knowledge of Jane Austen's biography, what we have gained far outweighs what we have lost.

WORKS CITED

Biography

Austen, Caroline, *My Aunt Jane Austen: A Memoir* (London: Spottiswoode, Ballantyne, 1952).

Reminiscences of Caroline Austen (Winchester: Jane Austen Society, 1986).

[Austen, Henry,] 'Biographical Notice of the Author', in *Northanger Abbey* and *Persuasion*, ed. R. W. Chapman (London: Oxford University Press, 1969).

Austen, Jane, *Jane Austen's Letters*, ed. Deirdre Le Faye (Oxford and New York: Oxford University Press, 1995).

Austen-Leigh, James Edward, *A Memoir of Jane Austen*, ed. R. W. Chapman (London: Oxford University Press, 1926).

Austen-Leigh, Mary Augusta, *James Edward Austen-Leigh: A Memoir by his Daughter* (privately printed, 1911).

Personal Aspects of Jane Austen (London: Murray, 1920).

Austen-Leigh, Richard A., ed., *Austen Papers, 1704–1856* (London: Spottiswoode, Ballantyne, 1942).

Austen-Leigh, William, and Richard A. Austen-Leigh, *Jane Austen: Her Life and Letters. A Family Record* (London: Smith, Elder, 1913).

Brabourne, Edward, 1st Lord, 'Introduction', *Letters of Jane Austen*, 2 vols. (London: Bentley, 1884).

Cecil, Lord David, *A Portrait of Jane Austen* (London: Constable, 1978).

Fergus, Jan, *Jane Austen: A Literary Life* (London: Macmillan; New York: St. Martin's Press, 1991).

Halperin, John, *The Life of Jane Austen* (Baltimore: Johns Hopkins University Press, 1984).

Hill, Constance, *Jane Austen: Her Homes and her Friends* (London and New York: Lane, 1902).

Hodge, Jane Aiken, *The Double Life of Jane Austen* (London: Hodder and

Stoughton, 1972); issued as *Only a Novel: The Double Life of Jane Austen* (New York: Coward, McCan, and Geohegan, 1972).

Honan, Park, *Jane Austen: Her Life* (London: Weidenfeld and Nicolson, 1987).

Hubback, J. H., and Edith Hubback, *Jane Austen's Sailor Brothers* (London and New York: Lane, 1906).

Jenkins, Elizabeth, *Jane Austen: A Biography* (London: Gollancz, 1938).

Laski, Marghanita, *Jane Austen and her World* (London: Thames and Hudson; New York: Viking, 1969).

Le Faye, Deirdre, *Jane Austen: A Family Record* (London: British Library, 1989).

Nicolson, Nigel, *The World of Jane Austen* (London: Weidenfeld and Nicolson, 1991).

Tucker, George Holbert, *A Goodly Heritage: A History of Jane Austen's Family* (Manchester: Carcanet, 1983).

Jane Austen the Woman: Some Biographical Insights (New York: St. Martin's Press, 1994).

Watkins, Susan, *Jane Austen's Town and Country Style* (London: Thames and Hudson; New York: Rizzoli, 1990).

Criticism to 1970

Austen, Jane, *The Novels of Jane Austen*, ed. R. W. Chapman, 5 vols. (Oxford: Clarendon Press, 1923; revised edition, 1965–6).

Minor Works, ed. R. W. Chapman, vol. 6 of *The Works of Jane Austen* (London: Oxford University Press, 1954; revised edition, 1969).

Babb, Howard S., *Jane Austen's Novels: The Fabric of Dialogue* (Columbus: Ohio State University Press, 1962).

Booth, Wayne C., *The Rhetoric of Fiction* (Chicago: University of Chicago Press, 1961).

Bradley, A. C., 'Jane Austen: A Lecture', *Essays and Studies by Members of the English Association*, 2 (1911), 7–36.

Farrer, Reginald, 'Jane Austen, *ob*. July 18 1817', *Quarterly Review*, 228 (October 1917), 1–30.

'Female Novelists', *New Monthly Magazine*, 95 (May 1852), 17–23; cited from Southam, *Jane Austen: The Critical Heritage*, pp. 131–9.

Forster, E. M., 'Jane Austen', in *Abinger Harvest* (London: Arnold, 1936), pp. 3–14.

Harding, D. W., 'Regulated Hatred: An Aspect of the Work of Jane Austen', *Scrutiny*, 8 (1939–40), 346–62; cited from Watt, *Jane Austen: A Collection of Critical Essays*, pp. 166–79.

Iddesleigh, Walter Stafford, 2nd Earl of, 'A Chat about Jane Austen's Novels', *Nineteenth Century*, 47 (1900), 811–20.

Lascelles, Mary, *Jane Austen and her Art* (Oxford: Clarendon Press, 1939).

Litz, A. Walton, *Jane Austen: A Study of her Artistic Development* (London: Chatto and Windus; New York: Oxford University Press, 1965).

Moler, Kenneth L., *Jane Austen's Art of Allusion* (Lincoln: University of Nebraska Press, 1968).

Mudrick, Marvin, *Jane Austen: Irony as Defense and Discovery* (Princeton: Princeton University Press; London: Oxford University Press, 1952).

[Scott, Sir Walter,] review of *Emma*, *Quarterly Review*, 14 (October 1815), 188–201; cited from Southam, *Jane Austen: The Critical Heritage*, pp. 58–69.

[Simpson, Richard,] review of J. E. Austen-Leigh, *A Memoir of Jane Austen*, *North British Review*, 52 (April 1870), 129–52; cited from Southam, *Jane Austen: The Critical Heritage*, pp. 241–65.

Southam, B. C., *Jane Austen's Literary Manuscripts: A Study of the Novelist's Development through the Surviving Papers* (London: Oxford University Press, 1964).

Southam, B. C., ed., *Critical Essays on Jane Austen* (London: Routledge and Kegan Paul; New York: Barnes and Noble, 1968).

Jane Austen: The Critical Heritage (London: Routledge and Kegan Paul; New York: Barnes and Noble, 1968).

Tanner, Tony, 'Introduction', *Mansfield Park* (Harmondsworth: Penguin, 1966).

'Introduction', *Sense and Sensibility* (Harmondsworth: Penguin, 1969).

Trilling, Lionel, '*Mansfield Park*', *Encounter*, 3, No. 3 (September 1954), 9–19, and *Partisan Review*, 21 (1954), 492–511; reprinted in his *The Opposing Self: Nine Essays in Criticism* (London: Secker and Warburg; New York: Viking, 1955), pp. 206–30.

'*Emma*', *Encounter*, 8, No. 6 (June 1957), 49–59; reprinted in his *Beyond Culture: Essays on Literature and Learning* (New York: Viking, 1965; London: Secker and Warburg, 1966), pp. 31–55.

Van Ghent, Dorothy, *The English Novel: Form and Function* (New York: Holt, Rinehart, and Winston, 1953).

Watt, Ian, ed., *Jane Austen: A Collection of Critical Essays* (Englewood Cliffs, NJ: Prentice-Hall, 1963).

[Whateley, Richard,] review of *Northanger Abbey* and *Persuasion*, *Quarterly Review*, 24 (January 1821), 352–76; cited from Southam, *Jane Austen: The Critical Heritage*, pp. 87–105.

Wiesenfarth, Joseph, *The Errand of Form: An Assay of Jane Austen's Art* (New York: Fordham University Press, 1967).

Woolf, Virginia, 'Jane Austen at Sixty', *Nation and Athenaeum*, 34 (1923), 433–4.

'Jane Austen', in *The Common Reader* (London: Hogarth, 1925), pp. 168–83; cited from Watt, *Jane Austen: A Collection of Critical Essays*, pp. 15–24.

Criticism since 1970

Armstrong, Nancy, *Desire and Domestic Fiction: A Political History of the Novel* (London and New York: Oxford University Press, 1987).

Auerbach, Nina, *Communities of Women: An Idea in Fiction* (Cambridge, MA, and London: Harvard University Press, 1978).

Brown, Julia Prewitt, *Jane Austen's Novels: Social Change and Literary Form* (Cambridge, MA: Harvard University Press, 1979).

Brown, Lloyd W., *Bits of Ivory: Narrative Techniques in Jane Austen's Fiction* (Baton Rouge: Louisiana State University Press, 1973).

Brownstein, Rachel, *Becoming a Heroine: Reading about Women in Novels* (New York and London: Viking, 1982).

Burrows, J. F., *Computation into Criticism: A Study of Jane Austen's Novels and an Experiment in Method* (Oxford: Clarendon Press, 1987).

Bush, Douglas, *Jane Austen* (London and New York: Macmillan, 1975).

Butler, Marilyn, *Jane Austen and the War of Ideas* (Oxford: Clarendon Press, 1975).

Collins, Irene, *Jane Austen and the Clergy* (London: Hambledon, 1994).

Copeland, Edward, *Women Writing about Money: Women's Fiction in England, 1790–1820* (Cambridge: Cambridge University Press, 1995).

De Rose, Peter L., and S. W. McGuire, *A Concordance to the Works of Jane Austen*, 3 vols. (New York: Garland, 1983).

Devlin, D. D., *Jane Austen and Education* (London: Macmillan, 1975).

Doody, Margaret Anne, 'Introduction', *Sense and Sensibility* (Oxford and New York: Oxford University Press, 1990).

Duckworth, Alistair M., *The Improvement of the Estate: A Study of Jane Austen's Novels* (Baltimore and London: Johns Hopkins University Press, 1971).

Dussinger, John, *In the Pride of the Moment: Encounters in Jane Austen's World* (Columbus: Ohio State University Press, 1990).

Evans, Mary, *Jane Austen and the State* (London and New York: Tavistock, 1987).

Fergus, Jan, *Jane Austen and the Didactic Novel: 'Northanger Abbey', 'Sense and Sensibility', and 'Pride and Prejudice'* (London: Macmillan; Totowa, NJ: Barnes and Noble, 1983).

Gard, Roger, *Jane Austen's Novels: The Art of Clarity* (New Haven: Yale University Press, 1992).

Gilbert, Sandra M., and Susan Gubar, *The Madwoman in the Attic: The Woman Writer and the Nineteenth Century Literary Imagination* (New Haven: Yale University Press, 1979).

Gillie, Christopher, *A Preface to Jane Austen* (London: Longman, 1974).

Gilson, David, *A Bibliography of Jane Austen* (Oxford: Clarendon Press, 1982).

Grey, J. David, *The Jane Austen Companion* (New York: Macmillan, 1986); issued as the *Jane Austen Handbook* (London: Macmillan, 1986).

Jane Austen's Beginnings: The Juvenilia and Lady Susan (Ann Arbor, MI: UMI Research Press, 1989).

Halperin, John, ed., *Jane Austen: Bicentenary Essays* (Cambridge: Cambridge University Press, 1975).

Handler, Richard, and Daniel Segal, *Jane Austen and the Fiction of Culture: An Essay on the Narration of Social Realities* (Tucson: University of Arizona Press, 1990).

Hardy, Barbara, *A Reading of Jane Austen* (London: Owen; New York: New York University Press, 1976).

Hardy, John, *Jane Austen's Heroines: Intimacy in Human Relationships* (London: Routledge and Kegan Paul, 1984).

Harris, Jocelyn, *Jane Austen's Art of Memory* (Cambridge: Cambridge University Press, 1989).

Horwitz, Barbara, *Jane Austen and the Question of Women's Education* (New York: Lang, 1991).

Johnson, Claudia L., *Jane Austen: Women, Politics, and the Novel* (Chicago: University of Chicago Press, 1988).

Equivocal Beings: Politics, Gender, and Sentimentality in the 1790s: Wollstone-

craft, Radcliffe, Burney, Austen (Chicago and London: University of Chicago Press, 1995).

Kaplan, Deborah, Jane Austen among Women (Baltimore: Johns Hopkins University Press, 1994).

Kirkham, Margaret, Jane Austen: Feminism and Fiction (Brighton: Harvester; Totowa, NJ: Barnes and Noble, 1983).

Koppel, Gene, The Religious Dimension in Jane Austen's Novels (Ann Arbor, MI: UMI Research Press, 1988).

Kroeber, Karl, Styles in Fictional Structures: The Art of Jane Austen, Charlotte Brontë, and George Eliot (Princeton: Princeton University Press, 1971).

Lane, Maggie, Jane Austen and Food (London: Hambledon, 1995).

Lauber, John, Jane Austen (New York: Twayne, 1993).

MacDonagh, Oliver, Jane Austen: Real and Imagined Worlds (New Haven: Yale University Press, 1991).

Mansell, Darrel, The Novels of Jane Austen: An Interpretation (London: Macmillan, 1973).

McMaster, Juliet, ed., Jane Austen's Achievement: Papers Delivered at the Jane Austen Bicentennial Conference at the University of Alberta (London: Macmillan, 1976).

Jane Austen on Love (Victoria, BC: University of Victoria Press, 1978).

Jane Austen the Novelist: Essays Past and Present (London: Macmillan, 1995).

McMaster, Juliet, and Bruce Stovel, eds., Jane Austen's Business: Her World and her Profession (London: Macmillan, 1996).

Moers, Ellen, Literary Women (New York: Doubleday, 1976).

Monaghan, David, Jane Austen: Structure and Social Vision (London: Macmillan, 1980).

Monaghan, David, ed., Jane Austen in a Social Context (London: Macmillan; Totowa, NJ: Barnes and Noble, 1981).

Mooneyham, Laura G., Romance, Language, and Education in Jane Austen's Novels (London: Macmillan; New York: St. Martin's Press, 1988).

Morgan, Susan, In the Meantime: Character and Perception in Jane Austen's Fiction (Chicago and London: University of Chicago Press, 1980).

Nardin, Jane, Those Elegant Decorums: The Concept of Propriety in Jane Austen's Novels (Albany: State University of New York Press, 1973).

Odmark, John, An Understanding of Jane Austen's Novels: Character, Value, and Ironic Perspective (Oxford: Blackwell, 1981).

Page, Norman, The Language of Jane Austen (Oxford: Blackwell, 1972).

Phillipps, K. C., Jane Austen's English (London: André Deutsch, 1970).

Piggott, Patrick, The Innocent Diversion: Music in the Life and Writings of Jane Austen (London: Cleverdon, 1979).

Pinion, F. B., A Jane Austen Companion: A Critical Survey and Reference Book (London: Macmillan, 1973).

Poovey, Mary, The Proper Lady and the Woman Writer: Ideology as Style in the Works of Mary Wollstonecraft, Mary Shelley, and Jane Austen (Chicago: University of Chicago Press, 1984).

Roberts, Warren, Jane Austen and the French Revolution (New York: St. Martin's Press, 1979).

Roth, Barry, *An Annotated Bibliography of Jane Austen Studies, 1973–1983* (Charlottesville: University of Virginia Press, 1985).

Roth, Barry, and Joel Weinsheimer, *An Annotated Bibliography of Jane Austen Studies, 1952–1972* (Charlottesville: University of Virginia Press, 1973).

Sales, Roger, *Jane Austen and Representations of Regency England* (London and New York: Routledge, 1994).

Showalter, Elaine, *A Literature of their Own: British Women Novelists from Brontë to Lessing* (Princeton: Princeton University Press, 1977).

Smith, Leroy W., *Jane Austen and the Drama of Woman* (New York: St. Martin's Press, 1983).

Southam, B. C., ed., *Jane Austen: The Critical Heritage, Volume II: 1870–1940* (London: Routledge and Kegan Paul; Totowa, NJ: Barnes and Noble, 1987).

Spacks, Patricia Meyer, *The Female Imagination: A Literary and Psychological Investigation of Women's Writing* (New York: Knopf, 1975).

Spencer, Jane, *The Rise of the Woman Novelist: From Aphra Behn to Jane Austen* (Oxford: Blackwell, 1986).

Stewart, Maija, *Domestic Realities and Imperial Fictions: Jane Austen's Novels in Eighteenth-Century Contexts* (Athens, GA: University of Georgia Press, 1993).

Sulloway, Alison G., *Jane Austen and the Province of Womanhood* (Philadelphia: University of Pennsylvania Press, 1989).

Tanner, Tony, 'Introduction', *Mansfield Park* (Harmondsworth: Penguin, 1966).
'Introduction', *Sense and Sensibility*, (Harmondsworth: Penguin, 1969).
'Introduction', *Pride and Prejudice* (Harmondsworth: Penguin, 1972).
Jane Austen (Cambridge, MA: Harvard University Press, 1986).

Tave, Stuart M., *Some Words of Jane Austen* (Chicago and London: University of Chicago Press, 1973).

Thompson, James, *Between Self and World: The Novels of Jane Austen* (University Park, PA: Pennsylvania State University Press, 1988).

Todd, Janet, ed., *Jane Austen: New Perspectives* (New York: Homes and Meier, 1983).

Wallace, Robert K., *Jane Austen and Mozart: Classical Equilibrium in Fiction and Music* (Athens, GA: University of Georgia Press, 1983).

Wallace, Tara Ghoshal, *Jane Austen and Narrative Authority* (New York: St. Martin's Press, 1995).

Weinsheimer, Joel, ed., *Jane Austen Today* (Athens, GA: University of Georgia Press, 1975).

Williams, Michael, *Jane Austen: Six Novels and their Methods* (London: Macmillan, 1986).

Williams, Raymond, *The Country and the City* (London and New York: Oxford University Press, 1973).

Wiltshire, John, *Jane Austen and the Body: 'The Picture of Health'* (Cambridge: Cambridge University Press, 1992).

INDEX

Note: only those proper names and place names cited in the essays are listed below. See the 'Chronology' for others.

Prior, Matthew
  'Henry and Emma' 210
Publishing
  general conditions 12–15
  process of 15–17
  market 17–19
  See also Crosby; Egerton; Murray;
    individual works of JA

Quarterly Review, The 19, 155, 187

Rabelais, François 92
Radcliffe, Ann
  contemporary of JA 13, 14
  politics of 152
  tradition of 39, 173, 179, 192, 206
  The Italian 187, 202
  The Mysteries of Udolpho 40, 205
  The Romance of the Forest 14, 16
Radcliffe, William 14
Raleigh, Walter 214
Reeve, Clara 192
Regency, the
  dress fashions 85–6
  politics 85–6, 87
  style 86–9, 93, 96, 98
Regency romances 87
  See also Heyer, Georgette
Religion 149–69
  Anglican romance, the 163–7
  Church of England 149–50, 154
  Dissenters 150, 154
  politics and 152–4, 159
  See also individual works by JA
Repton, Humphry 73
Richardson, Samuel 50, 90, 192–3, 197, 203,
  206, 207, 234
  Clarissa 35, 85, 112
  Pamela 35, 111–12, 128
  Sir Charles Grandison 112, 174, 198,
    205–6
Roberts, Warren 168, 234
Robertson, William 204
Robinson, Mary Darby 28, 152
Roche, Regina Maria 206
Roth, Barry and Joel Weinsheimer 238
Rousseau, Jean Jacques 94
  Emile 95
  Julie, ou la nouvelle Héloïse 94
Roworth, Charles
  printer of Sense and Sensibility 20
Royal Society of Literature 214, 219
  See also Janeites

Said, Edward 66, 169
Sales, Roger 168, 235
Sanditon
  literary references in 206–7
  money in 138, 144–5, 146
  progress of 11, 27, 82–3
  social ranks in 117
Schorer, Mark 222
Scott, Walter (Sir) 18, 50, 96, 152, 173, 175,
  178, 183, 187, 192, 200–1, 206, 207, 231
  reviews by 95, 187
  Marmion 200
  Waverley 18, 24, 201
Sedgwick, Eve 222
Selwyn, E. G. 168
Sense and Sensibility 42–9
  literary references in 204–5
  money in 133, 135, 136, 137–8
  progress to publication 8, 9, 12, 17, 19–21,
    85
  reviews of 18
  social ranks in 116, 119, 120, 126, 129
Shakespeare, William 77, 190, 192, 196–7,
  206, 209, 232, 234
  Romeo and Juliet 197
Sheridan, Richard Brinsley 208
  The School for Scandal 175
Sherlock, Thomas 165, 206
Showalter, Elaine 236
Simpson, Richard 232
Sleath, Elinor
  The Nocturnal Minstral 190
  The Orphan of the Rhine 190
Smith, Charlotte 13, 14, 152, 173
  Desmond 14
  Emmeline 187
  The Young Philosopher 187
Smith, Leroy W. 236
Smollett, Tobias 192–3
Southam, Brian 13, 29, 168, 224, 231, 234
Southampton 2, 4, 8, 228
Southey, Robert
  Letters from England 200
Spacks, Patricia Meyer 236
Spectator, The 205
Spencer, Jane 236
Spring, David 132, 146
Spurgeon, Caroline 213
Stafford, Walter 227
Stanton, Judith Phillips 13, 29
Staves, Susan 147
Stern, G. B. and Sheila Kaye-Smith 221
Sterne, Laurence 102, 106, 108, 192